THE GROLIER LIBRARY
OF
SCIENCE BIOGRAPHIES

VOLUME 9

Salk–Tsui

Grolier Educational
Sherman Turnpike, Danbury, Connecticut 06816

Published 1997 by
Grolier Educational
Danbury Connecticut 06816

Copyright © 1996 by Market House Books Ltd.
Published for the School and Library market exclusively
by Grolier Educational, 1997

Compiled and Typeset by Market House Books Ltd, Aylesbury, UK.

General Editors
    John Daintith BSc, PhD
    Derek Gjertsen BA

Market House Editors
    Elizabeth Martin MA
    Anne Stibbs BA
    Fran Alexander BA
    Jonathan Law BA
    Peter Lewis BA, DPhil
    Mark Salad

Picture Research
    Linda Wells

Contributors
    Eve Daintith BSc
    Rosalind Dunning BA
    Garry Hammond BSc
    Robert Hine BSc, MSc
    Valerie Illingworth BSc, MPhil
    Sarah Mitchell BA
    Susan O'Neill BSc
    W. J. Palmer MSc
    Roger F. Picken BSc, PhD
    Carol Russell BSc
    W. J. Sherratt BSc, MSc, PhD
    Jackie Smith BA
    B. D. Sorsby BSc, PhD
    Elizabeth Tootill BSc, MSc
    P. Welch DPhil
    Anthony Wootton

Published by arrangement with
The Institute of Physics Publishing
Bristol BS1 6NX
UK

ISBN   Volume 9   0-7172-7635-X
           Ten-Volume Set   0-7172-7626-0
Library of Congress Catalog Number: 96-31474
Cataloging Information to be obtained directly from Grolier Educational.
First Edition
Printed in the United States of America

CONTENTS

PREFACE

ABOUT THE GROLIER LIBRARY OF SCIENCE BIOGRAPHIES

The 19th-century poet and essayist Oliver Wendell Holmes wrote:

> Science is a first-rate piece of furniture for a man's upper chamber, if he has common sense on the ground floor.
>
> *The Poet at the Breakfast-Table* (1872)

While it has been fashionable in this century to assume that science is capable of solving all human problems, we should, perhaps, pause to reflect on Holmes's comment. Scientific knowledge can only be of value to the human race if it is made use of wisely by the men and women who have control of our lives.

If this is true, all thinking people need a solid piece of scientific furniture in their upper chambers. For this reason the editors and publishers of this series of books have set out to say as much about science itself as about the scientists who have created it.

All the entries contain basic biographical data – place and date of birth, posts held, etc. – but do not give exhaustive personal details about the subject's family, prizes, honorary degrees, etc. Most of the space has been devoted to their main scientific achievements and the nature and importance of these achievements. This has not always been easy; in particular, it has not always been possible to explain in relatively simple terms work in the higher reaches of abstract mathematics or modern theoretical physics.

Perhaps the most difficult problem was compiling the entry list. We have attempted to include people who have produced major advances in theory or have made influential or well-known discoveries. A particular difficulty has been the selection of contemporary scientists, in view of the fact that of all scientists who have ever lived, the vast majority are still alive. In this we have been guided by lists of prizes and awards made by scientific societies. We realize that there are dangers in this – the method would not, for instance, catch an unknown physicist working out a revolutionary new system of mechanics in the seclusion of the Bern patent office. It does, however, have the advantage that it is based on the judgments of other scientists. We have to a great extent concentrated on what might be called the "traditional" pure sciences – physics, chemistry, biology, astronomy, and the earth sciences. We also give a more limited coverage of medicine and mathematics and have included a selection of people who have made important contributions to engineering and technology. A few of the entries cover workers in such fields as anthropology and psychology, and a small number of philosophers are represented.

A version of this book was published in 1993 by the Institute of Physics, to whom we are grateful for permission to reuse the material in this set. Apart from adding a number of new biographies to the Institute of Physics text, we have enhanced the work with some 1,500 photographs and a large number of quotations by or about the scientists themselves. We have also added a simple pronunciation guide (the key to which will be found on the back of this page) to provide readers with a way of knowing how to pronounce the more difficult and unfamiliar names.

Each volume in this set has a large biographical section. The scientists are arranged in strict alphabetical order according to surname. The entry for a scientist is given under the name by which he or she is most commonly known. Thus the American astrophysicist James Van Allen is generally known as Van Allen (not Allen) and is entered under V. The German chemist Justus von Liebig is commonly referred to as Liebig and is entered under L. In addition, each volume contains a section on "Sources and Further Reading" for important entries, a glossary of useful definitions of technical words, and an index of the whole set. The index lists all the scientists who have entries, indicating the volume number and the page on which the entry will be found. In addition scientists are grouped together in the index by country (naturalized nationality if it is not their country of origin) and by scientific discipline. Volume 10 contains a chronological list of scientific discoveries and publications arranged under year and subject. It is intended to be used for tracing the development of a subject or for relating advances in one branch of science to those in another branch. Additional information can be obtained by referring to the biographical section of the book.

JD
DG 1996

PRONUNCIATION GUIDE

A guide to pronunciation is given for foreign names and names of foreign origin; it appears in brackets after the first mention of the name in the main text of the article. Names of two or more syllables are broken up into small units, each of one syllable, separated by hyphens. The stressed syllable in a word of two or more syllables is shown in **bold** type.

We have used a simple pronunciation system based on the phonetic respelling of names, which avoids the use of unfamiliar symbols. The sounds represented are as follows (the phonetic respelling is given in brackets after the example word, if this is not pronounced as it is spelled):

a *as in* bat
ah *as in* palm (pahm)
air *as in* dare (dair), pear (pair)
ar *as in* tar
aw *as in* jaw, ball (bawl)
ay *as in* gray, ale (ayl)
ch *as in* chin
e *as in* red
ee *as in* see, me (mee)
eer *as in* ear (eer)
er *as in* fern, layer
f *as in* fat, phase (fayz)
g *as in* gag
i *as in* pit
I *as in* mile (mIl), by (bI)
j *as in* jaw, age (ayj), gem (jem)
k *as in* keep, cactus (**kak**-tus), quite (kwIt)
ks *as in* ox (oks)
ng *as in* hang, rank (rangk)
o *as in* pot

oh *as in* home (hohm), post (pohst)
oi *as in* boil, toy (toi)
oo *as in* food, fluke (flook)
or *as in* organ, quarter (**kwor**-ter)
ow *as in* powder, loud (lowd)
s *as in* skin, cell (sel)
sh *as in* shall
th *as in* bath
th as in feather (**fe*th***-er)
ts *as in* quartz (kworts)
u *as in* buck (buk), blood (blud), one (wun)
u(r) *as in* urn (but without sounding the "r")
uu *as in* book (buuk)
v *as in* van, of (ov)
y *as in* yet, menu (**men**-yoo), onion (**un**-yon)
z *as in* zoo, lose (looz)
zh *as in* treasure (**tre**-zher)

The consonants b, d, h, l, m, n, p, r, t, and w have their normal sounds and are not listed in the table.

In our pronunciation guide a consonant is occasionally doubled to avoid confusing the syllable with a familiar word, for example, -iss rather than -is (which is normally pronounced -iz); -off rather than -of (which is normally pronounced -ov).

Sa

Salk, Jonas Edward

(1914–1995)

AMERICAN MICROBIOLOGIST

We are on our way to a new age of immunization throughout the world. I even look forward to the day when the principle of the killed virus will be used in a single vaccine against virtually all the virus diseases of man.
—On the future of immunization

The people – could you patent the sun?
—On being asked who owned the patent on his polio vaccine.
Quoted by S. Bolton in *Famous Men of Science*

Salk was born in New York City, the son of a garment worker. He was educated at the City College of New York and at New York University Medical School, where he obtained his MD in 1939. In 1942 he went to the University of Michigan where he worked as a research fellow on influenza vaccine under Thomas Francis. In 1947 he moved to the University of Pittsburgh, serving as professor of bacteriology from 1949 onward. Here Salk began the work that eventually led to the discovery of a successful polio vaccine in 1954. After this breakthrough Salk was invited in 1963 to become director of the Institute for Biological Studies at San Diego, California, known more simply as the Salk Institute – soon to emerge as one of the great research centers of the world.

Salk was not the first to develop a vaccine against polio for in 1935 killed and attenuated vaccines were tested on over 10,000 children. It turned out, however, that not only were the vaccines ineffective, but they were also unsafe and probably responsible for some deaths and a few cases of paralysis.

By the time Salk began his work in the early 1950s a number of crucial advances had been made since the 1935 tragedy. In 1949 John Enders and his colleagues had shown how to culture the polio virus in embryonic tissue. Another essential step was the demonstration, in 1949, that there were in fact three types of polio virus with the inconvenient consequence that vaccine effective against any one type was likely to be powerless against the other two.

Salk had to develop a vaccine that was safe but potent. To ensure its safety he used virus exposed to formaldehyde for up to 13 days and afterward tested for virulence in monkey brains. This, in theory, allowed a large safety margin, for Salk could detect no live virus after only three days.

To test its potency Salk injected children who had already had polio and noted any increase in their antibody level. When it became clear that high antibody levels were produced by the killed vaccine, Salk moved on to submitting it to the vital test of a mass trial. Two objections were raised to this. One from Albert Sabin that killed vaccine was simply the wrong type to be used and a second, from various workers, who claimed to find live virus in the supposedly killed vaccine.

Despite such qualms Salk continued with the trial, administering in 1954 either a placebo or killed vaccine to 1,829,916 children. The evaluation of the trial was put into the hands of the virologist Thomas Francis, who, in March 1955, reported that the vaccination was 80–90% effective. The vaccine was released for general use in the United States in April 1955.

Salk became a national hero overnight and plans went ahead to vaccinate 9 million children. However, within weeks there were reports from California in which children developed paralytic polio shortly after being vaccinated. After a period of considerable confusion it became clear that all such cases involved vaccine prepared in a single laboratory.

After several days of almost continuous debate, the decision was taken to proceed and, by the end of 1955, 7 million doses had been administered. Further technical improvements were made in the production process. These safeguards would either eliminate any further cases of live vaccine or if a live virus did manage to penetrate all defenses it should make its presence known long before its use in a vaccine.

The courage shown by Salk in persisting with his vaccine was clearly justified by the results for the period 1956–58 – 200 million injections without a single case of vaccine-produced paralysis.

Samuelsson, Bengt Ingemar

(1934–)

SWEDISH BIOCHEMIST

Born at Halmstad in Sweden, Samuelsson (**sam**-oo-el-son) was educated at the Karolinska Institute, Stockholm, where he gained his MD in 1961. He continued to work there until 1966, when he moved to the Royal Veterinary College, Stockholm as professor of medical chemistry. In 1972 he returned to the Karolinska Institute as professor of medicine and physiological chemistry.

Samuelsson has worked extensively on the hormonelike prostaglandins first identified by Ulf von Euler in the 1930s. With Sune Bergström in the 1950s he worked out the structure of several prostaglandins and went on to explore some of their physiological properties. Later work by Samuelsson and his colleagues indicated a relationship between prostaglandins and the chemicals involved in transmitting nerve impulses. He discovered the prostaglandin PGA_2, thromboxane, which causes blood vessels to contract and platelets to clump. A second prostaglandin, PGE_2, inhibits the release of norepinephrine, a neurotransmitter of the sympathetic nervous system, and thereby blocks the transmission of nerve impulses.

Samuelsson also worked out the structure of a number of prostaglandins. They were shown to be closely related and synthesized in the body from a number of polyunsaturated fatty acids. All prostaglandins were found to be 20-carbon carboxylic acids with a five-member carbon ring. They are divided into three series – PG_1, PG_2, and PG_3 – depending on whether they have one, two, or three double bonds. The different prostaglandins could be distinguished by the location of an oxygen atom or a hydroxyl group (OH). For his work on prostaglandins Samuelsson shared the 1982 Nobel Prize for physiology or medicine with John Vane and Sune Bergström.

Sanctorius, Sanctorius

(1561–1636)

ITALIAN PHYSIOLOGIST

> No medical book has attained this perfection.
> —Herman Boerhaave on Sanctorius's
> *De statica medicina* (On
> Medical Measurement)

Sanctorious (sangk-**tor**-ee-us), who was born at Capodistria (now in Croatia), graduated in medicine from the University of Padua in 1582. It is believed he may then have spent some years in Poland serving the king and his court. On his return he was appointed professor of theoretical medicine at the University of Padua from 1611 until 1624 when he retired to devote himself to private research.

Sanctorius was a highly original and creative scientist whose work was characterized by a determination to introduce measurement and quantification into physiology. Thus in 1612 he was probably the first to describe and construct a clinical thermometer. This was just one of a number of instruments designed by him. He also devised a "pulsilogium," which measured the pulse rate by means of a pendulum.

With his battery of instruments Sanctorius conducted a series of classic experiments that, recorded in his *De statica medicina* (1614; On Medical Measurement), virtually founded the modern study of animal metabolism. Starting from Galen's proposal that the skin "breathed" an "insensible perspiration," Sanctorius introduced an experimental setup incorporating a chair attached to a large balance in which such changes could be accurately measured. By recording his weight before and after various activities, he was able to demonstrate the existence of "insensible perspiration" and to show that its production "was more extensive than all the visible and palpable excreta taken together," accounting for about 62% of weight loss.

His work, however, failed to have any great impact on contemporary science, one reason being that Sanctorious was somewhat ahead of his time, for there seemed little use to which his insights could be put in the context of 17th-century physiology.

Sandage, Allan Rex

(1926–)

AMERICAN ASTRONOMER

Born in Iowa City, Sandage graduated from the University of Illinois in 1948 and obtained his PhD in 1953 from the California Institute of Technology. He was on the staff of the Hale Observatories at Mount Wilson and Mount Palomar from 1952 when he began as an assistant to Edwin Hubble. He was professor of physics at Johns Hopkins University (1987–88) and is now on the staff of the Carnegie Observatories, Pasadena.

In 1960, using the 200-inch (5-m) reflecting telescope, Sandage in collaboration with Thomas Matthews succeeded in making the first optical identification of a quasar or quasi-stellar object. Quasars first came to the notice of astronomers when a number of compact, rather than extended, radio sources were detected by the Cambridge surveys of the radio sky carried out in the 1950s. Sandage and Matthews showed that 3C 48, a compact radio source from the third Cambridge survey, was at the same position as a faint apparently starlike object. Sandage and others succeeded in obtaining spectra of 3C 48 that were found to be quite unlike those of any other star. The mystery of these strange new objects was partially cleared up by Maarten Schmidt in 1963 when he showed that the spectral lines of a quasar have undergone an immense shift in wavelength.

Sandage continued to work on quasars and in 1965 introduced a method of identifying them by searching at an indicated radio position for objects emitting an excessive amount of ultraviolet or blue radiation. He found that many ultraviolet objects, which he named blue stellar objects or BSOs, were not radio emitters but could still be classed as quasars because they had the characteristic immense red shift first detected by Schmidt. He speculated that these might be older quasars that had passed beyond the radio phase of their life cycle. It is now known that the vast majority of quasars are not radio sources.

Following the work of Hubble on the expanding universe, Sandage has also tackled the difficult question of the age of the universe and whether it will continue to expand forever. He has claimed that the rate of expansion is slowing down so that the universe will eventually stop expanding and start contracting back to the original primal atom, at which point the cycle will begin again. The time scale of this "oscillating universe" he predicted as about 80 billion years: there would thus be about another 25 billion years of expansion to complete before beginning the 40 billion year contraction. Such theories, depending as they do on such difficult measurements as the density of matter in the universe as a whole, are difficult to test and are not surprisingly frequently revised.

Sänger, Eugen

(1905–1964)

AUSTRIAN ROCKET SCIENTIST

Sänger (**seng**-er) was born at Pressnitz (now Přisečnice in the Czech Republic) and was educated at the universities of Graz and Vienna, where he graduated in aeroscience in 1929. He taught at the Vienna Technical Institute before moving to Germany in 1936. He remained in Germany until 1945, serving at the Institute for Rocket Flight at Trauen and from 1942 at the Gliding Research Station, Ainring, Bavaria. From 1945 Sänger advised the French ministry of armaments until his appointment as head of the Jet Propulsion Institute, Stuttgart, in 1954. A dispute with the Federal Government led to his resignation and acceptance of a chair of space-travel research in 1963 at the Technical University, West Berlin.

Sänger was one of the leading pioneers of rockets and space travel. He published in 1933 the influential *Technique of Rocket Flight* and did much in the 1930s to work out both the theory and practice of liquid-propelled rockets. During the war he worked on the development of the ram jet and went on to draw up plans for his proposed "antipodal" plane capable of bombing New York from Berlin. Launched from a sled and flying at an altitude of 150 kilometers (93 mi), it had a planned range of 23,000 kilometers (14,300 mi). He also produced, with Irene Bredt, later to be his wife, the secret report *Rocket Propulsion of Long-Range Bombers*.

Sanger, Frederick

(1918–   )

BRITISH BIOCHEMIST

Sanger, a physician's son from Rendcombe in England, received both his BA and his PhD from Cambridge University (in 1939 and 1943 respectively). He continued his research at the university and from 1951 until 1983 was a member of the scientific staff of the Medical Research Council. In 1955, after some ten years' work, Sanger established the complete amino-acid sequence of the protein bovine insulin. This was one of the first protein structures identified, and Sanger received the Nobel Prize for chemistry in 1958 in recognition of his achievement. Sanger's work enabled chemists to synthesize insulin artificially and also generally stimulated research in protein structure.

In 1977 Sanger's team at the MRC laboratories, Cambridge, published the complete nucleotide (base) sequence of the genetic material (DNA) of the virus Phi X 174. This involves determining the order of 5,400 nucleotides along the single circular DNA strand. Moreover they found two cases of genes located within genes. Previously it had been thought that genes could not overlap. Sanger's research required the development of new techniques for splitting the DNA into different-sized fragments. These are radioactively labeled and then separated by electrophoresis. The base sequence can then be worked out because it is known which base is located at the end of each fragment due to the specificity of the enzymes (the so-called restriction enzymes) used to split the DNA. Sanger was awarded the Nobel Prize for chemistry a second time (1980) for his work on determining the base sequences of nucleic acids.

Sarich, Vincent

(1934–   )

AMERICAN BIOCHEMIST

Chicago-born Sarich was educated at the University of California, Berkeley, where he gained his PhD in 1967. He has remained at Berkeley, being appointed professor of biochemistry in 1981.

Sarich was struck by the range of dates, from 4 million to 30 million years ago, within which anthropologists of the early 1960s placed the origin of the split between the hominids and the great apes. He began work, in collaboration with his Berkeley colleague Allan Wilson, to see if there was a more precise method of dating using the genetic relationship between man and apes. They chose to work with proteins, which closely reflect genes, choosing the blood-serum protein, albumin. As man and apes diverged further from their common ancestor, their albumins would also have diverged and would now be recognizably different.

Serum samples from apes, monkeys, and man were purified and then injected into rabbits to produce antiserums. A rabbit immunized against a human sample (antigen) will also react to other anthropoid antigens, only not as strongly. As antigenic differences are genetically based, response differences will therefore measure genetic differences between species. Sarich chose to work with a group of proteins found in blood serum known collectively as the "complement system." Antigens tend to attract and fix some of the complement. The amount of complement fixed could be measured precisely. Thus differences in complement-fixation rates produced by the albumin of man and gorilla when injected into immunized rabbits would measure their immunological distance.

If it could be assumed that protein differences between species have evolved at a constant rate, then immunological distance would also be a measure of evolutionary separation. It remained to calibrate the clock. Sarich and Wilson took as their base line the date 30 million years ago marking the separation between the hominoids and the old-world monkeys. Thereafter it was a relatively easy matter to turn immunological distance into dates.

The results were clear but surprising. *Homo*, on this scheme, separated from the chimps and gorillas only 5 million years ago. This was a bold claim to make in 1967 as orthodox opinion, argued for example by David Pilbeam, placed the split between hominids and hominoids closer to 15 million years. What is more they had the skull of *Ramapithecus*, dating from this period, to prove their point. Initially, therefore, Sarich's views were rejected out of hand by paleontologists. Slowly, however, Sarich made converts. He argued, "I know my molecules have ancestors, you must prove your fossils had descendants." They found it more and more difficult to do so. Consequently, when it became clear that *Ramapithecus* was the ancestor not of man but the orang-utan, opposition to Sarich largely disappeared.

Saussure, Horace Bénédict de

(1740–1799)

SWISS PHYSICIST AND GEOLOGIST

> In my youth, when I had crossed the Alps only a few times, I believed I had grasped all the facts...Since then, further explorations of different parts of the mountain chain have shown me that the only constant thing in the Alps is their great variety.
>
> —*Voyages dans les Alpes* (1779–96; Travels in the Alps)

Saussure (soh-**soor**) was the son of an agriculturist. He was educated at the university in his native city of Geneva, graduating in 1759, and became professor of physics and philosophy at the Geneva Academy (1762–86).

He was the first to make a systematic and prolonged study of the Alps, his work being published in his classic *Voyages dans les Alpes* (1779–96; Travels in the Alps). He began as a disciple of Abraham Werner, accepting that the mass of the Alps had crystallized from the primitive ocean. However, 17 years of studying the convolutions and folds of the Alps led him to state in 1796 that such folds could only be produced by some force acting from below, or that they must have actually been laid down folded. Both alternatives preclude deposition by water. He was unwilling to decide in favor of the plutonist theories of James Hutton and thus to introduce fire as an agent, for he could recognize no sign of it.

He also collected considerable meteorological data and developed, in 1783, an improved hygrometer to measure humidity, using a human hair. He made the second ascent of Mont Blanc (1787) and at the summit took many scientific recordings. He also made nocturnal recordings and, in 1788, stayed for 17 days on the 11,000-foot (3,358 m) summit of Col du Géant.

Savery, Thomas

(*c.* 1650–1715)

BRITISH ENGINEER AND INVENTOR

> ...vessells or engines for raiseing water or occasioning motion to any sort of millworks by the impellent force of fire.
> —Terms of Savery's patent for his steam pump (1698)

Little is known of Savery's early life except that he was born at Shilstone in England and that he probably trained as a military engineer. During the 1690s he tried to find a solution to the problem of pumping water from mines and built the first steam engine to be used during the Industrial Revolution. In order to pump water from coal mines, he developed a way of creating a vacuum in a closed vessel by filling it with steam and then condensing the steam with a spray of cold water. His water-raising engine was patented in 1698. The engine could not be used with high-pressure steam and could raise water by only 20 feet (6 m), but the design was improved by Thomas Newcomen, with whom he later went into partnership.

Schaefer, Vincent Joseph

(1906–1993)

AMERICAN PHYSICIST

Schaefer, who was born at Schenectady in New York, graduated from the Davey Institute of Tree Surgery in 1928. He was appointed as assistant to Irving Langmuir at the research laboratory of the General Electric Company in 1931 and remained there until 1954, becoming a research associate in 1938. In 1954 he was appointed director of research at the Munitalp Foundation, where he remained until 1959 when he was appointed to a chair of physics at the State University of New York, Albany. He retired in 1976.

In 1946 Schaefer was the first to demonstrate that it was possible to induce rainfall. Tor Bergeron had earlier argued that the presence of ice crystals in the atmosphere was a necessary precondition for the formation of rain. During World War II Schaefer had worked on atmospheric research and, more specifically, the problem of airplane wings icing up, and had discovered that he could produce a snow storm in the laboratory by dropping dry ice (solid carbon dioxide) into a container filled with a supercooled mist. In 1946 he seeded clouds over Massachusetts with dry ice pellets and produced the first man-made precipitation.

Following the success of this experiment the atmospheric research program known as Project Cirrus was established during which Bernard Vonnegut discovered the effectiveness of silver iodide as a cloud-seeding material.

Schally, Andrew Victor

(1926–)

POLISH–AMERICAN
PHYSIOLOGIST

Schally (**shal**-ee), who was born at Wilno in Poland, left his native country for Britain in 1939. After graduating from the University of London, he worked at the National Institute for Medical Research from 1949 until 1952 when he moved to Canada. There he worked at McGill University, Montreal, obtaining his PhD in biochemistry in 1957, before joining the staff of Baylor University Medical School, Houston. In 1962 he became head of the endocrine and polypeptide laboratories at the Veterans Administration Hospital, New Orleans.

Like his great rival Roger Guillemin, Schally spent much of his early career trying to confirm the hypothesis of Geoffrey Harris on the existence and role of hypothalamic hormones. It was not in fact until he had been donated a million pig's hypothalami by a meat packer that, independently of Guillemin, he isolated some 3 milligrams of the thyrotropin-releasing factor in 1966.

He followed this in 1971 by detecting the luteinizing releasing factor, showing it to be a decapeptide and working out its sequence of ten amino acids, thus permitting its synthesis.

For his work on the hypothalamic hormones Schally shared the 1977 Nobel Prize for physiology or medicine with Guillemin and Rosalyn Yalow.

Schank, Roger Carl

(1946–   )

AMERICAN COMPUTER SCIENTIST

Schank, a New Yorker by birth, was educated at the University of Texas where he obtained his PhD in 1969. After working at Stanford until 1974, Schank moved to Yale, becoming professor of computing science and psychology in 1976. In 1989 he was appointed professor of computer science at Northwestern University, Evanston, Illinois; he is currently director of the Institute for the Learning Sciences there.

Schank's work has concerned the fundamental problem of understanding natural language. One difficulty is the way in which simple verbs like "gave" are highly ambiguous in such uses as:

John gave Mary a book.

John gave Mary a hard time.

John gave Mary a night on the town.

John gave up.

and many more. While the computer can be instructed to infer from "John gave Mary a book" the conclusion: "Mary now possesses a book," it must not be allowed to infer "Mary now possesses a hard time" from "John gave Mary a hard time." Such complications seem endless.

Schank sought to avoid this particular problem by identifying different classes of verbs. Among action verbs he defined the class PTRANS, which stands for the ways objects can be transferred by such processes as carrying or throwing. Another class, MTRANS, describes the ways in which mental information is transferred by such methods as reading or writing. Knowing which class a verb belongs to, and some of the rules governing its use, computers are less likely to be misled by pervasive ambiguities.

In addition to this ambiguity, there are more fundamental differences between the way in which a computer "understands" and the way a person understands. For instance, a computer can be told that John went to a restaurant, ordered a meal, paid the check, and left, without being aware that John actually ate the meal. It can of course be informed of this fact. But if everything implicit in language must be made explicit, then programming a computer to deal with language would become an impossible task. Schank tried to deal with this by educating computers with the aid of various "scripts," which give the computer information about the "real world." In the case of the restaurant, the computer lacks a restaurant script. Schank filled the gap by telling the computer the props met with in restaurants (menus, plates, etc.), the players (cooks, waiters, etc.) and, among other items, some results (customer no longer hungry, has less money, etc.).

Are computers programmed in this way any more intelligent or knowledgeable? One difficulty, Schank has noted, is that it is impossible "to write down scripts for all the things stories and texts can be about." What is needed is a computer that can recognize its own ignorance and know where to find the data it needs. But, Schank notes, although "such a system is possible theoretically, we are still very far from developing one."

Schaudinn, Fritz Richard

(1871–1906)

GERMAN ZOOLOGIST

Schaudinn (**show**-din), who was born at Röseningken (now in Poland), took a doctorate in zoology at the University of Berlin (1894), where he became lecturer (1898). In 1904 he was appointed director of the protozoology laboratory in the Imperial Office, Berlin, and was subsequently director of the department of protozoological research in the Hamburg Institute for Tropical Diseases.

Some of Schaudinn's most important work was in his studies of those protozoans (notably trypanosomes) that cause tropical diseases in man. He distinguished between the amoeboid cause of tropical dysentery, *Entamoeba histolytica*, and its innocuous relative *Escherichia coli*, which lives in the lining of the intestine where it is actually beneficial in engulfing bacteria.

With the dermatologist Erich Hoffmann he isolated (1905) the spirochete cause of syphilis (*Treponema pallidum*, formerly *Spirochaeta pallida*) and, confirming an earlier conjecture, proved that hookworm infection occurs through the skin.

Schaudinn also carried out research into human and animal (bird) malaria, providing the basis for subsequent researchers to discover the causative blood parasite. Schaudinn's other work included the demonstration of an alternation of generations in the Foraminifera (rhizopod protozoans) and the Coccidae (scale insects).

Schawlow, Arthur Leonard

(1921–   )

AMERICAN PHYSICIST

> To do successful research you don't need to know everything. You just need to know of the one thing that isn't known.
> —Springer house magazine

Born in Mount Vernon, New York, Schawlow was educated at the University of Toronto and worked at Columbia (1949–51) and at the Bell Telephone Laboratories (1951–61). He became professor of physics at Stanford University in 1961, retiring in 1991.

Schawlow is noted for his work on the development and use of lasers. He collaborated with Charles Townes in early work on maser principles and is generally credited as a coinventor of the laser. Although he did not share in Townes's Nobel award (1964), Schawlow did share the 1981 Nobel Prize for physics with Nicholaas Bloembergen for their (independent) research in laser spectroscopy. In particular, Schawlow, with Theodor Hänsch, has used tunable dye lasers for high-resolution spectroscopy.

Scheele, Karl Wilhelm

(1742–1786)

SWEDISH CHEMIST

I realized the necessity to learn about fire...
But I soon realized that it was not possible to form an opinion on the phenomena of fire as long as one did not understand air.
—On his studies of the composition of air.
Letter to Anders Retzius (1768)

Scheele (**shay**-le), who came from a poor background in Straslund (now in Germany), received little schooling and was apprenticed to an apothecary in Göteborg when he was 14 years old. In 1770 he moved to Uppsala to practice as an apothecary. He met and impressed Torbern Bergman, the professor of chemistry there, and was elected to the Stockholm Royal Academy of Sciences in 1775. Also in 1775 he moved to Köping where he established his own pharmacy.

In 1777 Scheele published his only book, *Chemical Observations and Experiments on Air and Fire*. In this work he stated that the atmosphere is composed of two gases, one supporting combustion, which he named "fire air" (oxygen), and the other preventing it, which he named "vitiated air" (nitrogen). He was successful in obtaining oxygen in about 1772, two years before Joseph Priestley. He also discovered chlorine, manganese, barium oxide, glycerol, silicon tetrafluoride, and a long list of acids, both organic and inorganic, including citric, prussic, and tartaric acids. One further piece of work that had unexpectedly important consequences was his demonstration of the effects of light on silver salts.

Despite receiving many lucrative offers from Germany and England, Scheele remained at Köping for the rest of his life devoting himself to his chemical researches. Although his work must have suffered from his isolation, and he lost priority in many discoveries owing to delay in publication, he is still frequently referred to as the greatest experimental chemist of the 18th century.

Scheiner, Christoph

(1575–1650)

GERMAN ASTRONOMER

Scheiner (**shI**-ner), a Jesuit who became professor of mathematics and Hebrew at the university in his native city of Ingolstadt, claimed to be the discoverer of sunspots. In 1611 Scheiner was observing the Sun telescopically through a thick mist when he discovered "several black drops." His observations were published in 1612. Galileo replied with his *Letters on the Solar Spots* (1613) claiming that he had first observed such spots in 1610. He also argued against Scheiner's interpretation of such spots as small planets circling the Sun. Scheiner, although a Copernican, campaigned against the publication of Galileo's dialogues and did much to turn the Jesuits against Galileo. In 1615 he made the first Keplerian telescope and in 1630 he published his basic treatise on sunspots *Rosa ursina* (The Red Bear).

Schiaparelli, Giovanni Virginio

(1835–1910)

ITALIAN ASTRONOMER

> The meteor showers are the product of the dissolution of the comets and consist of very minute particles.
> —On the origin of meteors.
> Letter, December 1872

Schiaparelli (skyah-pa-**rel**-ee) was born at Savigliano in Italy. After graduating from Turin in 1854, he studied under Johann Encke in Berlin and Friedrich Struve in St. Petersburg. In 1860 he became director of the Brera Observatory, Milan, where he remained until he retired in 1900.

Schiaparelli worked mainly on the solar system, discovering the planetoid Hesperia in 1861. He contributed to the theory of meteors when he showed in 1866 that they follow cometary orbits. He also made careful studies of Mars, Venus, and Mercury. In 1877 Mars approached Earth at its nearest point, a mere 35 million miles. He observed what he called "canali." In Italian this means not "canals" but "channels," but the word was mistranslated into English as the former, which led to much controversy. Schiaparelli himself was neutral as to their origin. He would not rule out that they were constructed rather than natural but nor would he conclude from their geometrical precision that they were buildings, for he pointed out that other examples of regularity, such as Saturn's rings, had not been man-made. It was other astronomers, such as Percival Lowell and Camille Flammarion, who made extravagant claims about the "canals," not Schiaparelli.

After detailed observations of Venus and Mercury he announced that their period of axial rotation was the same as their sidereal period (the time taken to orbit the Sun, relative to the stars). Thus they would always keep the same face to the Sun. It was not until the early 1960s that this view was disproved, and then only by the use of sophisticated radar techniques.

Schickard, Wilhelm

(1592–1635)

GERMAN SCIENTIST

The son of a carpenter from Herrenberg in Germany, Schickard (**shik**-art) was educated at the local monastery school and the University of Tübingen. After several years working as a Lutheran pastor, Schickard returned to Tübingen as professor of oriental languages. His interests also extended to the natural sciences, a combination of interests not uncommon in the 17th century.

Schickard became a friend of the great Johannes Kepler when he visited Tübingen in 1617. In a 1623 letter to Kepler he spoke of a machine he had constructed "consisting of eleven complete and six incomplete sprocket wheels which can calculate." He promised to send one to Kepler but later apologized that it had been destroyed in a fire. He also referred to his invention as a "calculating clock." Little more is known about his life other than that he succeeded Michael Mastlin as professor of astronomy at Tübingen in 1631 and that he died of bubonic plague in 1635.

At this point Schickard was ignored for three centuries. In 1935 Fritz Hammer came across Schickard's sketch of his calculating clock while going through Kepler's papers. Many years later, in 1956, Hammer found another diagram and some instructions in Schickard's papers in Stuttgart. Hammer published his finds in 1957. Upon hearing of this a modern Tübingen professor, Bruno von Freytag, produced a working model of Schickard's invention.

The device consisted of six numbered dials connected to six axles. Tens were carried or borrowed by installing a single toothed gear on each axle, linked by an intermediate gear to the adjacent axle. The machine is of considerable interest to historians as it preceded the work of Pascal – long thought to have invented the first mechanical calculator – by twenty years.

Schiff, Moritz

(1823–1896)

GERMAN PHYSIOLOGIST

Schiff (shif), the son of a merchant from Frankfurt am Main in Germany, obtained his doctorate from the University of Göttingen in 1844. After working in the Frankfurt Zoological Museum, Schiff moved to Bern in 1854 as professor of comparative anatomy where he remained until 1863 when he was appointed to the chair of physiology in Florence. A campaign against vivisection forced Schiff to leave Florence in 1876 when he accepted the professorship of physiology at Geneva.

In 1856 Schiff demonstrated that removal of the thyroid gland in dogs and guinea pigs resulted in their death. He also showed, in 1885, that the effect could be postponed by grafting a piece of the gland elsewhere in the animal before its removal. The relief was however only temporary as the gland was absorbed by the body. Unfortunately Schiff's earlier work was unknown to surgeons like Theodor Kocher when, in the early 1870s, they began to perform thyroidectomies in humans, operations that often led to tragic ends.

Schiff had also worked in the 1850s on nervous control of the blood supply. By cutting the brainstem he was able to show the existence of special centers in the brain for the control of vasomotor nerves, nerves that narrow or widen blood vessels as the body's demand rises and falls. The same results were independently obtained by Claude Bernard.

Schimper, Andreas Franz Wilhelm

(1856–1901)

GERMAN PLANT ECOLOGIST

Schimper (**shim**-per) was born at Strasbourg, which is now in France. He first became interested in natural history while on excursions with his father, Wilhelm Philipp, who was professor of natural history and geology at the University of Strasbourg. Andreas entered the university in 1874, obtained his doctorate in natural philosophy in 1878, and in 1880 earned a fellowship to Johns Hopkins University. He returned to Germany in 1882 and became lecturer and eventually professor at the University of Bonn (1886), where he remained until in 1898 he was appointed professor of botany at the University of Basel.

While at Strasbourg Schimper made an important study of the nature and growth of starch grains showing that they arise in specific organelles, which he named chloroplasts. However, it is to the study of plant geography and ecology that he made his most significant contributions. During travels to the West Indies in 1881 and 1882–83, Brazil (1886), Ceylon (Sri Lanka) and Java (1889–90), and the Canary Islands, Cameroons, East Africa, Seychelles, and Sumatra (1898–99) with the *Valdivia* deep-sea expedition, he made ecological studies of tropical vegetation. His results led to publication of important papers on the morphology and biology of epiphytes and littoral vegetation, culminating with his masterpiece, *Pflanzengeographie auf physiologischer Grundlage* (1898; Plant Geography Upon a Physiological Basis), which relates the physiological structure of plants to their type of environment.

Schleiden, Matthias Jakob

(1804–1881)

GERMAN BOTANIST

As a popularizer he was a model, as a scientist an initiator.
—L. Errera, *Revue scientifique de la France et de l'étranger*
(1882; Scientific Review of France and Other Countries)

Schleiden (**shlI**-den) was born at Hamburg in Germany and studied law at Heidelberg; he then returned to Hamburg to practice as a lawyer. However, he soon became fully occupied by his interest in botany and graduated in 1831 from the University of Jena, where he became professor of botany in 1839.

Instead of becoming involved in plant classification – the pursuit of most of his botanical contemporaries – Schleiden studied plant growth and structure under the microscope. This led to his *Contributions to Phytogenesis* (1838), which stated that the various structures of the plant are composed of cells or their derivatives. He thus formulated the cell theory for plants, which was layer eleborated and extended to animals by the German physiologist Theodor Schwann. Schleiden recognized the significance of the cell nucleus and sensed its importance in cell division, although he thought (wrongly) that new cells were produced by budding from its surface. He was one of the first German biologists to accept Darwinism.

Schmidt, Bernhard Voldemar

(1879–1935)

ESTONIAN TELESCOPE MAKER

Schmidt (shmit), who was born on the island of Naissaar, in Estonia, received little education. After working in Gothenburg, Sweden, he went in 1901 to study engineering at Mittweida in Germany, near Jena. He set up his own workshop in 1904 in Mittweida and manufactured high-grade mirrors to be used in telescopes. He also built some reflecting telescopes, including one for the Potsdam Astrophysical Observatory, and set up his own observatory. In 1926 he moved to the Hamburg Observatory in Bergedorf. As a master craftsman he worked unaided even though he had lost his right arm as a boy. He was also an alcoholic and claimed to have his best ideas after prolonged drinking bouts. He died in a mental hospital.

His name is known to all astronomers as the designer of one of the most basic items of observatory equipment, the Schmidt telescope. This was built to overcome some of the penalties inherent in the design of the large parabolic reflectors like the Mount Wilson 100-inch (2.5-m) telescope. Parabolic mirrors are used rather than spherical ones in telescopes to correct the optical defect known as spherical aberration and thus allow the light from an object to be accurately and sharply focused. This accurate focusing only occurs, however, for light falling on the center of a parabolic mirror. Light falling at some distance from the center is not correctly focused owing to a different optical distortion in the image, known as coma.

This limits the use of parabolic reflectors to a narrow field of view and thus precludes them from survey work and the construction of star maps. Schmidt replaced the primary parabolic mirror with a spherical mirror, which though coma-free did however suffer from spherical aberration, thus preventing the formation of a sharp image. To overcome this fault Schmidt introduced a "corrector plate" through which the light passed before reaching the spherical mirror. It was so shaped to be thickest in the center and least thick between its edges and the center. In this way a comparatively wide beam of light passing through it is refracted in such a way as to just compensate for the aberration produced by the mirror and produce an overall sharp image on a (curved) photographic plate.

Schmidt's first hybrid reflector/refractor was ready and installed in the Hamburg Observatory in the early 1930s. Observatories have since used the Schmidt telescope to photograph large areas of the sky. The whole sky has now been surveyed with these instruments and the results, which include the very faintest objects down to a magnitude of 21, are published in the Palomar Sky Survey and the Southern Sky Survey.

Schmidt, Ernst Johannes

(1877–1933)

DANISH BIOLOGIST

Schmidt was born at Jaegerspris in Denmark and became director of the Carlsberg Physiological Laboratory, Copenhagen. He is chiefly known for his discovery of the breeding ground and life history of the European eel in 1904. Schmidt attained this end by a careful compilation of statistics of the length of eel larvae (leptocephali) found at different points and at different times in the Atlantic. From these he was able to link together leptocephali of similar size, radiating from a central area, the smaller and younger nearer the center. The center of radiation, and the breeding ground of all European eels, proved to be the Sargasso Sea, near Bermuda. Schmidt also carried out research and produced publications on bacteria and the flora of the island of Ko Chang, Thailand.

Schmidt, Maarten

(1929–   )

DUTCH–AMERICAN ASTRONOMER

Born in Groningen in the Netherlands, Schmidt graduated from the university there in 1949 and obtained his PhD in 1956 from Leiden University. After working at the Leiden Observatory from 1953 to 1959, he moved to America, taking up an appointment at the California Institute of Technology as a staff member of the Hale Observatories. He was made professor of astronomy in 1964 and also served as director of the Hale Observatories from 1978 to 1980.

Schmidt has investigated the structure and dynamics of our Galaxy and the formation of stars but he is best known for his research on quasars, or quasi-stellar objects. In 1960 Alan Sandage and Thomas Matthews identified a compact radio source, known as 3C 48, with a 16th-magnitude starlike object that was found to have a most curious spectrum. Soon, other optical identifications were made, including that of 3C 273 with a 13th-magnitude object that had an equally puzzling spectrum. These objects became known as quasars. In 1963 Schmidt was the first to produce a satisfactory interpretation of the spectrum of a quasar.

Schmidt realized that certain broad emission lines in the spectrum of 3C 273 were the familiar hydrogen lines but shifted in wavelength by an unprecedented amount. According to the Doppler effect, light emitted from a source that is moving away from an observer increases its wavelength, i.e., its spectral lines shift toward the red end of the spectrum. The faster an object is moving away, the greater the so-called red shift. Hubble had assumed that the red shift of the galaxies was explained by the Doppler effect: the galaxies were receding as the universe expanded and that as the velocity and hence the distance of a galaxy increased, its red shift increased accordingly. 3C 273 had an immense red shift. Assuming it to be a Doppler shift resulting from the expansion of the universe, Schmidt was amazed when he found that 3C 273 must be a billion light-years away. In that case, how could such a small source be visible at such an enormous distance? It would need to be as luminous as a hundred galaxies and it was by no means clear what physical mechanism could yield so much energy from such a compact source. Schmidt's work was soon confirmed by the red-shift interpretation of the spectra of other quasars; they all possessed unusually large red shifts. There arose a long debate as to whether the Doppler effect did explain the quasar red shift but it is now generally accepted that this is the case.

By the end of the 1960s many quasars had been discovered and their distribution mapped in the heavens. Schmidt realized that this allowed him to test the cosmological steady-state doctrine of Thomas Gold and others, which assumes that the universe on a large scale looks the same at all times and all places. He found, however, on examining the distribution of quasars and using the Doppler interpretation of their red shifts, that their numbers increase with distance and that they are indeed the most distant objects in the universe. Assuming that the big-bang rather than the steady-state theory is correct, they are also the youngest objects in the universe.

The discovery of the quasars with the problems they posed produced an enormous growth in astronomical research that led to the discovery of even stranger objects, such as pulsars, and the continued search for black holes. Huge black holes are indeed thought to be the source of the prodigious energy of quasars.

Schönbein, Christian Friedrich

(1799–1868)

GERMAN CHEMIST

Schönbein (**shu(r)n**-bIn) was born at Metzingen in Germany. After studying at the universities of Tübingen and Erlangen, he took up an appointment at the University of Basel in 1828, staying there for the rest of his life.

Many stories relate how he discovered nitrocellulose (guncotton) in 1846. In all of them a bottle in which he had been distilling nitric and sulfuric acids broke on the floor of the kitchen. In some stories, as he was forbidden by his wife to experiment in the kitchen, he is supposed to have panicked and wiped the mess up with his wife's cotton apron. In others he is unable to find a mop and uses the nearest thing to hand, his wife's cotton apron. Put to dry over the stove it flared up without smoke: Schönbein had discovered the first new explosive since gunpowder. (He was nearly anticipated in his discovery of guncotton: Théophile Pelouze had obtained an inflammable material in 1838 by treating cotton with nitric acid, but he failed to follow it up.)

Schönbein saw what a valuable commodity he had and quickly secured the appropriate patents on it. He gave exclusive rights of manufacture to John Hall and Sons in Britain but, unfortunately, their factory at Faversham blew up in July 1847, killing 21 workers. Similar lethal explosions occurred in France, Russia, and Germany. Its properties were too valuable to allow chemists to abandon it altogether: it was smokeless and four times more powerful than gunpowder; properly controlled it would make an ideal propellant. It was finally modified by Frederick Abel and James Dewar later in the century in the forms of Poudre B and cordite.

In 1840 Schönbein discovered ozone, the allotropic form of oxygen. Investigating the curious smell that seemed to linger around electrical equipment, he traced it to a gas (O_3) that he named after the Greek word for smell (*ozon*).

Schramm, David Norman

(1945–   )

AMERICAN PHYSICIST

Born in St. Louis, Missouri, Schramm was educated at the Massachusetts Institute of Technology and the California Institute of Technology, where he took his PhD in 1971. After a four-year spell at the University of Texas, he moved to the University of Chicago, becoming professor of physics in 1977.

Cosmology has long been a subject rich in speculation but poor in experimental control. Schramm has sought to bridge the gap through a union between cosmology and particle physics. From one side, Schramm saw, cosmology could offer insights to physics. Thus he noted physicists spoke of what happened at high energies well beyond the reach of any actual accelerator. They were not, however, beyond the capacity of the big bang. Hence the study of the big bang could perhaps throw light on and control the speculations of high-energy physicists.

Conversely, a well-established theory of elementary particles could test speculative cosmological theory. For example, Schramm has argued, from the nuclear reactions occurring when the universe was one second old, it follows that the number of fundamental particles must be small. Because of the amount of helium-4 in the universe, a consequence of the big bang, there can be no more than four families of quarks and leptons. Three are currently known.

Schrieffer, John Robert

(1931–   )

AMERICAN PHYSICIST

Born in Oak Park, Illinois, Schrieffer was educated at the Massachusetts Institute of Technology and the University of Illinois, where he obtained his PhD in 1957. After serving as a postdoctoral fellow in Europe at Birmingham and Copenhagen he worked at the University of Illinois from 1959 until 1962 when he moved to the University of Pennsylvania, Philadelphia, being appointed professor of physics there in 1964. He was professor of physics at the University of California, Santa Barbara (1980–91), moving to the Florida State University, Tallahassee, in 1992.

Schrieffer worked on superconductivity. In 1972 he was awarded the Nobel Prize for physics with John Bardeen and Leon N. Cooper for their formulation in 1957 of the first successful theory of superconductivity, the BCS theory.

Schrödinger, Erwin

(1887–1961)

AUSTRIAN PHYSICIST

> Thus the task is not so much to see what no one has yet seen; but to think what nobody has yet thought, about that which everybody sees.
>
> —Quoted by L. Bertlanffy in
> *Problems of Life* (1952)

Schrödinger (**shru(r)**-ding-er or **shroh**-ding-er), the son of a prosperous Viennese factory owner, was educated at both the gymnasium and the university in his native city, where he obtained his doctorate in 1910. After serving as an artillery officer in World War I, he taught at various German-speaking universities before he succeeded Max Planck as professor of physics at the University of Berlin in 1927.

Before long, however, Schrödinger's bitter opposition to the Nazis drove him, in 1933, into his first period of exile, which he spent in Oxford, England. Homesick, he allowed himself to be tempted by the University of Graz in Austria in 1936 but, after the Anschluss in 1938, he found himself once more under a Nazi government which this time was determined to arrest him. Schrödinger had no alternative but to flee. He was however fortunate in that the prime minister of Eire, Eamonn De Valera, himself a mathematician, was keen to attract him to a newly established Institute of Advanced Studies in Dublin. Working there from 1939 Schrödinger gave seminars that attracted many eminent foreign physicists (as well as the frequent presence of De Valera) until his retirement in 1956 when he returned to Austria.

Starting from the work of Louis de Broglie, Schrödinger in the period 1925–26 developed wave mechanics, one of the several varieties of quantum theory that emerged in the mid-1920s. He was deeply dissatisfied with the early quantum theory of the atom developed by Niels Bohr, complaining of the apparently arbitrary nature of a good many of the quantum rules. Schrödinger took the radical step of eliminating the particle altogether and substituting for it waves alone.

His first step was to derive an equation to describe the behavior of an electron orbiting an atomic nucleus. The de Broglie equation giving the wavelength $\lambda = h/mv$ (where h is the Planck constant and mv the momentum) presented too simple a picture for in reality, particularly with the inner orbits, the attractive force of the nucleus would result in a very complex and variable configuration. He eventually succeeded in establishing his famous wave equation, which when applied to the hydrogen atom yielded all the results of Bohr and de Broglie. It was for this work that he shared the 1933 Nobel Prize for physics with Paul Dirac.

Despite the considerable predictive success of wave mechanics, as the theory became known, there remained two problems for Schrödinger. He still had to attach some physical meaning to ideas of the nature of an electron, which was difficult if it was nothing but a wave; he also had to interpret the ψ function occurring in the wave equation, which described the wave's amplitude. He tried to locate the electron by constructing stable "wave packets" from many small waves, which it was hoped would behave in the same way as a particle in classical mechanics. The packets were later shown to be unstable.

Nor was his interpretation of the ψ function as a measure of the spread of an electron any more acceptable. Instead the probabilistic interpretation of Max Born soon developed into a new orthodoxy. Schrödinger found such a view totally unacceptable, joining those other founders of quantum theory, Einstein and de Broglie, in an unrelenting opposition to the indeterminism entering physics.

In 1944 Schrödinger published his *What Is Life?*, one of the seminal books of the period. Partly due to its timely publication it influenced a good many talented young physicists who, disillusioned by the bombing of Hiroshima, wanted no part of atomic physics. Schrödinger solved their problem by revealing a discipline free from military applications, significant and, perhaps just as important, largely unexplored. He argued that the gene was not built like a crystal but that it was rather what he termed an "aperiodic solid." He went on to talk of the possibility of a "code" and observed that "with the molecular picture of the gene it is no longer inconceivable that the miniature code should precisely correspond with a highly complicated and specified plan of development." It is not surprising that such passages,

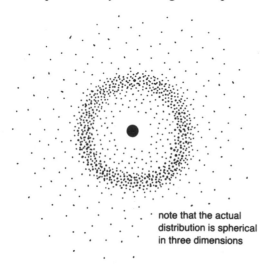

note that the actual distribution is spherical in three dimensions

HYDROGEN ATOM The hydrogen atom according to Erwin Schrödinger.

written with more insight than that contained in most contemporary biochemical works, inspired a generation of scientists to explore and decipher such a code.

Schrötter, Anton

(1802–1875)

AUSTRIAN CHEMIST

Schrötter (**shru(r)**-ter) was the son of an apothecary from Olomouc (now in the Czech Republic). He taught chemistry at Graz and the Vienna Polytechnical Institute. From 1845 he was master of the Austrian mint.

Schrötter was the first to recommend hydrogen peroxide for bleaching hair but his greatest achievement was the discovery in 1845 of red phosphorus. Until this time white phosphorus had been used in the production of matches. This was highly flammable and also toxic, producing inflammation and eventual necrosis of the jaw, a condition popularly known as "phossy jaw."

Schrötter found that if ordinary phosphorus was heated in an enclosed vessel the allotrope, red phosphorus, would be produced. This had the advantage of being neither spontaneously flammable nor toxic. He lectured on his discovery in Birmingham, England, in 1849 and Arthur Albright, the British phosphorus producer, quickly introduced the new process into his Oldbury factory. Schrötter's discovery was eventually given legal backing in Britain under the White Phosphorus Prohibition Act of 1908.

Schultze, Max Johann Sigismund

(1825–1874)

GERMAN ZOOLOGIST

Schultze (**shuult**-se) was born at Freiberg in Germany. He was educated at the University of Griefswald, where his father was professor of anatomy, and the University of Berlin. After a brief period on the staff of the University of Halle he moved in 1859 to Bonn where he served as professor of zoology until his sudden death in 1874 from a perforated ulcer.

In 1861 Schultze, who had worked on the cellular structure of a wide variety of animals, published a famous paper in which he emphasized the role of protoplasm in the workings of the cell. Cells, he argued, were "nucleated protoplasm" or "the physical basis of life," the protoplasm and not the cell wall being the important constituent. This he illustrated by pointing out that some cells, for example those of the embryo, do not have bounding membranes.

In 1866 Schultze went on to formulate the so-called duplicity theory of vision. He had noticed that in diurnal birds the retina consisted mainly of cones but nocturnal birds possessed a retina with an abundance of rods. This led him to propose that cones must respond to colored light while rods should be more sensitive to black and white.

Schuster, Sir Arthur

(1851–1934)

BRITISH PHYSICIST AND
SPECTROSCOPIST

Schuster (**shoo**-ster) was the son of a Frankfurt textile merchant and banker who, unwilling to remain in the city after its annexation by Prussia in the wake of the 1866 war, moved with his family to Manchester, England. Schuster became a British citizen in 1875 and studied physics at Owens College, Manchester, and the University of Heidelberg where he obtained his doctorate in 1873. Schuster then spent the period 1875–81 at the Cavendish Laboratory, Cambridge, but returned to Manchester to serve first as professor of applied mathematics and from 1889 to 1907 as professor of physics. His somewhat premature retirement at the age of 56 was spent on his own research and the formation of the International Research Council, which he served as first secretary from 1919 to 1928.

Initially Schuster worked as a spectroscopist. In 1881 he refuted the speculation of George Stoney that spectral lines could be regarded as the harmonics of a fundamental vibration. This was done by a statistical analysis of the spectral lines of five elements in which he showed their random distribution. Somewhat discouraged by this result he turned to the study of the passage of an electric current through a gas.

In the 1880s he was the first to show that an electric current is conducted by ions. He went on to propose how the ratio between the charge and the mass of cathode rays could be calculated and in fact described the technique later used by J. J. Thomson in his determination of the charge on the electron. He further proposed, in 1896, that the new x-rays of Wilhelm Röntgen were in fact transverse vibrations of the ether of very small wavelength.

One of Schuster's greatest achievements was the physics department of Manchester University. He raised funds to construct a new laboratory in 1897, was bold enough to create new departments, such as that of meteorology in 1905, and made ample provisions for research. He also had the insight to pick as his successor Ernest Rutherford who, despite invitations from the Smithsonian, Yale, and King's College, London, recognized the value of Schuster's achievement by preferring the Manchester invitation.

Schwann, Theodor

(1810–1882)

GERMAN PHYSIOLOGIST

> The treatise [is] worthy to be ranked among the most important steps by which the science of physiology has ever been advanced.
> —Henry Smith, from the introduction to the first English edition (1847) of Schwann's *Mikroskopische Untersuchungen* (1839; Microscopical Researches)

Born at Neuss in Germany, Schwann (shvahn) was educated at the universities of Bonn, Würzburg, and Berlin where he obtained his MD in 1834. He worked with Johannes Müller in Berlin from 1834 until 1838 when he moved to Belgium, serving as professor of anatomy first at Louvain (1838–47) and thereafter at Liège until his death.

Schwann's first experiments at Berlin were on muscle contraction. He showed that the mechanism of contraction could be explained without invoking any vital principles – a marked departure from the teachings of Müller. This mechanistic philosophy was fruitfully developed by Schwann's successors at Berlin, Emil du Bois-Reymond and Hermann von Helmholtz. Schwann next conducted some experiments to disprove (again) the theory of spontaneous generation, which was enjoying a renaissance in the mid 1830s. One unexpected outcome of his experiments on putrefaction and fermentation was his discovery in 1836, independently of Cagniard de la Tour, that yeast is involved in fermentation. The same year Schwann also discovered the digestive enzyme pepsin.

His most memorable achievement however is his *Mikroskopische Untersuchungen* (1839; Microscopical Researches) in which he first formulated, at the same time as Matthias Schleiden, the most important of all ideas in modern biology, namely that "cellular formation might be a widely extended, perhaps a universal principle for the formation of organic substances."

In 1838 Schleiden had proposed that all plant tissue was composed of nucleated cells. Using the newly introduced achromatic microscope Schwann went on to examine a variety of tissues taken from several different animals. He surmised that fibers, ducts, etc., do not form directly from molecules but rather are built up from cells. The process of cell formation he saw as something like that of crystallization: cells were not formed from other cells but somehow condensed out of intercellular "nutrient liquid." One further radical misconception was that the cellular material, Schwann's cytoblastema, was devoid of structure.

Despite such errors the cell theory met with rapid acceptance. Improvements were soon made. Robert Remak first described cell division in 1841 and by 1855 Rudolf Virchow could issue the new dogma *omnis cellula e cellula* (all cells come from cells). The cytoblastema also came in for revision; renamed protoplasm, it was shown by Max Schultze in 1861 to have definite properties and a structure.

Despite these successes Schwann's work on fermentation was savagely criticized by leading chemists of the time, notably Justus von Liebig and Friedrich Wöhler. A particularly damaging paper by the pair was published in 1839 after which Schwann found it impossible to continue his career in Germany. In Belgium he conscientiously carried out his professional duties and invented some useful equipment for the mining industry. His brilliant contributions to physiology, however, virtually ceased. Not until Pasteur's work in the 1850s was Schwann vindicated.

Schwartz, Melvin

(1932–   )

AMERICAN PHYSICIST

Schwartz was born in New York and educated at Columbia University, where he obtained his PhD in 1958. He remained at Columbia until 1966, when he was appointed to the chair of physics at Stanford, California.

In 1961 Schwartz, in collaboration with his Columbia colleagues Leon Lederman and Jack Steinberger, performed what has since come to be known as the two-neutrino experiment. All three shared the 1988 Nobel Prize for physics.

Long before his Nobel award Schwartz had abandoned academic science. Physics, he said, in the earlier days had been "a lot of fun." But after the bureaucrats moved in and set up committees to control finance and direct research, he found his work obstructed and his time spent less and less on physics and more and more on the preparation of reports. Consequently he left Stanford in 1979, moved to "Silicon Valley" in California, and set up his own company, Digital Pathways, specializing in computer security. He returned to academic life in 1991, when he was appointed professor of physics at Columbia, New York.

Schwarz, John Henry

(1941–)

AMERICAN MATHEMATICAL PHYSICIST

Born in North Adams, Massachusetts, Schwarz was educated at Harvard and the University of California, Berkeley, where he completed his PhD in 1966. After working at Princeton until 1972, he moved to the California Institute of Technology and was appointed professor of theoretical physics there in 1985.

In 1970 Yoichiro Nambu had proposed that elementary particles may not be particles at all but could be vibrating rotating strings. Schwarz saw in this idea a way to explain the behavior of hadrons – i.e., particles such as protons and neutrons, which respond to the strong nuclear force. Hadrons were known to be composed of quarks and, in the new model, the quarks could be seen as joined by stringlike connections. The theory required space to have 26 dimensions, the existence of a massless particle, and the presence of tachyons (particles supposedly able to travel faster than light). More significantly, however, string theory had to compete with the more plausible account of hadrons proposed by Sheldon Glashow and others, known as quantum chromodynamics (QCD). Against competition from this source string theory withered away.

Schwarz, however, continued to work on string theory and in collaboration with Michael Green reduced the dimensions demanded by early theories to ten. They also eliminated the need for tachyons. As for the massless particle, it seemed to possess precisely the properties demanded by Einstein's theory of general relativity for the carrier of the gravitational force, a fact that was of interest to cosmologists.

Further, the new theory carried other implications. It exhibited a deep symmetry, known as supersymmetry, which seemed able to unify two fundamentally different categories of particles: fermions and bosons. Bosons are not conserved and have an integral spin; fermions are conserved and have a spin of one half. Schwarz demonstrated how they could be seen as waves moving in a closed loop, with fermions moving in one direction and bosons in the other direction.

The fact that the theory needs space–time to have ten dimensions rather than the four observed is explainable if the six "extra" dimensions are extremely small, curled into six-dimensional balls with a diameter of about 10^{-35} meter.

Schwarz has published a full account of his work, in collaboration with Green and Ed Witten, in *Superstring Theory* (1987, 2 vols.).

Schwarzschild, Karl

(1873–1916)

GERMAN ASTRONOMER

The greatest German astronomer of the last 100 years.
—Berlin Academy of Sciences dedication on inaugurating the Karl Schwarzschild telescope (1960)

Schwarzschild (**shvarts**-shilt or **shworts**-chIld) was the son of a prosperous Jewish businessman from Frankfurt am Main in Germany. His interest in astronomy arose while he was at school and he had published two papers on binary orbits by the time he was 16. Following two years at the University of Strasbourg, he went in 1893 to the University of Munich, obtaining his PhD in 1896. He worked at the Kuffner Observatory in Vienna from 1896 to 1899 and after a period of lecturing and writing became in 1901 associate professor, later professor, at the University of Göttingen and director of its observatory. In 1909 he was appointed director of the Astrophysical Observatory in Potsdam. He volunteered for military service in 1914 at the beginning of World War I and was invalided home in 1916 with a rare skin disease from which he died.

Schwarzschild's practical skill was demonstrated by the instruments he designed, the measuring techniques he devised, and the observations he made. In the 1890s, while the use of photography for scientific purposes was still in its infancy, he developed methods whereby the apparent magnitude, i.e., observed brightness, of stars could be accurately measured from a photographic plate. At that time stellar magnitudes were usually determined by eye. He was then able to establish the photographic magnitude of 3,500 stars brighter than magnitude 7.5 and lying between 0° and 20° above the celestial equator. He also determined the magnitude of the same stars visually, demonstrating that the two methods do not yield identical results. This difference between the visual and photographic magnitude of a star, measured at a particular wavelength, is known as its color index.

Schwarzschild also made major contributions to theoretical astronomy, the subjects including orbital mechanics, the curvature of space, and the surface structure of the Sun. In 1906 he published a paper showing that stars could not just be thought of as a gas held together by its own gravity. Questions of thermodynamics arise, concerning the transfer of heat within the star both by radiation and convection, that need a full mathematical treatment.

Einstein's theory of general relativity was published in 1916. While serving in Russia, Schwarzschild wrote two papers on the theory, which were also published in 1916. He gave a solution – the first to be found – of the complex partial differential equations by which the theory is expressed mathematically and introduced the idea of what is now called the *Schwarzschild radius*. When a star, say, is contracting under the effect of gravity, if it attains a particular radius then the gravitational potential will become infinite. An object will have to travel at the velocity of light to escape from the gravitational field of the star. The value of this radius, the Schwarzschild radius, SR, depends on the mass of the body. If a body reaches a radius less than its SR nothing, including light, will be able to escape from it and it will be what is now known as a "black hole." The SR for the Sun is 3 kilometers while its actual radius is 700,000 kilometers. The theoretical study of black holes and the continuing search for them has become an important field in modern astronomy.

Schwarzchild's son, Martin, is also a noted astronomer.

Schwinger, Julian Seymour

(1918–1994)

AMERICAN PHYSICIST

Schwinger, who was born in New York City, developed his prowess for mathematics and physics at an early age. At 14 he entered the City College of New York, but later transferred to Columbia University. He received his BA degree from Columbia at the age of 17 (1936) and his doctorate three years later. Moving to the University of California at Berkeley, he worked as a research associate under J. Robert Oppenheimer. In the war years (1943–45) he worked at the Metallurgical Laboratory of the University of Chicago and at the Radiation Laboratory of the Massachusetts Institute of Technology. In 1945 he joined the faculty of Harvard as an associate professor of physics, and the next year was made full professor, one of the youngest in Harvard's history. He became professor of physics at the University of California, Los Angeles, in 1972.

Schwinger's most notable contribution to physics was in the fusion of electromagnetic theory and quantum mechanics into the science of quantum electrodynamics (the foundations of which had been laid by Paul Dirac, Werner Heisenberg, and Wolfgang Pauli). During World War II, Schwinger, and others such as Richard Feynman, Sin-Itiro Tomonaga, and Frank Dyson, developed the mathematical formulation of quantum electrodynamics in a way that was consistent with Einstein's theory of relativity. The new theory led to a better understanding of the interactions between charged particles and electromagnetic fields and proved useful in measuring and explaining the behavior of atomic and subatomic particles. Schwinger, Feynman, and Tomonaga, who had conducted their work independently – Feynman at the California Institute of Technology and Tomonaga at the Tokyo Education University – were subsequently rewarded with the 1965 Nobel Prize for physics.

Schwinger also conducted significant research into the properties of synchrotron radiation, produced when a fast moving charged particle is diverted in a magnetic field. He was the author of *Particles Sources and Fields* (1970).

Scott, Dukinfield Henry

(1854–1934)

BRITISH PALEOBOTANIST

Scott, the son of the architect Gilbert Scott, was born in London and studied classics at Oxford University before studying engineering for three years. He finally decided to pursue a career in botany rather than architecture and studied for his doctorate under Julius von Sachs at the University of Wurzburg. Scott gained his PhD in 1882 and was appointed to an assistantship at University College, London. He held various junior posts before becoming director of research at the Jodrell Laboratory, Kew, in 1892, a post he held until his retirement in 1906 after which he devoted himself to full-time research.

In 1889 Scott met William Williamson who awoke in him a passion for paleobotany. He worked mainly on the plants of the Carboniferous but also published such general works as his *Extinct Plants and Problems of Evolution* (1924). With Williamson and Albert Seward, Scott was one of the founders of the scientific study of fossil plants, a task as crucial to the study of evolution as better-known searches for fossil vertebrates.

Seaborg, Glenn Theodore

(1912–)

AMERICAN NUCLEAR CHEMIST

> People must understand that science is inherently neither a potential for good nor for evil. It is a potential to be harnessed by man to do his bidding.
> —Associated Press interview with Alton Blakeslee, 29 September 1964

Born in Ishpeming, Michigan, Seaborg graduated in 1934 and gained his doctorate in 1937 at the University of California. He rose to become full professor in the Berkeley faculty in 1945.

Over the period 1948–58 Seaborg and his collaborators extended the periodic table beyond uranium (element 92) – hence the term "transuranics" applied to artificial elements with atomic numbers higher than 92. Chief among his collaborators in the early days was Edwin McMillan (with whom he shared the Nobel Prize for chemistry in 1951), who with Philip Abelson had discovered the first transuranic element – neptunium (element 93) – in the spring of 1940. Neptunium was found to be a beta-particle emitter and it was thus expected that its decay product should be a transuranic element – the next in the series. In December 1940 Seaborg, McMillan, and their collaborators isolated element 94 – plutonium. It was realized that the transuranics formed a special series – the actinide transition series of elements, similar to the lanthanide series of rare-earth elements. Thus Seaborg and his coworkers were able to predict the chemical properties of further then-unknown transuranics and enabled them to be isolated. Seaborg's name is associated with the discovery or first isolation of a number of transuranics:

Element 93 neptunium 1940
Element 94 plutonium 1940
Element 95 americium 1944
Element 96 curium 1944
Element 97 berkelium 1949

Element 98 californium 1950
Element 101 mendelevium 1955
Element 102 nobelium 1958

It should be noted that all of these discoveries are correctly attributed to groups or teams of researchers and that attribution has been disputed in the past. In particular the first, unconfirmed, report of element 102 was in 1957 by an international group of physicists working at the Nobel Institute in Stockholm. The Berkeley team subsequently confirmed the discovery the next year. Similar work to Seaborg's was done in the former Soviet Union by Georgii Flerov.

Another discovery with which Seaborg is associated is the isolation of the isotope uranium–233 from thorium (1941). This may be an alternative source of fuel for nuclear fission – a route to nuclear energy that is still relatively unexplored.

The work on elements was directly relevant to the World War II effort to develop an atomic bomb, and from 1942 until 1946 Seaborg was on leave to the University of Chicago metallurgical laboratory, where he was made head of the laboratory's chemical-separation section. It is said that he was influential in determining the choice of plutonium rather than uranium in the first atomic-bomb experiments.

Seaborg went on to become chancellor of the University of California from 1958 to 1962 and was then chair of the U.S. Atomic Energy Commission until 1971. Element 106, synthesized in 1974, was named seaborgium in his honor.

Secchi, Pietro Angelo

(1818–1878)

ITALIAN ASTRONOMER

> Who knows whether or not an intimate relationship may exist between certain solar phenomena and some terrestrial ones?
> —*Le soleil* (1875–77; The Sun)

Secchi (**sek**-ee), who was born at Reggio in Italy, was a Jesuit who lectured in physics and mathematics. He spent some time abroad when the Jesuits were expelled from Rome, being at one time professor of physics at Georgetown University, Washington. He returned to Italy in 1849, becoming professor of astronomy and director of the observatory of the Roman College, which he rebuilt and reequipped.

He researched in stellar spectroscopy and his main work was done on spectral types. He introduced some order into the mass of new observations that was pouring in from the early spectroscopists. In 1867 he proposed four spectral classes. Class 1 had a strong hydrogen line and included blue and white stars; class 2 had numerous lines and included yellow stars; class 3 had bands rather than lines, which were sharp toward the red and fuzzy toward the violet and included both orange and red lines; finally, class 4 had bands that were sharp toward the violet and fuzzy toward the red and included red lines alone. These spectral types mark an important, and fairly straightforward, temperature sequence. Secchi's classification, as very much extended and modified by Edward Pickering and Annie Cannon, has become one of the basic tools of astrophysicists.

Sedgwick, Adam

(1785–1873)

BRITISH GEOLOGIST AND MATHEMATICIAN

Sedgwick was the son of the vicar of Dent in England. He graduated in mathematics from Cambridge University in 1808, was made a fellow in 1810, and was elected to the Woodwardian Chair of Geology in 1818, a post he retained until his death. He was made president of the Geological Society in 1829.

In 1831 he began a study of the Paleozoic rocks of Wales, choosing an older region than the Silurian recently discovered by Roderick Murchison. In 1835 he named the oldest fossiliferous strata the Cambrian (after Cambria, the ancient name for Wales). This immediately caused a problem for there was no reliable way to distinguish the Upper Cambrian from the Lower Silurian.

Sedgwick formed a close friendship with Murchison. The two made their most significant joint investigation with their identification of the Devonian System from studies in southwest England in 1839. The partnership between Sedgwick and Murchison was broken when Murchison annexed what Sedgwick considered to be his Upper Cambrian into the Silurian. The bitter dispute between the two over these Lower Paleozoic strata was not resolved until after Sedgwick's death, when Charles Lapworth proposed that the strata should form a new system – the Ordovician.

Sedgwick's works included *A Synopsis of the Classification of the British Paleozoic Rocks* (1855). In 1841, largely due to Sedgwick, a museum now bearing his name was opened to house the growing geological collection. Sedgwick was, throughout his life, a committed opponent of Darwin's theory of evolution.

Seebeck, Thomas Johann

(1770–1831)

ESTONIAN–GERMAN PHYSICIST

Seebeck (**zay**-bek or **see**-bek) was born into a wealthy family in Tallinn, the Estonian capital, and moved to Germany at the age of 17. He studied medicine in Berlin and in 1802 received an MD from the University of Göttingen. More interested in science than medical practice, he was wealthy enough to be able to devote his time to scientific research. In the early years of the 19th century he moved to Jena, where he became acquainted with an important intellectual circle of scientists and philosophers. His subsequent researches made him one of the most distinguished experimental physicists of his day.

Seebeck made investigations into photoluminescence (the luminescent emission from certain materials excited by light), the heating and chemical effects of different parts of the solar spectrum, polarization, and the magnetic character of electric currents. His most important work however came in 1822, after he had moved to Berlin. His discovery of thermoelectricity (the *Seebeck effect*) showed that electric currents could be produced by temperature differences. Seebeck joined two wires of different metals to form a closed circuit and applied heat to one of the junctions; a nearby magnetic needle behaved as if an electric current flowed around the circuit. He called this effect "thermomagnetism" (and later objected to the term thermoelectricity).

Sefström, Nils Gabriel

(1787–1845)

SWEDISH CHEMIST

Born at Ilsbo in Sweden, Sefström (**sev**-stru(r)m) studied under Jöns Berzelius in Stockholm, graduating in 1813. He taught chemistry at the School of Mines from 1820. While there he was informed that the local steelmakers were able to predict whether iron ore delivered at the foundries would produce steel that was brittle or not. On investigation he found that they tested the ore by dissolving it in hydrochloric acid and if a black powder resulted the steel was likely to be brittle. Sefström investigated and found that what was important in the test was the presence or absence in the ore of a new element. In 1830 he isolated the new element, which he named vanadium after the Norse goddess Vanadis. This proved to be identical to the metal discovered by Andrès Del Rio in 1801 and named erythronium. Del Rio had been dissuaded that this was in fact a new element and had abandoned his claim.

Segrè, Emilio Gino

(1905–1989)

ITALIAN–AMERICAN PHYSICIST

Segrè (se-**gray**), who was born at Tivoli in Italy, studied at the University of Rome under Enrico Fermi and obtained his doctorate there in 1928. He worked with Fermi until 1936, when he was appointed director of the physics laboratory at Palermo. He was dismissed for political reasons in 1938 and moved to America where he worked at the University of California, Berkeley, from 1938 to 1972, apart from the years 1943–46, which he spent at Los Alamos working on the development of the atom bomb. He became a professor in 1945.

Segrè made a number of significant discoveries in his career. In 1937 he filled one of the gaps in the periodic table at atomic number 43 when he showed that some molybdenum that had been irradiated with deuterium nuclei by Ernest Lawrence contained traces of the new element. As the first completely man-made element they gave it the appropriate name, technetium. Segrè played a part in the detection of element 85, astatine, and also plutonium in 1940.

His main achievement however was the discovery of the antiproton with Owen Chamberlain in 1955, for which they shared the 1959 Nobel Prize for physics. Segrè calculated that producing an antiproton would require about 6 billion electron-volts (Bev), which could be provided by the recently constructed bevatron at the University of California. He therefore went on to bombard copper with protons that had been accelerated to 6 Bev, thus yielding a large number of particles. As only one antiproton was produced to about 40,000 other particles his next problem was to detect this rare event.

This was done by noting that the antiproton would travel much faster than the other particles and at such speeds it would give off Cherenkov radiation in certain media and could thus be detected. The few particles that produced this radiation could more easily be screened to see if any of them possessed the necessary properties. Before long Segrè had identified antiprotons at the rate of about four per hour. The work of the California group was soon confirmed by Italian physicists who began to detect the tracks of antiprotons on photographic plates.

Seleucus

(about 2nd century BC)

BABYLONIAN ASTRONOMER

According to Strabo, Seleucus (se-**loo**-kus) was a Babylonian, an inhabitant of Seleucia on the Tigris (in modern Iraq). He is unique in that he is the only named astronomer in antiquity who followed Aristarchus of Samos in believing that the Earth moves. What his precise belief was is unclear. He is reported by Plutarch as asserting that the Earth rotates on its axis but whether he also accepted the annual motion around the Sun is still a matter of speculation. He is also reported as writing on the theory of the tides. He attributed the tides to the movement of the Moon, thinking that its motion pushed the air between it and the Earth, which in turn pushed the seas and oceans to produce the tides.

Semenov, Nikolay Nikolaevich

(1896–1986)

RUSSIAN CHEMIST

Semenov (sye-**myen**-of) was born in Saratov in Russia and educated at the University of Petrograd (now St. Petersburg). After working in various institutes in St. Petersburg he moved to Moscow University in 1944 as head of the department of chemical kinetics.

It was for work in this field that Semenov was awarded the 1956 Nobel Prize for chemistry, the first Russian to be so honored. He shared the prize with Sir Cyril Hinshelwood. His particular contribution was in the study of chemical chain reactions – an idea introduced by Max Bodenstein in 1913. Semenov investigated the idea of a chain reaction in the 1920s and was able to show that such reactions can lead to combustion and violent explosions when the chain branches, spreading with explosive rapidity. In 1934 he published a book on the subject, which was translated into English the following year, *Chemical Kinetics and Chain Reactions*.

Semmelweis, Ignaz Philipp

(1818–1865)

HUNGARIAN PHYSICIAN

Semmelweis (**zem**-el-vIs), the son of a storekeeper in Buda (now Budapest in Hungary), graduated in medicine from the University of Vienna in 1844. He specialized in obstetrics, being appointed assistant under J. Klein in the clinic of the Vienna General Hospital. Here he became concerned about the high incidence of puerperal fever, a streptococcal infection then endemic throughout 19th-century maternity wards. Although 5–10% of women in such wards died from the disease, particularly virulent outbreaks could more than treble such appalling figures. Few physicians had any idea of the cause of the complaint; although theories that emphasized an "atmosphere of infection" were known, they were largely discounted by the Viennese authorities.

Semmelweis began searching through the excellent hospital records maintained by the Hapsburg bureaucracy. He soon came across a striking statistic. Obstetric services of the hospital were provided by two distinct clinics, one staffed mainly by medical students and the other staffed by midwives. The mortality rate from puerperal fever in the former was three times higher than in the latter. Moreover Semmelweis pointed out that mortality figures had significantly increased with the appointment of Klein as professor of obstetrics in 1822, an observation that led to Semmelweis's virtual demotion.

Semmelweis tested many theories to account for such figures. The answer came to him early in 1847 when he heard of the death of his colleague Jakob Kolletschka, professor of forensic medicine, from an infection arising from a scalpel wound incurred during a postmortem. Semmelweis realized that the symptoms of Kolletschka's disease had been identical to puerperal fever. He proposed that "cadaveric particles" had fatally infected Kolletschka, the same particles that would be found on the hands of medical students (but not midwives) who routinely moved from assisting in postmortems to aid in the delivery ward. In May 1847 he made all students and doctors wash their hands thoroughly in a solution of chlorinated lime at the entrance of the wards. In 1848 deaths from puerperal fever had dropped from just under 10% to 1.27%.

His impressive results still failed to convince many of his colleagues and, disheartened, Semmelweis returned to his native Buda in 1850. He took up an appointment at the St. Rochus Hospital where his ideas were accepted. However, in later years his mind became unbalanced and he was committed to an asylum where, ironically, he died within a matter of days of an infection variously described as gangrene or puerperal fever. It was left to the more conventional Joseph Lister to rediscover the results of Semmelweis in the very year of his death.

Serre, Jean-Pierre

(1926–   )

FRENCH MATHEMATICIAN

Serre (sair), one of the outstanding French mathematicians of his generation, was born at Bages in France and studied at the Ecole Normale Supérieure. He has been a professor at the Collège de France since 1956 and a member of the French Academy of Sciences since 1976, as well as teaching at both the University of Nancy and Princeton University.

Serre's mathematical work began with a collaboration with Henri Cartan in which they were able to bring about a decisive reorientation of the theory of a complex variable. What Serre and Cartan did was to reformulate, in a completely original way, the central problems and results of the subject in terms of what is known as cohomology theory. Serre himself also did work of great originality and importance on the homotopy theory of spheres.

Homotopy and homology theory have been the area of his greatest mathematical achievements. Before his revolutionary work, the two subjects had been thought of as quite unconnected and unrelated. But Serre was able to show how to associate the homotopy group of a space with the homology groups of suitably constructed auxiliary spaces. By forging this link he succeeded in bringing to bear purely algebraic methods and techniques on the central problems of homotopy theory in a way that was entirely new and immensely fruitful.

In recognition of this fundamental work in revolutionizing homotopy theory Serre, aged only 28, was awarded a Field's Medal in 1954.

Sertürner, Friedrich Wilhelm Adam Ferdinand

(1783–1841)

GERMAN APOTHECARY

Sertürner (zair-**toor**-ner), whose father was Austrian, was a civil engineer in the service of the prince of Paderborn. Sertürner was born at Neuhaus (now in Germany) and on the death of his father was apprenticed to the court apothecary. Eventually, in 1820, he became the town pharmacist of Hameln.

In 1805 Sertürner published an account of a substance he had separated from opium. It turned out to be the sleep-inducing factor he was searching for so he consequently named it morphine after the Roman god of sleep, Morpheus. His paper received little attention and it was not until he republished his results in 1817 that it was picked up by physicians and rapidly entered their pharmacopoeia. The term was first reported in England as early as 1828.

Servetus, Michael

(1511–1553)

SPANISH PHYSICIAN

I shall burn, but this is a mere incident. We shall continue our discussion in eternity.
—Comment to his judges on being condemned to be burned at the stake as a heretic

Servetus (ser-**vee**-tus), the son of a notary, was born at Tudela in Spain and studied law in Toulouse and medicine at the University of Paris. After practicing medicine in Lyons for some years he considered it prudent to leave France for Italy but, for reasons never explained, he decided to travel via Calvin's Geneva where, in 1553, he was burned at the stake as a heretic. Servetus appears as the kind of man who once having seen the strength of a particular idea could never let it go. Thus when it struck him sometime in the late 1520s that the word "trinity" appears nowhere in the Bible he was a lost man, and he further invited disaster by sending his heretical works to Calvin in 1546. Calvin swore that if Servetus ever visited Geneva he would not get out alive.

However, before Calvin was allowed to fulfill his threat Servetus had made a noteworthy contribution to science by describing in *Christianismi restitutio* (1553; Restoring Christianity) the lesser circulation. This was the proposal that blood traveled from the right to the left side of the heart via the lungs and not, as had been supposed since Galen, through some minute perforations in the dividing wall or septum. It is not clear what led Servetus to this conclusion but it was certainly not derived from anatomical dissection.

As it was contained in but a few lines of a bulky theological work that was declared heretical and suffered in most cases the same fate as the author (only three copies have survived), it is not surprising that his views were virtually unknown in his own day and had no effect on the work of William Harvey.

Seward, Albert Charles

(1863–1941)

BRITISH PALEOBOTANIST

Seward, the son of a hardware dealer from Lancaster in northwest England, studied natural sciences at Cambridge University. After graduating in 1886 he spent a year in Manchester with William Williamson. Seward then spent his whole career at Cambridge, beginning in 1890 as a lecturer in botany and serving from 1906 until his retirement in 1936 as professor of botany. He had also held, from 1915, the office of master of Downing College.

With Dukinfield Scott, Seward did much to establish the foundations of the new discipline of paleobotany. Although he began with the study of Paleozoic plants he switched to the Mesozoic when invited by the British Museum (Natural History) to catalog their collection. The results were his *Jurassic Flora* (1900–1904) and his four volumes of *Fossil Plants for Students of Botany and Geology* (1898–1919). Seward also published a more discursive and popular work, *Plant Life through the Ages* (1931).

Seyfert, Carl Keenan

(1911–1960)

AMERICAN ASTRONOMER

Seyfert was born in Cleveland, Ohio, and studied at Harvard where he graduated in 1933 and obtained his PhD in 1936. He worked at the McDonald Observatory in Texas from 1936 to 1940, the Mount Wilson Observatory in California from 1940 to 1942 and the Case Institute of Technology in Cleveland, Ohio from 1942 to 1946. Seyfert then moved to the Vanderbilt University in Tennessee as associate professor and where from 1951 until his death he was director of the Dyer Observatory.

In 1943, while observing at Mount Wilson, Seyfert discovered an unusual class of spiral galaxies that have since been named for him. Optically they presented a very small intensely bright nucleus; spectroscopically they had very broad emission lines indicating the presence of very hot gas moving at considerable velocities.

Since their discovery Seyfert galaxies have become even more puzzling as they are now recognized to be emitters of prodigious amounts of energy from a very compact area. Energy is released not just in the form of light but also as x-rays and radio and infrared waves. It is felt that they are related in some way to quasars, discovered in the 1960s, although possessing a less powerful source of energy.

Shannon, Claude Elwood

(1916–   )

AMERICAN MATHEMATICIAN

Born in Gaylord, Michigan, Shannon graduated from the University of Michigan in 1936. He later worked both at the Massachusetts Institute of Technology and the Bell Telephone Laboratories. In 1958 he returned to MIT as Donner Professor of Science, a post he held until his retirement in 1978.

Shannon's greatest contribution to science has been in laying the mathematical foundations of communication theory. The central problem of communication theory is to determine the most efficient ways of transmitting messages. What Shannon did was to show a precise way of quantifying the information content of a message, thus making the study of information flow amenable to exact mathematical treatment. He first published his ideas in 1948 in *A Mathematical Theory of Communication*, written in collaboration with Warren Weaver. The resulting theory found wide application in such wide-ranging fields as circuit design, computer design, communication technology in general, and even in biology, psychology, semantics, and linguistics. Shannon's work made extensive use of the theory of probability; he also extended the concept of entropy from thermodynamics and applied it to lack of information.

Shannon has also made important contributions to computer science. In his paper *A Symbolic Analysis of Relay and Switching Circuits* (1938) he drew the analogy between truth values in logic and the binary states of circuits. He also coined the term "bit" for a unit of information.

Shapley, Harlow

(1885–1972)

AMERICAN ASTRONOMER

Shapley came from a farming background in Nashville, Missouri. He began his career as a crime reporter on the *Daily Sun* of a small Kansas town when he was 16. He entered the University of Missouri in 1907 intending to study journalism but took astronomy instead, gaining his MA in 1911. He then went on a fellowship to Princeton where he studied under Henry Russell and gained his PhD in 1913. From 1914 to 1921 he was on the staff of the Mount Wilson Observatory in California. Finally Shapley was appointed in 1921 to the directorship of the Harvard College Observatory where he remained until 1952, also serving for the period 1922–56 as Paine Professor of Astronomy.

Shapley's early work, under Russell, on eclipsing binaries proved that the group of stars, known as Cepheids, were not binary but were single stars that changed their brightness as they changed their size. Cepheids were thus the first "pulsating variables" to be discovered, the theory of the pulsation being supplied subsequently by Arthur Eddington.

Once at Mount Wilson, Shapley began to study Cepheids in globular clusters, huge spherical groups of closely packed stars. From this stemmed his fundamental work on the size and structure of our Galaxy. In 1915 he was able to make a bold speculation about the galactic structure. Using the relation between the period of Cepheids and their observed brightness, discovered in 1912 by Henrietta Leavitt, he was able to map the relative distances of clusters from us and from each other. To his surprise he found that they were widely and randomly distributed both above and below the plane of the Milky Way and appeared to be concentrated in one smallish area in the direction of the constellation Sagittarius. He argued that such a distribution would make sense if the Galaxy had the shape of a flattened disk with the clusters grouped around the galactic center. This required that the solar system be displaced from its accepted central position by a considerable distance.

Thus Shapley had found the general structure of the Galaxy but not its size. Here the Cepheids were of limited use as they could only provide a relative scale. Absolute distances could at that time only be determined for small distances. In order to calibrate his galactic structure Shapley needed to measure the distance of a few Cepheids. He used a statistical method pioneered by Ejnar Hertzsprung in 1913. Since the intrinsic brightness, or luminosity, of stars can be determined once their distance is known, Shapley's measurements allowed him to produce a quantified form of the relationship between Cepheid period and observed brightness, i.e., a period-luminosity relationship. This P-L relationship meant that a measure of the period of any Cepheid would reveal its luminosity and hence its distance and the distance of the stars surrounding it.

By 1920 Shapley felt that he had finally cracked the fundamental problem of the scale of the Galaxy. The Sun, he declared, was some 50,000 light-years from the center of the Galaxy while the diameter of the galactic disk could be perhaps 300,000 light-years. Actually Shapley's calculations were too generous as he was unaware of the interstellar matter that absorbs some of the light from stars and thus affects determinations of stellar brightness. Consequently his figures were later revised to 30,000 light-years for the distance to the galactic center and 100,000 light-years for the diameter.

Shapley was however less successful with his work on the scale of the universe. In 1920 he took part with Heber Curtis in a famous debate organized by the National Academy of Sciences at the Smithsonian in Washington. Using the brightness of novae in the Andromeda nebula, Curtis gave an estimate approaching 500,000 light-years for its distance and maintained that it was an independent star system. Shapley, misled by the measurements of Adriaan van Maanen, argued that this distance was far too great and that the Andromeda nebula and the other spiral nebulae lay within the Galaxy. It was left to Edwin Hubble to show, some years later, that Curtis had in fact underestimated rather than overestimated the distance of the Andromeda nebula and that it was in fact a separate star system.

Not the least of Shapley's achievements was his development of the Harvard Observatory into one of the major research institutions of the world. He introduced a graduate program and attracted a distinguished and much increased permanent staff. During his time there his interest turned to "galaxies," as he called them, or "extragalactic nebulae" in Hubble's terminology. Northern and southern skies were surveyed for galaxies and tens of thousands were recorded. In 1932 he produced a catalog, with Adelaide Ames, of 1,249 galaxies, which included over a thousand galaxies brighter than 13th magnitude. In 1937 he published a survey of 36,000 southern galaxies. He also studied the Magellanic Clouds and identified the first two dwarf galaxies, the Fornax and Sculptor systems, which are members of the Local Group of galaxies.

Shapley wrote several books on astronomy and left an account of his scientific life in his informal *Through Rugged Ways to the Stars* (1969).

Sharp, Phillip Allen

(1944–   )

AMERICAN MOLECULAR BIOLOGIST

Born in Falmouth, Kentucky, Sharp was educated at Union College, Kentucky, and the University of Illinois, Urbana, where he obtained his PhD in 1969. After spending short periods as a postdoctoral fellow at Caltech and Cold Spring Harbor Laboratory, New York, Sharp joined the Massachusetts Institute of Technology in 1974 and was appointed professor of biology in 1979.

Much of the early work in molecular genetics had been carried out on prokaryotes, cells which lack a nucleus. It was found that continuous stretches of DNA were converted into various proteins. The DNA was first transcribed into a continuous sequence of messenger RNA (mRNA), triplets of which coded for one of the amino acids from which proteins were assembled:

DNA	CCC	TGA	TCG	AAA	ATA	CAG	...
mRNA	GGG	ACU	AGC	UUU	UAU	GUC	...
amino acid	gly	thr	ser	phe	tyr	val	...

It was automatically assumed that similar mechanisms would be found to operate in eukaryotic cells, cells with a nucleus.

In 1977, however, Sharp demonstrated that this assumption was baseless. Sharp worked with adenoviruses, the viruses responsible for, among other things, the common cold. He explored the process of protein production by forming double stranded hybrids of adenovirus DNA and mRNA. The hybrids were then displayed on an electron micrograph. To Sharp's surprise the mRNA hybridized with only four regions of DNA, and these were separated by long stretches of DNA looping out from the hybrid. The intervening loops, later to be termed "introns" by Walter Gilbert, it was presumed, were later snipped off and the four remaining groups, "exons" in Gilbert's terminology, would be spliced together to form the mature mRNA. This mature mRNA would then leave the cell's nucleus and serve as the template upon which proteins could be assembled.

Sharp's work was confirmed independently by Richard Roberts. The "split genes" identified in adenoviruses by Sharp were quickly shown to be fairly standard in eukaryotic cells. The phenomenon has proved highly puzzling. In some organisms as much as 90% of nuclear DNA is snipped away as introns and consequently seems to serve no purpose at all. Why there should be so much "junk" DNA as it has sometimes been described remains a mystery.

For his discovery of split genes Sharp shared the 1993 Nobel Prize for physiology or medicine with Richard Roberts.

Sharpey-Schäfer, Sir Edward Albert

(1850–1935)

BRITISH PHYSIOLOGIST

Schäfer (**shay**-fer), the son of a city merchant in London, qualified in medicine at University College there in 1874. He joined the staff of the college and served as Jodrell Professor of Physiology from 1883 until 1899. He then moved to a similar chair at the University of Edinburgh where he remained until his retirement in 1933.

In 1896 Schäfer, working with George Oliver, discovered that an extract from the medulla of the adrenal gland produced an immediate elevation of blood pressure when injected into animals. The substance, adrenaline (epinephrine), was later isolated and crystallized by Jokichi Takamine in 1901. Schäfer also worked on pituitary extracts. He is further remembered in the field of endocrinology for his proposal that the active pancreatic substance in the islets of Langerhans should be called "insuline," some eight years before its discovery by Frederick Banting and Charles Best.

Schäfer published two influential works: *Essentials of Histology* (1885) and *Endocrine Organs* (1916). He also founded the important *Quarterly Journal of Experimental Physiology* in 1898.

Schäfer had named one of his two sons Sharpey after his much admired anatomy teacher, William Sharpey, at University College. But after the tragic death of both his sons in World War I Schäfer changed his own name to the hyphenated Sharpey-Schäfer.

Shaw, Sir William Napier

(1854–1945)

BRITISH METEOROLOGIST

Born in the English Midlands city of Birmingham, Shaw studied at Cambridge University, England. After graduating in 1876 he was appointed as a lecturer in experimental physics in the Cavendish Laboratory, Cambridge. In 1900 he took the post of secretary of the Meteorological Council, later becoming (1905) director of the Meteorological Office. After his retirement in 1920 he was appointed professor of meteorology at Imperial College, London.

Shaw established the Meteorological Office as an efficient organization and demonstrated the use of meteorology as an applied science. He carried out research into air currents and in his *Life History of Surface Air Currents* (1906) anticipated the "polar front" theory of cyclones later developed by Jacob Bjerknes. He also worked on the upper atmosphere using instrumented balloons. After he retired from teaching in 1924 he produced a major account of the discipline in his four-volume *Manual of Meteorology* (1926–31). He was knighted in 1915.

Shemin, David

(1911–1991)

AMERICAN BIOCHEMIST

Shemin was born in New York City and educated at the City College there before obtaining his PhD from Columbia in 1938. He served as professor of biochemistry at Columbia from 1953 until 1968, when he moved to a similar post at Northwestern University in Chicago, which he held until 1979.

In the 1940s Shemin and his colleagues succeeded in working out some of the details of porphyrin synthesis. Several biologically important molecules, including hemoglobin and chlorophyll, are porphyrins, i.e., they contain a porphyrin ring in their structure. This consists of carbon and nitrogen atoms forming four pyrrole rings, which are linked by carbon atoms and joined to a metal atom in the center – iron in the case of hemoglobin and magnesium in chlorophyll.

Using radioactive tracers, Shemin and his coworkers were able to show that all the carbon and nitrogen atoms of the porphyrin ring are derived from glycine and succinyl-CoA. Such work is not merely of academic interest, since errors in the metabolism of porphyrin are responsible for a number of diseases. Porphyria, an excess of porphyrins in the blood affecting the nervous system, was possibly responsible for the madness of the English king, George III.

Shen Kua

(about 1031–1095)

CHINESE SCIENTIST AND SCHOLAR

As for the waxing and waning of the moon, although some phenomena such as pregnancy and the tides are tied to them, they have nothing to do with seasons or changes of climate.

—*Meng ch'i pi t'an* (*c.* 1086; Dream Pool Essays)

Shen Kua (shen kwah) spent his life in government service in his native China, working variously as an ambassador, a military commander, and a director of water systems. In around 1086 he completed his *Meng ch'i pi t'an* (Dream Pool Essays) in which he recorded the scientific observations made on his extensive travels, the results of his own researches, and the general scientific activity of his day.

One of the work's most important parts is its description of the discovery of the magnetic compass. This is first reported in Europe in the 12th century but Shen Kua described it a century before. He also discussed fossils that he had been shown, giving an accurate account of their origin. Other passages in the book contain detailed descriptions of meteorological phenomena he had seen, experiments done on mirrors, and mathematical problems.

Sherman, Henry Clapp

(1875–1955)

AMERICAN BIOCHEMIST

Sherman, one of ten children, was born on a farm in Ash Grove, Virginia. He attended Maryland Agricultural College, graduating in 1893 in general science and chemistry. He then went to Columbia University, where he received his doctorate in chemistry and physiology in 1897, and he remained working in the chemistry department at Columbia for the rest of his career.

His most important work was on the development of quantitative biological methods for assaying the vitamin content of food. He studied enzyme chemistry, producing experimental evidence for the protein nature of digestive enzymes and contributing to the development of greater precision in measuring amylase activity. He investigated the calcium and phosphorus requirements of the body, showing that both are needed in an appropriate ratio and that rickets can be induced on a low-phosphorus diet even when calcium supplies are more than adequate.

Sherrington, Sir Charles Scott

(1857–1952)

BRITISH PHYSIOLOGIST

Like this old Earth that rolls through sun and shade,
Our part is less to make than to be made.

—Man on his Nature (1955)

Sherrington, a Londoner by birth, was educated at Cambridge University and St. Thomas's Hospital, London, gaining his BA in natural science in 1883 and his MB in 1885. He then traveled to Europe to study under Rudolf Virchow and Robert Koch in Berlin. After lecturing in physiology at St. Thomas's Hospital, Sherrington was superintendent of the Brown Institute (1891–95), a veterinary hospital of the University of London. He then became professor of physiology, firstly at the University of Liverpool (1895–1913) and then at Oxford University, holding the latter post until his retirement in 1935.

Sherrington's early medical work was in bacteriology. He investigated cholera outbreaks in Spain and Italy and was the first to use diphtheria antitoxin successfully in England, his nephew being the patient. During the war he tested antitetanus serum on the wounded and also worked (incognito) as a laborer in a munitions factory. He then turned his attention to studies of the reflex actions in man, demonstrating their effect in enabling the nervous system to function as a unit and anticipating Ivan Pavlov in his discovery of the "conditioned reflex." These researches culminated in his most celebrated publication, *The Integrative Action of the Nervous System* (1906), a landmark in modern physiology. Sherrington also did much work on decerebrate rigidity and the renewal of nerve tissue. For their work on the function of the neuron, Sherrington and Edgar Adrian were jointly awarded the Nobel Prize for physiology or medicine in 1932. Sherrington was knighted in 1922.

Shibukawa, Harumi

(1639–1715)

JAPANESE ASTRONOMER

> Barbarians who may have theories but cannot prove methods.
> —On Western astronomers

Shibukawa (shee-buu-**kah**-wah) was born at Kyoto in Japan, the son of a professional go player. Initially he followed his father's career, even adopting for a time his father's name, Yasoi Santetsu II. He also studied mathematics and astronomy and became increasingly interested in calendar reform.

In 862 Japan had adopted the Chinese T'ang calendar, the Hsuan-Ming, compiled in 822 and unreformed in Japan until Shibukawa's time. As the Chinese calendar consisted of 12 lunar months (six of 30 days and six of 29 days) and 354 days it rapidly fell out of phase with the tropical year of 365.2422 days. The simplest solution to the problem was to add intercalary months when needed. Thus seven months added in a 19-year cycle would be no more than six hours out of phase. But, six hours per 19 years does mount up and, by the time of Shibukawa, the calendar had become useless for eclipse prediction and could not even establish the date of the winter solstice.

Shibukawa began to make observations with a gnomon to determine the precise solstice date. In 1684 he resigned his position as go master but remained at court as head of a new department, the Tenmongata (or Bureau of Astronomy). In this office he was largely responsible for the annual production of the civil calendar. His new system, the Jujireki, was based upon the Shou-shih calendar of the Yuan dynasty (1279–1368) corrected for the differences in latitude and longitude between Peking and Kyoto. However, as Shibukawa's instruments were inferior to those used by the Yuan astronomers, discrepancies soon arose and Shibukawa's system remained in force only until 1754.

Shizuki, Tadao

(1760–1806)

JAPANESE ASTRONOMER AND TRANSLATOR

> The cause of gravity is quite inscrutable. Even with advanced Western instruments and mathematics, the fundamental cause is indeterminable.
> —*Rekisho Shinsho* (1802; New Treatise on Calendrical Phenomena)

Born in Nagasaki, the son of an interpreter, Shizuki (shee-**zuuk**-ee) studied under another interpreter, Motoki Ryoei. By the end of the 17th century the only foreign ideas allowed to enter Japan were traditional ones from China. Trade was permitted with the Dutch and Portuguese but since 1641 was confined to the island of Dejima. No other intellectual contact was permitted.

Some relaxation, however, was allowed during the reign of Yoshimune (1716–45), and Western texts on such subjects as astronomy and gunnery began to circulate in Japan in Chinese translation. Shizuki took advantage of the more liberal regime and began work in the 1780s on the translation of *Introductio ad veram physicam et veram astronomiam* (1739; Introduction to True Physics and True Astronomy), a commentary by John Keill (1671–1721) on Newtonian physics. Shizuki worked from a 1741 Dutch translation by Johan Lulof. The work was completed by 1802 and published under the title *Rekisho Shinso* (New Treatise on Calendrical Phenomena) and was in fact the first book on modern physics and astronomy to be published in Japanese. It contained an elementary account of universal gravitation, the laws of motion, and the properties of ellipses.

Shockley, William Bradford

(1910–1989)

BRITISH–AMERICAN PHYSICIST

Shockley, born the son of a mining engineer in London, was educated at the California Institute of Technology and at Harvard, where he obtained his PhD in 1936. He started work at the Bell Telephone Laboratories in 1936. In 1963 he took up an appointment as professor of engineering at Stanford University.

Shockley is noted for his early work in the development of the transistor – an invention that has had a profound effect on modern society. He collaborated with John Bardeen and Walter Brattain in their work on the point-contact transistor (1947). The following year Shockley developed the junction transistor.

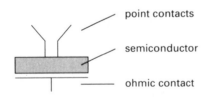

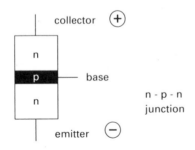

TRANSISTORS   Point-contact and junction transistors.

In semiconductors such as germanium and silicon the electrical conductivity is strongly affected by impurities. The germanium and silicon atoms have four outermost electrons and an impurity such as arsenic, with five outer electrons, contributes extra electrons to the solid. In such materials the current is carried by negative electrons and the conductivity is said to be n-type. Alternatively, impurities such as boron, with three outer electrons, have a different effect in that they introduce "holes" – i.e., "missing" electrons. An electron on an adjacent atom can move to "fill" the hole, leaving another hole. By this mechanism electrical conduction is by movement of positive holes through the solid – the conductivity is said to be *p*-type.

Shockley experimented with junctions of *p*- and *n*-type material, showing how they act as rectifiers. He formed the first junction transistor of a thin layer of *p*-type material sandwiched between two *n*-type regions. This *n–p–n* junction transistor could be used to amplify current. Shockley shared the 1970 Nobel Prize for physics with Bardeen and Brattain.

Shull, Clifford Glenwood

(1915–)

AMERICAN PHYSICIST

Shull, who was born in Pittsburgh, Pennsylvania, was educated at the Carnegie Institute of Technology and New York University, where he obtained his PhD in 1941. He began as a research physicist working first for the Texas Company, from 1941 to 1946, and then with the Oak Ridge National Laboratory from 1946 until 1955, when he entered academic life as professor of physics at the Massachusetts Institute of Technology. He remained at the institute until his retirement in 1986.

Shull's main research interest has been in the diffraction of slow neutrons by crystals. Just as x-rays can be diffracted by a crystal lattice, neutron beams of suitable energy also show diffraction effects. In the case of x-rays, diffraction is mainly by the electrons in the atom, whereas in neutron diffraction the nuclei scatter the neutrons. From about 1946 onward Shull applied neutron diffraction to determining crystal structure, showing that the method could indicate the position of light atoms such as hydrogen (which are not detected by x-ray methods).

Shull also showed that an additional effect occurred in neutron diffraction – magnetic scattering by interaction of the neutron's magnetic moment with that of the atom. He demonstrated antiferromagnetism in manganese(II) oxide using this technique in 1949. He has subsequently done considerable work in "magnetic diffraction" of neutrons and in other aspects of neutron interaction with matter. For his work on neutron diffraction Shull shared the 1994 Nobel Prize for physics with Bertram Brockhouse.

Sidgwick, Nevil Vincent

(1873–1952)

BRITISH CHEMIST

Sidgwick, who was born in Oxford, England, came from a distinguished intellectual family; both his father and an uncle were Oxford classicists and another uncle was a professor of moral philosophy at Cambridge University. He was educated at Oxford University obtaining first class degrees in both chemistry (1895) and classics (1897). After further study in Germany, during which he obtained his PhD in 1901 from Tübingen, he returned to Oxford as a fellow and spent the remainder of his life there.

Sidgwick began his career working on organic compounds and in 1910 he produced *The Organic Chemistry of Nitrogen*, a classic text on the subject. In 1914 Sidgwick attended a meeting of the British Association in Australia and there he met Ernest Rutherford with whom he formed a lasting friendship. The meeting marked a turning point in his career; he became interested in atomic structure and tried to explain chemical reactions through this.

Sidgwick's theory was eventually published in 1927 in his *Electronic Theory of Valency*, which established his international reputation. The significance of his work was that it extended the idea of valency developed by Gilbert Lewis and Irving Langmuir to inorganic compounds, emphasizing the necessity of assuming the Bohr–Rutherford model of the atom. He introduced what he termed a coordinate bond in which, unlike the covalent bond of Lewis, both electrons are donated by one atom and accepted by the other. This explained the coordination compounds of Alfred Werner.

In his later years Sidgwick worked on his two-volume *The Chemical Elements and their Compounds* (1950), a massive work that attempted to demonstrate the adequacy of valency theory by showing that it applied to all compounds. The work took 25 years of Sidgwick's life and for it he was reported to have examined 10,000 scientific papers.

Siebold, Karl Theodor Ernst von

(1804–1885)

GERMAN ZOOLOGIST AND PARASITOLOGIST

Instead of being able to relax in my later years, I have to learn just as much – no, even more – than I did during all my younger days. If you reflect that in old age it is much harder to learn than to forget, you will bear with me.
—Letter to Ernst Haeckel, 16 February 1874

Siebold (**zee**-bohlt), who came from a family of physicians in Würzburg, Germany, began his academic education by studying medicine at Berlin and Göttingen. He later practiced briefly in Danzig. In his spare time he studied marine fauna and it was largely owing to his published research on these animals that he became elected to the chair of anatomy and physiology at Erlangen in 1840. Siebold later held professorships at Freiburg, Breslau, and Munich. Apart from some work on the salamanders and freshwater fish of central Europe, Siebold devoted his attention almost entirely to the invertebrates, especially the vermiform parasites. Of particular importance was his demonstration that the various stages in the life cycles of parasites develop in different host animals, proving, for example, that the sheep disease of the brain known as "gid" or "the staggers" is caused by the adolescent stage of the tapeworm that passes its adult life in the intestine of the dog. Siebold also studied insect parthenogenesis, proving that drone (male) bees develop from unfertilized eggs, and made valuable contributions to invertebrate classification, especially with regard to the Protozoa. Siebold's major publication, which he produced in collaboration with Hermann Stannius, is *Lehrbuch der vergleichenden Anatomie* (1846; Textbook of Comparative Anatomy). Embracing both invertebrates (Siebold) and vertebrates (Stannius), it is regarded as one of the first important texts on comparative anatomy, based as it is on observed facts rather than abstruse philosophy. In 1848 Siebold founded, with Rudolph von Kölliker, the prestigious *Zeitschrift für wissenschaftliche Zoologie* (Journal of Scientific Zoology).

Siegbahn, Kai Manne Börje

(1918–   )

SWEDISH PHYSICIST

Siegbahn (**seeg**-bahn), who was born at Lund in Sweden, was the professor of physics at the Royal Institute of Technology, Stockholm, from 1951 to 1954. He taught at the University of Uppsala from 1954 to 1984. Here he worked on the emission of electrons from substances irradiated with x-rays. Siegbahn's technique was to subject a specimen to a narrow beam of x-rays with a single wavelength (i.e., energy) and measure the energy spectrum of the ejected electrons by magnetic or electrostatic deflection. The spectrum shows characteristic peaks formed by electrons ejected from different inner energy levels of atoms. Moreover, the positions of these peaks depend to a slight extent on the way in which the atom is linked to other atoms in the molecule. These "chemical shifts" allow the technique to be used as an analytical tool – Siegbahn has named it ESCA (electron spectroscopy for chemical analysis). He has also worked on the related technique of ultraviolet photoelectron spectroscopy developed by David Turner.

Siegbahn is the son of Karl Manne Siegbahn, who won the Nobel Prize for physics in 1924. Kai Siegbahn was awarded the Nobel Prize in 1981.

Siegbahn, Karl Manne Georg

(1886–1978)

SWEDISH PHYSICIST

Siegbahn, who was born at Örebro in Sweden, was educated at the University of Lund, where he studied astronomy, mathematics, physics, and chemistry, obtaining his doctorate in 1911. In 1914 he turned his attention to the new science of x-ray spectroscopy. It had already been established from x-ray spectra that there were two distinct "shells" of electrons within atoms, each giving rise to groups of spectral lines, labeled "K" and "L." In 1916 Siegbahn discovered a third, or "M," series. (More were to be found later in heavier elements.)

Through successive refinement of his x-ray equipment and technique, Siegbahn was able to achieve a significant increase in the accuracy of his determinations of spectral lines. This allowed him to make corrections to Bragg's equation for x-ray diffraction to allow for the finer details of crystal diffraction. Besides working with crystals, he performed x-ray spectroscopy at longer wavelengths using gratings. Here again his accurate measurements revealed discrepancies that were later shown to result from inaccuracies in the value assumed for the electronic charge.

In 1920 Siegbahn was made professor and head of the physics department at the University of Lund and in 1923 he moved to the University of Uppsala to become chairman of the physics department. In 1924 he received the Nobel Prize for physics, cited for "his discoveries and research in the field of x-ray spectroscopy," and the following year saw publication of his influential book *Spectroscopy of X-rays* (1925). In the same year Siegbahn and his colleagues showed that x-rays are refracted as they pass through prisms, in the same way as light.

When, in 1937, the Swedish Royal Academy of Sciences created the Nobel Institute of Physics at Stockholm, Siegbahn was appointed its first director. In the same year he became professor of physics at the University of Stockholm, retaining this post until his retirement in 1964. He was responsible for the building of accelerators, laboratory spectrometers, and other equipment at the Nobel Institute.

Siemens, Ernst Werner von

(1816–1892)

GERMAN ENGINEER

To measure is to know.

—Attributed

The son of a farmer from Lenthe in Germany, Siemens (**zee**-mens) was the eldest of fourteen highly talented children, who included William Siemens. In 1834 he joined the Prussian army and spent three years in Berlin receiving a thorough training in science and mathematics. Afterward duties were so light as to allow him to pursue his growing interest in chemistry and electricity. From this work he derived his first invention, a new system of electroplating sold by his brother William in London for 1,600 pounds in 1843.

In 1847 Siemens founded, with Johann Halske (1814–90), the firm of Siemens and Halske, later to become one of the major industrial concerns in Europe. Initially Siemens hoped to move into the rapidly growing telegraphy business. In 1847 he built the Berlin–Frankfurt line, insulating the underground cables with the newly introduced gutta-percha. Unfortunately for Siemens the gutta-percha had been vulcanized and the copper wire and sulfur destroyed the insulation. Contracts were canceled and, for a time, Siemens found it necessary to work outside Germany. The period, nonetheless, gave Siemens time to experiment, refine, and improve on the basic principles of telegraphy. He was consequently selected to construct the telegraph line connecting London to Calcutta, a distance of 11,000 kilometers, which was completed in 1870.

Siemens's other main interest lay in power generation. The early electric generators were cumbersome machines using large steel permanent magnets and delivering very little power. In 1867 Siemens proposed to replace them with the self-activating dynamo. The permanent magnets were replaced by electromagnets and these were fed by a current obtained from an armature and commutator. Once the dynamo had been perfected it made possible the many manifestations of electric power – lighting, both domestic and public, transport, heating, cooling, and so on. The Siemens companies were well placed to take advantage of the commercial and industrial revolution created by the dynamo. Perhaps the clearest measure of the achievements of Siemens could once have been found in Berlin, where the suburb in which the firm's factories were located and where 120,000 men were employed was named Siemensstadt.

Siemens, Sir William

(1823–1883)

BRITISH ENGINEER

Born Carl Wilhelm in Lenthe, Germany, Siemens (**see**-menz or **zee**-mens) was the son of a tenant farmer and a younger brother of Ernst Werner Siemens. He was educated at Göttingen and first visited Britain in 1843 as an agent of his brother Ernst Werner. He settled in England shortly afterwards, becoming a naturalized citizen in 1859.

Siemens worked in two main areas, namely, heat and electricity. In the age of Joule he was aware of the potential value to be gained by conserving heat. Early attempts to redesign the steam engine proved impractical. More successful was his introduction, aided by his younger brother Friedrich (1826–1904), of the regenerator furnace (1856). In the Siemens furnace the hot combustion gases were not simply discharged into the air but used to heat the air supply to the chamber. The process was first used in the manufacture of steel by an open-hearth process known as the *Siemens–Martin process* (after the French engineer Pierre Blaise Emile Martin, 1824–1915) in the 1860s. It proved to be the first serious challenge to the Bessemer process and by the century's end had become the favored method of steel production. On the strength of this a steel foundry was opened at Landore, South Wales, in 1869. As it failed to prosper it was abandoned in 1888.

He was more successful with his work in electric telegraphy. Siemens designed the cable-laying ship *Faraday* for laying a new trans-Atlantic cable in 1874. He also worked on electric lighting and on the Portrush electric railway in Northern Ireland. He died suddenly from a heart attack in 1883. When, forty years before, he had first arrived in Britain his English had been so poor that he looked for legal advice from an undertaker. Since then, it was said of him, he made three fortunes: one he lost, one he gave away, and one he bequeathed to his brothers. The electrical unit of conductance, the *siemens*, is named in his honor.

Sierpiński, Waclaw

(1882–1969)

POLISH MATHEMATICIAN

The son of a physician, Sierpiński (sher-**pin**-ye-skee or seer-**pin**-skee) was educated at the university in his native city of Warsaw. After first teaching at Lvov University he moved in 1919 to the University of Warsaw, where he remained for the rest of his career.

Although Sierpiński had written 600 papers on set theory and another 100 on number theory, his name only became widely known when popular books on chaos began to talk about *Sierpiński carpets*. The carpet begins with a square divided into nine equal squares. The central square is removed and the operation is repeated on the eight other squares, and the process is continued indefinitely. The figure is a fractal with a dimension of log 8/log 3 = 1.8928.

Silliman, Benjamin

(1779–1864)

AMERICAN CHEMIST

Born at North Stratford (now Trumbull) in Connecticut, Silliman graduated in law from Yale and was called to the bar in 1802. Instead of taking up law he was appointed professor of chemistry and natural history at Yale. To prepare himself he spent two years at the University of Pennsylvania studying chemistry before taking up his appointment in 1804.

Silliman did much to stimulate the interest in and growth of science in 19th-century America. He also prepared and founded the organizational structure of American science in anticipation of its later growth. He was a great teacher and popularizer willing to lecture on most aspects of science. In 1813 he introduced lectures on geology at Yale and in 1818 founded the *American Journal of Science*, the only journal at the time which had a nationwide distribution as well as being read in Europe. In 1830 he published his textbook *Elements of Chemistry*. He became (1840) the first president of the Association of American Geologists, an organization which later became the American Association for the Advancement of Science. He was also a founder member of the National Academy of Science in 1863. His son, Benjamin Jr., succeeded him to his chair at Yale.

Simon, Sir Francis Eugen

(1893–1956)

GERMAN–BRITISH PHYSICIST

Simon, the son of a wealthy Berlin merchant, was educated at the universities of Munich, Göttingen, and Berlin, where he worked with Walther Nernst and obtained his doctorate in 1921. He moved to Breslau in 1931 to take the chair of physical chemistry but the rise of Hitler forced him into exile in 1933. He was invited by Frederick Lindemann to the Clarendon Laboratory in Oxford and was made reader in thermodynamics there in 1935. He succeeded Lindemann as professor in 1956 but died a month later.

Under Simon, Oxford became one of the leading centers in the world for low-temperature physics. Shortly before his death a temperature of 0.000016 kelvin was achieved in his laboratory – less than 1/200,000 of a degree above absolute zero – using the method of magnetic cooling introduced by Francis Giauque and Peter Debye in 1926.

Simon was able to claim one further distinction, that he was the only man to hold the Iron Cross of Imperial Germany and a knighthood of the British Empire.

Simpson, Sir George Clark

(1878–1965)

BRITISH METEOROLOGIST

Simpson, who was born at Derby in England, was educated at Manchester University. After a year at Göttingen (1902) and fieldwork in Lapland investigating atmospheric electricity, he was appointed lecturer in meteorology at Manchester (1905), the first such post to be created in a British university. He was meteorologist on Scott's final expedition to the Antarctic in 1910, publishing his account of his researches in three volumes (1919–23). He succeeded William Napier Shaw as director of the Meteorological Office in 1920 and was knighted in 1935.

His main research was in the field of atmospheric electricity and he attempted to establish the process by which clouds and rain become electrified. He also improved the scale of wind speeds worked out by Francis Beaufort in 1806. The Beaufort scale was defined in numerical terms of the behavior of sails in varying winds. Simpson brought this up to date by standardizing Beaufort numbers against wind speeds in miles per hour at a height of 33 feet (10 m) above ground level. Thus force 10 on the Beaufort scale became the equivalent of 55–63 miles per hour (88–101 km per hour).

Simpson, George Gaylord

(1902–1984)

AMERICAN PALEONTOLOGIST

Simpson, born the son of a lawyer in Chicago, Illinois, was educated at the University of Colorado and at Yale where he obtained his PhD in 1926. He joined the staff of the American Museum of Natural History in the following year and after serving as curator from 1942 to 1959 moved to Harvard as Agassiz Professor of Vertebrate Paleontology at the Museum of Comparative Zoology, a post he retained until his retirement in 1970. In 1967 he became professor of geosciences at the University of Arizona, Tucson.

Simpson worked extensively on the taxonomy and paleontology of mammals. His main contribution was his elucidation of the history of the early mammals in the late Mesozoic and the Paleocene and Eocene. To this end, beginning with field trips to Patagonia and Mongolia in the 1930s, he traveled to most areas of the world. In addition to a number of monographs he produced, in 1945, *Principles of Classification and the Classification of Mammals,* a major reference work on the subject.

In such works as *The Meaning of Evolution* (1949) and *The Major Features of Evolution* (1949) he also did much to establish a neo-Darwinian orthodoxy, as did similar works by Theodosius Dobzhansky and Ernst Mayr. Such works brought together population genetics, paleontology, and chromosomal studies to establish for the first time a broad consensus concerning the nature and mechanism of evolution.

Simpson, Sir James Young

(1811–1870)

BRITISH OBSTETRICIAN

Simpson, a baker's son, was born at Bathgate in Scotland. He obtained his MD in 1832 from the University of Edinburgh, where, in 1839, he was appointed professor of midwifery.

On 21 December 1846 Robert Liston performed the first operation under anesthetic in Britain at University College Hospital, London. Simpson immediately traveled to London to confirm the reports with Liston. On 19 January 1847 he used ether for the first time in a difficult delivery with complete success, establishing that the anesthetic did not, as had been feared, inhibit uterine contraction. He was not, however, completely satisfied with ether and later used chloroform (first tested on lower animals by Pierre Flourens) as an alternative. By the end of November 1847 he had not only used chloroform in three surgical cases but had also written and published an important pamphlet, *Account of a New Anaesthetic Agent*.

This pamphlet initiated a major controversy. There was little objection to performing major surgical operations under ether or chloroform but the extension to childbirth resulted in the publication of dozens of papers arguing both ingeniously and crudely against the innovation on supposed biblical and medical grounds. The practice became respectable when Queen Victoria decided in 1853 to permit John Snow to use chloroform during her eighth confinement.

Simpson was however less sympathetic to the introduction of antiseptic techniques proposed by Joseph Lister and saw hospital infection more as a problem of architectural design. He thus proposed replacing the large overcrowded hospitals with smaller units, open to the fresh air. The future however lay with Lister.

In 1866 Simpson was made a baronet, the first physician practicing in Scotland to be so honored.

Simpson, Thomas

(1710–1761)

BRITISH MATHEMATICIAN

> The ablest Analyst...that this country [Britain] can boast of.
> —R. Woodhouse, introduction to the 1823 edition of Simpson's
> *A New Treatise on Fluxions*

The son of a weaver from Market Bosworth in Leicestershire, England, Simpson was largely self-educated. His mathematical interests were aroused when a peddler gave him a copy of the popular textbook, *Cocker's Arithmetic*. He left home early, for by 1724 he was reported to be in nearby Nuneaton, practicing as an astrologer. By 1735 he had arrived in London where he worked initially as a weaver but also as a part-time teacher of mathematics. He soon became well known through a series of popular textbooks among which were *A New Treatise on Fluxions* (1737) and his *Treatise of Algebra* (1745). In 1743 he was appointed to the Royal Military Academy at Woolwich. He also served (1754–60) as editor of the *Ladies Diary* – a journal that sought to interest the "fair sex" in "Mathematicks and Philosophical Knowledge."

In mathematics he is best known for his formulation in 1743 of what has since been known as *Simpson's rule*, allowing the area under a curve to be approximated by using parabolic arcs.

Škoda, Josef

(1805–1881)

AUSTRIAN PHYSICIAN

The son of a poor Bohemian locksmith from Pilsen (now in the Czech Republic), Škoda (**shkaw**-dah), studied medicine at the University of Vienna where he obtained his doctorate in 1831. After some years in practice in Pilsen he returned to the University of Vienna and served as professor of internal medicine from 1846 onward.

In 1839 he published an important work on percussion and auscultation, which helped to establish the modern techniques of Leopold Auenbrugger and René Laënnec.

Škoda, with Ferdinand von Hebra, was one of the few members of the Viennese establishment actively to support the work of Ignaz Semmelweis on puerperal fever and it was owing to him that his colleague's claims were investigated, however incompetently, and first published in 1849.

Skolem, Thoralf Albert

(1887–1963)

NORWEGIAN MATHEMATICIAN

The son of a teacher, Skolem (**skoh**-lem) was born at Sandsvaer in Norway and educated at the University of Oslo. He joined the faculty in 1911 and was appointed professor of mathematics in 1938, a post he held until his retirement in 1950.

Skolem is best known for his work in mathematical logic, including his contribution to the proof of the *Lowenheim-Skolem theorem* and the construction of the *Skolem paradox*.

The Lowenheim theorem of 1915, as generalized by Skolem in 1920, simply states that any schema satisfiable in some domain is satisfiable in a denumerably infinite domain. Denunerably infinite domains, also known as countable domains, can be matched in a one–one correspondence with the domain of natural numbers. Clearly the natural numbers are denumerably infinite, as are the even numbers and the rational numbers. There are in fact just as many even numbers as natural numbers, as can be seen from the correspondences set out below:

2   4   6   8   10   12   14   16...
1   2   3   4   5   6   7   8...

There are, however, domains, such as the domain of the real numbers, which cannot be put into such a correspondence with the natural numbers. Such domains are nondenumerably infinite.

Skolem pointed out in 1922 that this result leads to a new paradox in set theory. There are sets, the set of real numbers for example, which are nondenumerable. Yet, by the Lowenheim-Skolem theorem, they must be satisfiable in a denumerably infinite domain. Skolem proposed to defuse the paradox by claiming that notions such as nondenumerability have no absolute meaning, but can only be understood within the confines a particular axiomatic system. Thus a set may be nondenumerable within a system and denumerable outside. Consequently, the paradox will fail to arise.

Skraup, Zdenko Hans

(1850–1910)

AUSTRIAN CHEMIST

Skraup (skrowp) was born in Prague (now in the Czech Republic) and educated at the university there. He worked at the University of Vienna and in the Mint before being appointed professor of chemistry at the Institute of Technology in Graz in 1886. He returned to the University of Vienna in 1906 to take the chemistry chair.

In 1880 Skraup synthesized quinoline, which had been discovered by Friedlieb Runge in 1834, by heating a mixture of aniline and glycerol with sulfuric acid and an oxidizing agent, nitrobenzene. Skraup also worked on carbohydrates and proteins.

Slipher, Vesto Melvin

(1875–1969)

AMERICAN ASTRONOMER

> It seems to me that with this discovery, the great question, if the spirals belong to the Milky Way or not, is answered with great certainty, to the end that they do not.
> —On Slipher's research into spiral nebulae. Ejnar Hertzsprung, letter to Slipher, 14 March 1914

Born in Mulberry, Indiana, Slipher graduated from the University of Indiana in 1901 and obtained his PhD there in 1909. He spent the whole of his career from 1901 to 1952 at Percival Lowell's observatory in

Flagstaff, Arizona, being made acting director on Lowell's death in 1916 and director in 1926.

Slipher was basically a spectroscopist. One of his major achievements was to determine the rotation periods of some of the planets by spectroscopic means. Thus in 1912, in collaboration with Lowell, he found that the spectral lines at the edge of the disk of Uranus were displaced by an amount corresponding to a speed of 10.5 miles (16.8 km) per second. Knowing the circumference it was easy to work out the rotation period as 10.8 hours. Although still the accepted figure, it is now thought that this rotation period could be considerably longer. Slipher also produced comparable data for Venus, Mars, Jupiter, and Saturn and showed that Venus's period was much longer than expected.

Slipher also studied the matter lying between the stars in our Galaxy. Like Johannes Hartmann he concluded in 1908 from his spectroscopic research that there must be gaseous material lying between the stars. He also studied the spectra of the luminous nebulae in the Pleaides cluster of stars and proposed in 1912 that they were illuminated by starlight reflected off dust grains. This was an early indication of the presence of solid material in nebulae and other interstellar clouds.

Slipher's most important achievement, however, was his determination of the radial velocities of spiral nebulae by the measurement of the displacement of their spectral lines. Such measurement relies on the Doppler effect by which the wavelength of light from an object moving away from an observer will be lengthened, i.e., shifted toward the red end of the spectrum, while light from an object moving toward an observer will have its wavelength shortened, i.e., moved toward the blue end of the spectrum. By measuring the change in wavelength, known as the Doppler shift, the velocity of the moving object can be determined easily.

Slipher's work produced two surprising results. The first was the immense speed of the Andromeda nebula (galaxy), which he first successfully measured in 1912. He found it to be moving toward the Earth with a velocity of nearly 300 kilometers per second, which was then the greatest velocity ever observed. Secondly, by 1917 he had obtained the radial velocities of 15 spiral nebulae of which it would have been thought that roughly half would be receding while the other half would be approaching. But he found that 13 out of the 15 were receding. What was equally significant was their velocity, which in many cases exceeded that of the 300 kilometers per second of the Andromeda nebula. Many astronomers questioned these findings. At that time there was considerable controversy over whether the spiral nebulae were part of our Galaxy or lay far beyond it as independent star systems. Slipher's work was, in retrospect, evidence both for the extragalactic hypothesis, since the velocities of the spiral nebulae were too great for them to be members of the Galaxy, and for the expanding universe, which was first proposed by Alexander Friedmann in 1922 and later shown to be correct by Edwin Hubble.

Smalley, Richard Errett

(1943–)

AMERICAN CHEMIST

Born in Akron, Ohio, Smalley was educated at Michigan University and at Princeton where he obtained his PhD in 1973. After spending the period from 1973 to 1976 at the James Franck Institute, Chicago, Smalley moved to Rice University, Houston, and was appointed professor of chemistry in 1981.

In 1981 Smalley devised a procedure to produce microclusters of a hundred or so atoms. The technique is to vaporize the metal by a laser. The released atoms are cooled by a jet of helium and condense into variously sized clusters. In 1985 a visiting British chemist, Harry Kroto, persuaded Smalley to direct his laser beam at a graphite target. Smalley knew that an Exxon group had already used graphite and produced carbon molecules with an even number of atoms. At first Smalley was reluctant to repeat this work but he was eventually persuaded. They soon had spectroscopic evidence for the presence of an apparently large, stable molecule of sixty carbon atoms – now known as buckminsterfullerene.

Smellie, William

(1697–1763)

SCOTTISH OBSTETRICIAN

Smellie was a medical practitioner in his native Lanark until 1739, when he moved to London. Here he studied obstetrics, becoming a close colleague of another Scottish obstetrician, William Hunter. In 1741 he began teaching midwifery and in 1745 he received a medical degree from Glasgow University. His *Treatise on the Theory and Practice of Midwifery* (1752) provided much-improved descriptions of labor and childbirth. Smellie gave his name to several obstetrical techniques, including a method of breech delivery and to a special type of delivery forceps.

Smith, Hamilton Othanel

(1931–   )

AMERICAN MOLECULAR BIOLOGIST

Born in New York City, Smith studied at the University of Illinois, graduated in mathematics (1952) from the University of California, Berkeley, and took his MD at Johns Hopkins in 1956. He taught at the University of Michigan from 1962 until 1967, when he returned to Johns Hopkins where later, in 1973, he became professor of microbiology.

In 1970 Smith succeeded in confirming the hypothesis of Werner Arber to explain the phenomenon of "host-controlled variation" in phages. He identified an enzyme extracted from the bacterium *Hemophilus influenzae*, later to be known as Hind II, which cut DNA at a specific site. This was the first of the so-called restriction enzymes to be identified – by 1978 over 80 were known. Such enzymes, by permitting the controlled splitting of genes, opened up the possibility of the genetic engineering so energetically pursued from the 1970s onward.

For his work on restriction enzymes Smith shared the 1978 Nobel Prize for physiology or medicine with Arber and Daniel Nathans.

Smith, Henry John

(1826–1883)

IRISH MATHEMATICIAN

> The bond of union among the physical sciences is the mathematical spirit and the mathematical method which pervades them.
> —*Nature*, Vol. VIII

Dublin-born Smith studied at Oxford and had a great interest in classics – it was only after a good deal of hesitation that he chose mathematics as a profession instead. He remained in Oxford in various capacities for most of the rest of his life. In 1860 he became Savilian Professor of Geometry there.

Smith's main work was in number theory and his greatest contribution was his development of a general theory of n indeterminates, which enabled him to establish results about the possibility of expressing positive integers as sums of five and seven squares. This achievement ought to have won Smith the prestigious prize offered in 1882 by the French Academy for their mathematical competition. However Smith, a notably unambitious man, did not enter and the prize was in fact given to Hermann Minkowski. When it was discovered that Minkowski had made use of crucial results published by Smith, the French Academy hastened to transfer the prize to Smith, but as he had unfortunately died in the meantime his fame was only posthumous. Smith also worked on the theory of elliptic functions.

Smith, Michael

(1932–)

CANADIAN BIOCHEMIST

Born in the Lancashire coastal town of Blackpool, England, Smith was educated at the University of Manchester where he obtained his PhD in 1956. He moved soon after to Canada working initially as a post-doctoral fellow at the University of British Columbia, Vancouver. From 1961 until 1966 Smith served with the Fisheries Research Board of Canada, Vancouver, but returned to the University of British Columbia in 1966 and was appointed professor of biochemistry in 1970.

In 1978 Smith introduced a basic new technique known as "site specific mutagenesis" into molecular biology. In order to establish the function of a particular protein or gene, it had long been an established procedure to induce a mutation in the gene and observe the consequences. Thus if changes to a gene prevented an organism from making a particular enzyme, then it was reasonable to conclude that the gene controlled some part of the production of that enzyme. The difficulty with this approach was that the available mutagens, radiation and chemicals, produced random and multiple mutations. The precise effects of a single mutant gene could seldom, therefore, be distinguished from the other consequences of the mutagens.

Smith demonstrated how to introduce specific mutations into genes. He worked with a single strand of viral DNA. A short segment of complementary DNA differing at a single site was assembled and allowed to bind to the original viral DNA. The second strand was then completed in the normal way and the double-stranded DNA inserted into the viral genome. The virus would develop with normal and mutated versions of the gene which would in turn produce normal and mutated proteins. When the different protein molecules were compared, the role of the initial mutation would become apparent.

The new technique has been widely used in protein chemistry and molecular biology. Smith himself has used it to investigate the role of cytochrome c in cellular respiration, and myoglobin in oxygen storage. For his work in this field Smith shared the 1993 Nobel Prize for chemistry with Kary Mullis.

Smith, Theobald

(1859–1934)

AMERICAN BACTERIOLOGIST

There was about him [Smith] an unobtrusive pride, a reserve tinged with austerity.
—H. Zinsser, *Biographical Memoirs of the National Academy of Sciences* (1936)

Smith, the son of a German immigrant tailor, was born in Albany, New York, and educated at Cornell and at Albany Medical College, where he obtained his MD in 1883. He began his career at the U.S. Bureau of Animal Husbandry but, dissatisfied with the recognition his work received, moved in 1895 to Harvard, where he served as professor of comparative pathology. In 1914 Smith was appointed director of animal pathology at the Rockefeller Institute, Princeton, a post he held until his retirement in 1929.

For more than a generation Smith was undoubtedly the leading American bacteriologist. He published numerous monographs on a wide variety of infections, beginning with his work on hog cholera in 1889. He went on in 1896 to distinguish between the bacilli responsible for bovine and human tuberculosis.

His name is mainly remembered, however, for his work in 1893 on Texas cattle fever, one of the earliest demonstrations of the transmission of a disease via a tick. He noted that northern cattle seemed to acquire their infection not from direct contact with southern diseased animals but by passing over territory previously occupied by such cattle. In 1889 he discovered a microorganism in the red blood cells of infected cattle and began to suspect the cattle tick, *Boophilus bovis*, of transmitting it. Smith went on to confirm his hypothesis in 1890 by noting that when ticks were placed on cattle there was a sudden fever and extensive loss of red cells that could not be explained by a mere loss of blood. Such work led to immediate and simple methods to control the disease. Smith published a full account of his work in *Nature, Causation and Prevention of Southern Cattle Fever* (1893).

Smith, William

(1769–1839)

BRITISH SURVEYOR AND
GEOLOGIST

In consideration of his being a great original discoverer in English Geology; and
especially for his having been the first, in this country, to discover and teach the
identification of strata, and to determine their succession by means of their
imbedded fossils.

—Citation on the award of the Wollaston Medal of the
Geological Society of London to Smith (1831)

Smith was born in Churchill, England, the son of the village black-smith. He was educated at local schools and in 1787 began work with the surveyor who had been commissioned to make a survey of his parish. This was at the time of the great canal boom and Smith soon found himself fully employed conducting surveys for proposed canals. He was also regularly employed to report on coal deposits in different parts of the country while making his canal surveys. During this work he traveled considerable distances throughout Britain.

From his surveying and observation of rock strata Smith formulated very clearly two basic principles of geology for which he is often known as the father of British geology. As early as 1791 he had noted that certain strata, wherever they occurred, all contained the same invertebrate fossils and that different strata could be distinguished by a difference in their fossil content. Previously geologists had relied upon the nature of the rocks to identify and discriminate between strata. This could work well in some favored cases but, in general, was far from reliable. Smith's other major theory was the law of superposition, which simply states that if one layer of sedimentary rocks overlays another then it was formed later, unless it can be shown that the beds have been inverted.

Smith never managed to produce a major book on the geology of Britain although he did publish two small pamphlets: *Strata Identified by Organized Fossils* (1816) and *Stratigraphical Systems of Organized Fossils* (1819). His major productions were instead in the field of maps.

In 1815 he produced the first geological map of England and Wales. This was published in 15 sheets at a scale of 5 miles to the inch. During the period 1819–24 he published a series of geological maps of 21 counties. The plates were still being used to produce maps as late as 1911.

Smith seems to have received little recognition and reward during his early life; he was forced to sell his collection of fossils to the British Museum to overcome his financial difficulties. However, in the 1830s he began to receive the recognition he deserved. In 1831 the Geological Society of London awarded him their first Wollaston medal and in 1835 he received an honorary LLD from Dublin.

Smithson, James

(1765–1829)

BRITISH GEOLOGIST

Smithson was born in France, the illegitimate son of Hugh Smithson Percy, duke of Northumberland. His mother, a cousin of his father's wife, had been twice married to wealthy husbands and was a descendant of Henry VII. Smithson was first known as James Lewis or Louis Macie, only taking his father's name after 1800. He was educated at Oxford University where he received his MA in 1786. He became interested in chemistry and mineralogy and published many papers in these fields, which were collected in 1879. Zinc carbonate was named smithsonite for him.

Smithson inherited a large fortune, chiefly from his mother's family, and in his will, drawn up in 1826, he left the income of this fortune (well over £100,000) to his nephew. If his nephew died without issue then, under the terms of the will, the capital was to be offered "to the United States of America, to found at Washington, under the name of the Smithsonian Institution, an establishment for the increase and diffusion of knowledge among men." Why he did this is not clear; he had never visited America although he was widely traveled in Europe. It was not immediately acceptable to the Americans. President Jackson ignored it and it was not until John Quincy Adams argued Congress into acceptance that the research institution was finally established by act of Congress in 1846 with Joseph Henry as its first secretary.

In 1904 Smithson's remains were removed to America where they were fittingly interred in the original Smithsonian building.

Smoot, George Fitzgerald III

(1945–)

AMERICAN ASTROPHYSICIST

> We now have direct evidence of the birth of the Universe and its evolution... ripples in space–time laid down earlier than the first billionth of a second. If you're religious, it's like seeing God.
>
> —*Wrinkles in Time* (1993)

Born at Yukon in Florida, Smoot was educated at the Massachusetts Institute of Technology where he took his PhD in physics in 1970. He moved to the University of California, Berkeley, in 1971 as a research physicist and in 1974 was appointed team leader for the differential microwave radiometers on board the Cosmic Background Explorer Satellite (COBE).

In 1965 Penzias and Wilson had discovered the cosmic background radiation. Initially it appeared to be perfectly isotropic, exactly the same whatever part of the universe it came from. Theorists found it difficult to account for such uniformity, and experimentalists began to wonder if it really was as uniform as it appeared.

The first disproof of isotropy came in 1977 from observations taken on board a high-flying U2 plane. The dipole anisotropy, as it was called, was small and was connected with the position of the Milky Way. Clearly further work was called for. After a number of delays, COBE was launched in 1989. Three instruments were carried. The differential microwave radiometer would measure differences in radiation from two points in the sky and could pick out differences between them of 1 part in 100,000. Also, a photometer measured the absolute brightness of the sky and searched for diffuse infrared radiation from the early universe. Finally, an interferometer measured the spectrum of the background radiation from 1 centimeter to 100 micrometers.

As the results emerged Smoot saw within the assumed uniformity "islands of structure." A year was spent checking the reliability of the data – prizes were offered to anyone on the team who could identify a significant flaw. Finally the material was checked against a list of all the systematic errors ever noted during the years of preparation. After four papers describing the initial results had been revised more than a hundred times, Smoot was ready to go public.

The results seemed to show that there were bright spots in the universe, 30 millionths of a degree warmer than the average temperature. This was precisely the result predicted by the inflationary model of Alan Guth. It might also be possible, Smoot considered, to find in the ripples in the radiation the galactic clusters that populate the universe. Smoot has published a valuable popular account of the COBE mission in his *Wrinkles in Time* (1993).

Smyth, Charles Piazzi

(1819–1900)

BRITISH ASTRONOMER

The son of William Henry Smyth (1788–1865), a naval officer and astronomer, Smyth was born at Naples in Italy and named after a friend of his father, the astronomer Giuseppe Piazzi (1746–1826). They returned to England in 1825 and settled in Bedford where William Smyth established his own observatory; he also published a pioneering work, *Sidereal Chromatics or Colours of Double Stars* (1864), as well as a catalog of 850 double stars, the *Bedford Catalogue* (1844).

Charles Smyth left school at sixteen and went straight to work at the Cape of Good Hope Observatory in South Africa as assistant to the director, Thomas Maclear, another friend of his father. William further exercised his influence in 1845 to make his son Astronomer Royal of Scotland, a post that carried with it the directorship of the Edinburgh Observatory and the position of Regius Professor of Practical Astronomy at Edinburgh University.

Much of Smyth's work was devoted to spectroscopy. In 1872 on an expedition to Sicily, he succeeded in obtaining the spectrum of the zodiacal light – a luminous triangular patch seen in the eastern sky just before sunrise and in the west just after sunset. The spectrum was continuous, from which he concluded that zodiacal light could not be the same as the Aurora, as was widely believed, which possessed a line spectrum. It is probably caused by the reflection of sunlight from cosmic dust.

Smyth also worked on the solar spectrum. He sought to show that not all the spectral lines were solar in origin; some originated in the Earth's atmosphere. On an expedition to Tenerife in 1856 he had noted that Fraunhofer's C band (the hydrogen alpha line) remained unchanged whatever the Sun's altitude; the red A and B bands grew visibly at lower altitudes. Similar results were obtained by Smyth in 1878 on an expedition to Lisbon.

In 1884 working on the spectrum of oxygen under high dispersion Smyth found that the single lines in the spectrum were in fact triplets when viewed at high resolution. He tried unsuccessfully to identify triplets in the solar spectrum. They were recorded photographically by F. McClean in 1897.

Smyth, like many an astronomer both before and after, became obsessed by the metrology of the Great Pyramid. He visited the pyramid in 1864 and made thousands of very accurate measurements, which he recorded in his *Life and Work at the Great Pyramid* (3 vols., Edinburgh, 1867).

Snell, George Davis

(1903–1996)

AMERICAN GENETICIST

With Snell's fundamental discoveries came the birth of transplantation immunology.
—Nobel Prize citation (1980)

Snell was born in Bradford, Massachusetts, and educated at Dartmouth and Harvard, where he obtained his doctorate in 1930. After brief appointments at Texas, Brown, and Washington University, St. Louis, he joined the staff of the Jackson Laboratory, Bar Harbor, Maine, in 1935 and remained there for his entire career, retiring finally in 1969.

Early in his career, while at the University of Texas, Snell was the first to show that x-rays can cause mutations in mammals, by his demonstration that x-rays induce chromosome translocations in mice. His main work concerned what he called the major histocompatibility complex. It had been known since the 1920s that although skin grafts between mice are generally rapidly rejected they survive best when made between the same inbred line. Snell's coworker Peter Gorer showed in 1937 that this was due to the presence of certain histocompatibility antigens found on the surface of mouse cells and since known as the H-2 antigens. In the 1940s Snell began a detailed study of the system.

His first task was to develop inbred strains of mice through back-crossing, genetically identical except at the H-2 locus. After much effort he was able to show that the H-2 antigens were controlled by the genes at the H-2 complex of chromosome 17, described by him as the major histocompatibility complex (MHC).

It was for this work that Snell shared the 1980 Nobel Prize for physiology or medicine with Jean Dausset and Baruj Benacerraf.

Snell, Willebrord van Roijen

(1580–1626)

DUTCH MATHEMATICIAN AND PHYSICIST

Snell, who was born at Leiden in the Netherlands, received his initial training in mathematics from his father, who taught at Leiden University. He traveled widely in Europe, visiting Paris, Würzburg, and Prague, and among the celebrated scientists he met were Johannes Kepler and Tycho Brahe. Once he had returned to Leiden, Snell published a number of editions of classical mathematical texts. On the death of his father (1613) Snell succeeded him as professor of mathematics at the university.

He was involved in practical work in geodesy and took part in an attempt to measure the length of the meridian. In this project he was one of the first to see the full usefulness of triangulation and published his method of measuring the Earth in his *Eratosthenes Batavus* (1617; The Dutch Eratosthenes). In 1621 Snell discovered his famous law of refraction, based on a constant known as the refractive index, after much practical experimental work in optics. Snell did not, however, publish his discovery and the law first reached print in Descartes's *La Dioptrique* (1637; Dioptrics). However, Descartes had arrived at the law in a totally different way from Snell and made no use of practical observation.

Snow, John

(1813–1858)

BRITISH PHYSICIAN

Snow was born at York in England and apprenticed to a surgeon in Newcastle-upon-Tyne from the age of 14. In 1836 he enrolled at the Great Windmill Street School of Medicine in London and also studied at Westminster Hospital, receiving his MD from the University of London in 1844.

Snow had harbored a concern for the causes and spread of cholera since working amid an outbreak of the disease in northeast England. In 1849 he published an essay in which he asserted that cholera was transmitted via a contaminated water supply. He advocated simple hygiene precautions, such as boiling drinking water, to avoid infection. Snow's reputation, however, rested upon his skill as an anesthetist. He introduced a device for the controlled administration of ether to patients and did likewise for chloroform when it superseded ether. Snow personally administered chloroform to Queen Victoria at the birth of two of her children.

Snyder, Solomon Halbert

(1938–   )

AMERICAN PSYCHOPHARMACOLOGIST

Snyder was born in Washington DC and educated at Georgetown University. After receiving his MD in 1962 he moved to the National Institute of Health, Bethesda, Maryland, as a research associate. He later

(1965) joined the staff of Johns Hopkins where he has served since 1970 as professor of psychiatry and pharmacology.

Many drugs, hormones, and neurotransmitters are effective at very low concentrations. The synthetic opiate etorphine produces euphoria and relieves pain in doses as low as one ten-thousandth of a gram. It was inferred from this that for such small doses to be effective they must bind to highly selective receptor sites. Snyder, in collaboration with C. Pert, began the search for such receptor sites using radioactively labeled opiates. By 1973, despite many complications, they were able to report the presence of receptors in the mammalian limbic system, a primitive region in the center of the brain associated with the perception and integration of pain and emotional experiences. To identify the receptors Snyder, working with Candice Pert, developed the widely used technique of "reversible ligand binding." Brain tissue was exposed to opiates labeled with radioactive isotopes. These were quickly washed away. The assumption was that, in low concentrations, opiates would first bind tightly to receptors. The opiates which would normally bind loosely with other tissue would be washed away. The binding sites could then be identified by locating the radioactive isotopes.

The implications of such a discovery were far-reaching for it is clear that opiate receptors had not evolved to await the isolation of morphine. The alternative is that there must be natural morphinelike substances in the brain that bind at these sites. Within a few years the first such enkephalins or endorphins, as they were named, were discovered by J. Hughes and Hans Kosterlitz.

In more recent work Snyder has claimed to have identified a new kind of neurotransmitter, namely, the unlikely and highly toxic nitric oxide (NO). In 1987 it had been discovered that NO diffused from blood-vessel walls causing adjacent muscles to relax and the vessels to dilate. Snyder set out to find if NO was made in the brain. He found NO present bound with iron in an enzyme, cyclic guanosine monophosphate (cGMP). NO acts in an unusual way by initiating a three-dimensional change in the shape of the enzyme. Snyder has also suggested that nitric oxide in the brain could be involved in changes connected with learning and memory processes. He has proposed that carbon monoxide may also belong to this novel class of neurotransmitters.

In another breakthrough in 1987 Snyder succeeded in cultivating *in vitro* human cerebral cortex tissue. For some unknown reason neurons, which do not normally divide, taken from a child undergoing an operation have continued to divide. "They have all the properties of neurons," Snyder emphasized, "they do everything that neurons do." Snyder has speculated that it might in the future be possible to implant such neurons in badly damaged brains.

Sobrero, Ascanio

(1812–1888)

ITALIAN CHEMIST

Born at Casal in Italy, Sobrero (soh-**brair**-oh) began by studying medicine but changed to chemistry, attending the universities at Turin, Paris, and Giessen. He became professor of chemistry at Turin in 1849, staying there until his retirement in 1882.

In 1846 – the year that Christian Schönbein discovered nitrocellulose – Sobrero discovered an even more powerful explosive, nitroglycerin. By slowly stirring drops of glycerin into a cooled mixture of nitric and sulfuric acids he produced a new but unpredictable explosive. Unlike Schönbein, Sobrero showed no desire to exploit the commercial value of his discovery. As it was liable to explode on receiving the slightest vibration there seemed to be no way to develop it, and its liquid nature made it difficult to use as a blaster. It was not utilized until 1866, when Alfred Nobel mixed it with the earth kieselguhr to produce a compound that could be transported and handled without too much difficulty. In this form – dynamite – it was used extensively in the great engineering programs of roads, railroads, and harbors of the late 19th century.

Socrates

(*c.* 469 BC–399 BC)

GREEK PHILOSOPHER

> It seemed to me a superlative thing to know the explanation of everything, why it comes to be, why it perishes, why it is.
> —Quoted by Plato in *Phaedo*

Through Plato's writings Socrates (**sok**-ra-teez), born the son of a stonemason in Athens, has become one of the best known figures of antiquity. Apart from a public life of service in the Peloponnesian War and membership of the council of 500, in 406 BC, Socrates's life appears to have been spent in discussion and debate with both the youth of Athens and the leading philosophers of his day. From such discussions emerged his reputation, confirmed by the Delphic oracle, as the wisest of all men. Socrates characteristically interpreted this to mean that his wisdom lay in his awareness of his own lack of wisdom. In 399 he was accused of neglecting the gods worshiped by the city and of corrupting the young, tried, found guilty, sentenced to death, and forced to drink hemlock – scenes fully described in some of the most remarkable pages in the whole corpus of Western literature in the *Apology* and *Phaedo* of Plato.

Socrates's innovations were dialectical rather than scientific. His interests lay in the behavior of man rather than the planets. Despite this he introduced a new critical spirit, a deliberate and methodical refusal to accept either established opinion or recognized authority, as important for the development of science as for any other discipline.

Soddy, Frederick

(1877–1956)

BRITISH CHEMIST

Soddy, born the son of a corn merchant in the coastal town of East-bourne, England, was educated at the University College of Aberystwyth and Oxford University. After working with Ernest Rutherford in Canada and William Ramsay in London, Soddy took up an appointment at Glasgow University in 1904. He moved to take the chair of chemistry at Aberdeen University in 1914 where he remained until 1919 when he accepted the post of Dr. Lee's Professor of Chemistry at Oxford.

Soddy's work was quite revolutionary in that he succeeded in overthrowing two deep assumptions of traditional chemistry. The first arose out of his period of collaboration with Rutherford, from 1901 to 1903. Together they established that radioactive elements could change into other elements through a series of stages.

Soddy's next major achievement was to make some kind of sense of the bewildering variety of new elements that had been found as decay products of radium, thorium, and uranium. The books of the period refer to such strange entities as mesothorium, ionium, radium A, B, C, D, E, and F, and uranium X. Such entities were clearly distinct for they had markedly different half-lives. But what they were and, more significantly, where they fitted in the periodic table were difficult questions. There were gaps in the periodic table but far too few to accommodate so many new elements. One further difficulty soon forced itself on chemists. Attempts to separate thorium from radiothorium by Otto Hahn in 1905 and radium D from lead by Georg von Hevesy a few years later had failed, as had numerous other attempts to separate various radioactive elements by chemical means.

Finally Soddy made the bold claim that the reason such substances could not be separated was because they were in fact identical. Consequently some kind of modification of the periodic table was called for. In his view (1913) "it would not be surprising if the elements...were mixtures of several homogeneous elements of similar but not completely identical atomic weights." He called such chemically identical elements, with slightly differing atomic weights, isotopes (from the Greek words meaning in the same place). He could thus assert that both radium D and thorium C were in fact isotopes of lead. Radium D has a half-life of 24 years and an atomic weight of 210 while thorium C has a half-life of 87 minutes and an atomic weight of 212; but, although they have different half-lives and differing weights, they were both chemically indistinguishable from lead.

Until the discovery of the neutron by James Chadwick a complete understanding of this enormously fruitful idea was not available to Soddy. All he could propose, somewhat vaguely, as an explanation was different numbers of positive and negative charges in the nucleus. As yet, no one seemed to suspect the existence of a neutral particle without a charge.

He did, however, go on to explain the transformation of atoms by his displacement law. In this the emission of an alpha particle, a helium nucleus of two protons and two neutrons, lowers the atomic weight by four while the emission of a beta particle, an electron, raises the atomic number by one. Given these rules Soddy could show how, for example, uranium and thorium could both decay, by different paths, to different isotopes of lead (Casimir Fajans independently suggested the same law).

Despite the award of the 1921 Nobel Prize for chemistry for his work on the origins and nature of isotopes Soddy became disillusioned with science and his place in it. After 1919 Soddy took no further part in creative science. He wrote a good deal, mainly in the fields of economic and social questions, which raised little interest or support. On the issue of energy, however, he was remarkably perceptive. As early as 1912 he could comment that "the still unrecognized 'energy problem'...awaits the future," continuing with the by now familiar refrain of our profligate use of hydrocarbons, "a legacy from the remote past," and concluding with what he saw as our only hope, atomic energy, which "could provide anyone who wanted it with a private sun of his own."

Sokoloff, Louis

(1921–   )

AMERICAN NEUROPHYSIOLOGIST

Born in Philadelphia, Pennsylvania, Sokoloff was educated at the University of Pennsylvania. After gaining his MD in 1946 he joined the staff of the medical school there, leaving in 1956 for the National Institute of Mental Health, Bethesda, Maryland, where he served from 1968 as chief of the Cerebral Metabolism Laboratory.

Sokoloff and his colleagues at the NIMH have recently established a relatively simple technique for determining which brain cells respond to experimental stimuli. The technique, described as opening up "an entirely new realm in brain research," depends on the fact that active neurons in brain cells absorb more glucose than inactive ones. The glucose is normally metabolized rapidly but if a similar sugar is substituted, 2-deoxyglucose, it tends to accumulate in the active neurons. When radioactively labeled, such accumulated deoxyglucose can be readily detected and measured.

The value of this new approach was shown by David Hubel and Torsten Weisel in 1978 when they succeeded in confirming much of their earlier work by obtaining from neurons of the visual cortex autoradiographs of the regions responsive to vertical lines.

Solvay, Ernest

(1838–1922)

BELGIAN INDUSTRIAL CHEMIST

Solvay (**sol**-vay) was born at Rebecq-Rognon in Belgium. As the son of a salt refiner and the nephew of a manager of a gas plant, he was introduced at an early age to the techniques and problems of the chemical industry. He devised several methods for purifying gases but is best known for the ammonia–soda process named for him.

For most of the 19th century soda was produced by the Leblanc process. This had a number of disadvantages: it produced toxic hydrochloric acid fumes and also a number of expensive and irrecoverable waste products. As early as 1811 Augustin Fresnel had proposed an ammonia–soda process. However, although chemists succeeded in the laboratory, when they tried to translate their results onto an industrial scale they invariably ended up like James Muspratt, who lost £8,000 in the period 1840–42. Solvay was the first to solve the engineering problems of the process. He later confessed that he was completely ignorant of all these earlier failures, adding that he would probably never have tried if he had known.

In 1861 Solvay took out his first patent for soda production and in 1863 set up his first factory at Charleroi, in partnership with his brother. The process involved mixing brine with ammonium carbonate, which produced sodium carbonate and ammonium chloride. The sodium carbonate yielded soda on being heated and the ammonium chloride, when mixed with carbon, regenerated the ammonium carbonate the process started from. Solvay's innovation was to introduce pressurized carbonating towers.

The system was soon adopted throughout the world and by 1900 95% of a greatly increased world production of soda came from the Solvay process. The price of soda fell by more than a half in the last quarter of the 19th century.

Solvay is also remembered for financing the great series of international conferences of physicists starting in 1911, in which much of the new nuclear and quantum physics was discussed.

Somerville, Mary

(1780–1872)

BRITISH ASTRONOMER AND PHYSICAL GEOGRAPHER

Mary Fairfax, as she was born in Jedburgh, Scotland, was the daughter of a naval officer. She received precisely one year of formal education before her marriage to a cousin in 1804 who was a captain in the Russian navy. After his death in 1807 she married another cousin, W. Somerville, an army physician, in 1812.

Somerville was unique in 19th-century British science as she was an independent female. Virtually all other women participated in science as the wife or sister of a husband or brother whom they assisted and sometimes went on to make some small contribution of their own. Her interest in science began when as a young girl she first heard of algebra and Euclid and satisfied her curiosity as to the nature of these subjects from books she purchased. She certainly received no encouragement from her father nor was her first husband much more sympathetic. She was more fortunate with her second husband, who encouraged and assisted her.

Living with her husband in London from 1816 she soon became a familiar and respected figure in the scientific circles of the capital. Her first significant achievement was her treatise on the *Mécanique céleste* (Celestial Mechanics) of Pierre Simon de Laplace. She was persuaded to undertake this difficult task by John Herschel and in 1831 750 copies of *The Mechanism of the Heavens* were published. The work was a great success and was used as a basic text in advanced astronomy for the rest of the century.

She followed this in 1834 with her *On the Connexion of the Physical Sciences*, a more popular but still serious work. In this she suggested that the perturbations of Uranus might reveal the existence of an undiscovered planet. Somerville was of course denied such obvious honors as a fellowship of the Royal Society as a result of her work. She was, however, granted a government pension of £300 a year in 1837.

From 1840, because of the health of her husband, she moved to Europe, living mainly in Italy. It was there that she produced her third and most original work, *Physical Geography* (1848). It was widely used as a university text book to the end of the century, although overshadowed by the *Kosmos* (Cosmos) of Friedrich von Humboldt, which came out in 1845.

She produced her fourth book, *On Molecular and Microscopic Science* (1869), at the age of 89 and was working on a second edition when she died.

When a hall was opened in Oxford in 1879 for the education of women it was appropriately named for her and was to produce sufficient talent to refute her own belief that genius was a gift not granted to the female sex.

Sommerfeld, Arnold Johannes Wilhelm

(1868–1951)

GERMAN PHYSICIST

The misuse of the word "national" by our rulers has thoroughly broken me of the habit of national feeling that was so pronounced in my case. I would now be willing to see Germany disappear as a power and merge into a pacified Europe.
— On the Nazi regime. Letter to Albert Einstein (1934)

Sommerfeld (zom-er-felt), the son of a physician, was born in Königsberg (now Kaliningrad in Russia) and educated at the university in his native city. He later taught at Göttingen, Clausthal, and Aachen before being appointed to the chair of theoretical physics at the University of Munich in 1906.

In 1916 Sommerfeld produced an important modification to the model of the atom proposed by Niels Bohr in 1913. In Bohr's model an atom consists of a central nucleus around which electrons move in definite circular orbits. The orbits are quantized, that is, the electrons occupy only orbits that have specific energies. The electrons can "jump" to higher or lower levels by either absorbing or emitting photons of the appropriate frequency. It was the emission of just those frequencies that produced the familiar lines of the hydrogen spectrum. Increasing knowledge of the spectrum of hydrogen showed that Bohr's model could not account for the fine structure of the spectral lines. What at first had looked like a single line turned out to be in certain cases a number of lines close to each other. Sommerfeld's solution was to suggest that some of the electrons moved in elliptical rather than circular orbits. This required introducing a second quantum number, the azimuthal quantum number, l, in addition to the principal quantum number of Bohr, n. The two are simply related and together permit the fine structure of atomic spectra to be satisfactorily interpreted.

Sommerfeld was the author of an influential work that went through a number of editions in the 1920s, *Atombau und Spektrallinien* (Atomic Structure and Spectral Lines).

Sondheimer, Franz

(1926–1981)

BRITISH CHEMIST

Sondheimer (**sond**-hI-mer) was born at Stuttgart in Germany but moved with his family to Britain in 1937. He was educated at Imperial College, London, where he obtained his PhD in 1948. After serving as a research fellow with Robert Woodward at Harvard from 1949 to 1952 he spent a brief period as associate director of chemical research with Syntex in Mexico City before being appointed in 1956 professor of organic chemistry at the Weizmann Institute, Rehovoth, Israel. In 1964 Sondheimer returned to Britain where he held a Royal Society research professorship first at Cambridge and from 1967 at University College, London.

In 1952, while with Syntex, Sondheimer collaborated with Carl Djerassi in the synthesis of an oral estronelike compound, the precursor of the contraceptive pill. In the 1960s Sondheimer deployed his synthetic skills on the annulenes, monocyclic hydrocarbons with alternating double and single bonds like the familiar benzene ring. Such molecules were important in theoretical chemistry following the formulation in 1931 by Erich Hückel of his rule claiming that compounds with monocyclic planar rings containing $(4n + 2)\pi$ electrons should be aromatic. The rule obviously held for benzene ($n = 1$).

In 1956 Sondheimer and his colleagues discovered a relatively simple way to synthesize large-ring hydrocarbons and by the early 1960s they had produced annulenes with 14 and 18 carbon atoms, $n = 2$ and $n = 4$ respectively. 14–annulene is a highly unstable compound, which is not planar because of the positions of the hydrogen atoms on the molecule. 18–annulene has a planar ring obeying the Hückel rule and does have aromatic properties. The group also synthesized 30–annulene – a planar compound ($n = 7$). In 1981 while a visiting professor at Stanford, Sondheimer was found dead in his laboratory beside an empty cyanide bottle. He had apparently been suffering from depression.

Sonneborn, Tracy Morton

(1905–1981)

AMERICAN GENETICIST

Born in Baltimore, Maryland, Sonneborn received his PhD from Johns Hopkins in 1928 and soon afterward joined the faculty there. In 1939 he moved to Indiana University, later serving as professor of zoology from 1943 until his retirement in 1976.

In 1937 Sonneborn made the important discovery of sexuality in the protozoan *Paramecium aurelia*. He reported the existence of two mating types between which conjugation could occur but within which conjugation is prohibited. This allowed Mendelian breeding experiments to be carried out with a unicellular organism and led to the demonstration that Mendelian principles, which had been established using higher animals and plants, are also applicable to microorganisms.

In 1943 Sonneborn announced that he had found evidence for what he believed to be cytoplasmic inheritance in *Paramecium*. He found two strains one of which was lethal to the other when mixed together, and yet both strains were identical genetically. He devised an experiment that showed the killer factor is inherited via the cytoplasm, and later found many different types of killer paramecia each with cytoplasmic particles containing a different killer gene. However, the killer trait still depended for its expression upon the presence of a certain gene in the nucleus.

From such work Sonneborn began to talk of the gene as consisting of two parts, one localized in the chromosome and responsible for replication while the other part was present in the cytoplasm and served the varied demands of cellular differentiation. Such latter bodies soon became known as plasmagenes, a term introduced by Cyril Darlington in 1944.

However, it was later shown that Sonneborn's cytoplasmic particles are in fact symbiotic bacteria. Nevertheless, Sonneborn's work is still of significance in showing that cellular cytoplasm is something more than a "playground for the genes."

Sorby, Henry Clifton

(1826–1908)

BRITISH GEOLOGIST

Not to pass an examination, but to qualify myself for a career of original investigation.
—The stated aim of his education

Sorby was born in Woodbourne, England, the only son of a cutlery manufacturer. He was educated at schools in Harrogate and Sheffield and under a private tutor, who stimulated his interest in science. On the death of his father (1847) he inherited sufficient money to allow him to set up a laboratory and devote himself to science.

Sorby became particularly interested in geology and he recognized the value of the microscope in the science. Using the Nicol prism introduced by William Nicol and thin slices of rock, about 0.001 inch (0.0025 cm) wide, he was able to study the microscopic structure of minerals and metals. By polishing steel, etching it, and then examining it under a microscope, he could see the crystalline structure of the metal and the presence of impurities, and he concluded that steel is a crystallized igneous rock. This has been referred to as the beginning of the technique of metallography, which is an essential feature of modern metallurgy. He also attempted to model geological processes in the laboratory; he tried to throw light on the process of sedimentation by examining in great detail the rate at which particles of different sizes settle in water.

Sørensen, Søren Peter Lauritz

(1868–1939)

DANISH CHEMIST

Sørensen (**su(r)**-ren-sen), the son of a farmer from Haurebjerg in Denmark, was educated at the University of Copenhagen, obtaining his PhD in 1899. After serving as a consultant chemist to the Royal Danish Laboratory from 1892 he became director of the Carlsberg Laboratory (1901).

Sørensen is noted for introducing the concept of pH (potential of hydrogen) as a measure of the acidity or alkalinity of solutions. The pH value is defined as $\log_{10}(1/[H^+])$, where $[H^+]$ is the concentration of hydrogen ions. On this scale, a neutral solution has a pH of 7; alkaline solutions have values higher than 7 and acidic solutions have values lower than 7.

Sosigenes

(about 1st century BC)

EGYPTIAN ASTRONOMER

Nothing seems to be known about Sosigenes (soh-**sij**-e-neez) apart from his design of the Julian calendar. By the time of Julius Caesar the Roman calendar was hopelessly out of alignment with the seasons. The Romans had traditionally had a lunar 12-month calendar of 355 days. To bring it into phase with the solar year an intercalary (inserted) month of 27 days was supposed to be added every other year to a reduced February of 23 or 24 days. In theory this should have produced a year of 366¼ days, which would have proved inaccurate in the long run but should have been controllable by skipping an intercalation whenever the discrepancy became too uncomfortable. For whatever reason the practice had not been followed and to cure the confusion Caesar felt in need of expert foreign advice. He called in Sosigenes, an Alexandrian Greek from Egypt. To restore the situation to normal he introduced two intercalary months between November and December totaling 67 days and one of 27 days after February producing the famous year of "ultimate confusion" of 445 days in 46 BC. To ensure that harmony would continue he introduced what was the basic Egyptian year of 365 days plus a leap year every four years. This is in fact eleven minutes too long but it is a tribute to Sosigenes that it lasted for 1,500 years before being modified.

Spallanzani, Lazzaro

(1729–1799)

ITALIAN BIOLOGIST

You have discovered more truths in five years than entire academies in half a century.
—Charles Bonnet, letter to Spallanzani

Spallanzani (spah-lan-**tsah**-nee) was born at Scandiano in Italy and educated at the Jesuit College, Reggio, before leaving to study jurisprudence at Bologna University. While at Bologna he developed an interest in natural history, which was probably encouraged by his cousin, Laura Bassi, who was professor of physics there. After receiving his doctorate he took minor orders and a few years later became a priest, although he continued to pursue his researches into natural history.

Spallanzani's most important experiments, published in 1767, questioned John Needham's "proof" 20 years earlier of the spontaneous generation of microorganisms. He took solutions in which microorganisms normally breed and boiled them for 30 to 45 minutes before placing them in sealed flasks. No microorganisms developed, demonstrating that Needham's broth had not been boiled for long enough to sterilize it. Opponents of Spallanzani asserted, however, that he had destroyed a vital principle in the air by prolonged boiling. While conducting these experiments, Spallanzani showed that some organisms can survive for long periods in a vacuum: this was the first demonstration of anaerobiosis (the ability to live and grow without free oxygen).

In 1768 he submitted papers to the Royal Society on his findings concerning the regeneration of amputated parts in lower animals, and on the strength of this was elected a fellow of the Royal Society. In the same year Maria Theresa of Austria appointed Spallanzani to the chair of natural history at Pavia, which at that time was under Austrian dominion, and here he remained until his death. He was also in charge of the museum at Pavia and made many journeys around the Mediterranean collecting natural-history specimens for the museum.

Spallanzani's research interests covered a wide area and during his career he made important contributions to the understanding of digestion, reproduction, respiration, and blood circulation, as well as sensory perception in bats. He also (in 1785) managed to accomplish the artificial insemination of a dog.

Spedding, Frank Harold

(1902–1984)

AMERICAN CHEMIST

Spedding was born at Hamilton, Ontario, in Canada and educated at the University of Michigan and Berkeley where he obtained his PhD in 1929. After working at Cornell from 1935 to 1937, he moved to Iowa State University, where he remained for the rest of his career. He was appointed professor of chemistry in 1941 and director of the Institute of Atomic Research from 1945 to 1968.

In 1942, at the request of Arthur Compton, Spedding and his Iowa colleagues devised new techniques for the purification of the uranium required urgently for the development of the atomic bomb. Their method reduced the price of uranium from $22 per pound to $1 per pound.

After the war Spedding put his new skills to separating the lanthanide elements, an extremely difficult task because of the similarity of their physical and chemical properties. The technique used on uranium, and later successfully applied to the lanthanides, was that of ion-exchange chromatography. A simple example is seen when hard water is allowed to percolate through a column of the mineral zeolite; calcium ions are absorbed by the mineral, which releases its own sodium ions into the water – in effect, an exchange of ions. In the late 1930s more efficient synthetic resins were introduced as ion exchangers.

Spedding passed lanthanide chlorides through an exchange resin that differentially absorbed the compounds present, thus allowing them to be separated. As a result, for the first time, chemists could deal with lanthanoids in substantial quantities.

In 1965 Spedding published, with Adrian Daane, an account of his work in his *Chemistry of Rare Earth Elements*.

Spemann, Hans

(1869–1941)

GERMAN ZOOLOGIST, EMBRYOLOGIST, AND HISTOLOGIST

Spemann (**shpay**-mahn), who was born at Stuttgart in Germany, worked for a time in his father's bookshop there before graduating in zoology, botany, and physics at the universities of Heidelberg, Munich, and Würzburg. He was first an assistant, then a lecturer, at the Zoological Institute of Würzburg (1894–1908) before becoming professor at Rostock (1909–14). He was then successively associate director of the Kaiser Wilhelm Institute of Biology, Berlin (1914–19), and professor of zoology at Freiburg (1919–35).

Spemann's concept of embryonic induction, based on a lifetime's study of the development of amphibians such as newts, showed that certain parts of the embryo – the organizing centers – direct the development of groups of cells into particular organs and tissues. He further demonstrated an absence of predestined organs or tissues in the earliest stages of embryonic development; tissue excised from one part of the embryo and grafted onto another part will assume the character of the latter, losing its original nature. Spemann's highly original work, for which he received the Nobel Prize in 1935, paved the way for subsequent recognition of similar organizing centers in other animals groups. It is elaborated in *Experimentelle Beiträge zu einer Theorie der Entwicklung* (1936; Embryonic Development and Induction).

Spence, Peter

(1806–1883)

BRITISH CHEMICAL INDUSTRIALIST

Born in Brechin, Scotland, Spence started his career as a grocer's apprentice. He was later employed in the Dundee gas plant before setting up as a small chemical manufacturer in London.

In 1845 his introduction of a new process revolutionized the production of potash alum (potassium aluminum sulfate), which was widely used as a mordant in the textile industry. It was obtained by burning shales sufficiently rich in alum, found near Guisborough and Whitby. Some of the waste from Scottish coal mines consisted of shales containing alum, which was extracted on a small scale, producing 2,000 tons a year by 1835.

Spence patented his new process in 1845 and established his factory in Manchester. He used sulfuric acid to treat a mixture of shale and iron pyrites (iron sulfide), producing alum and iron sulfate. The spent shale could be used in cement production. Spence became the world's largest producer of alum. In an early pollution case in 1857 he was prosecuted and forced to move his factory from Manchester.

Spencer, Herbert

(1820–1903)

BRITISH PHILOSOPHER

> Progress...is not an accident, but a necessity...it is part of nature.
> —*Social Statics*

> Science is organized knowledge
> —*Education*

Spencer was born in Derby, England, and educated by his father and uncle. Having turned down his uncle's offer to send him to Cambridge University, he worked instead as a railroad civil engineer. He began submitting articles on sociology and psychology to various papers in 1842 and later became a subeditor with *The Economist*.

Some years before the publication of Charles Darwin's *The Origin of Species*, Spencer had formulated his own theory of evolution and applied it to the development of human societies. A generation earlier, Karl von Baer had demonstrated that heterogenous organs develop from homogenous germ layers in the embryo. Spencer adopted this observation, applying it to the development of animal species, industry, and culture, defining evolution as the progression from "an indefinite incoherent homogeneity to a definite coherent heterogeneity." He believed in the inheritance of acquired characteristics, but adapted his views when *The Origin* was published, integrating the theory of natural selection into his scheme and popularizing the term "survival of the fittest."

Even though it was quite inappropriate to apply Darwin's theory to social development, Spencer's "social Darwinism" was very influential outside scientific circles and was used to justify many industrial and social malpractices. Darwin himself remarked that Spencer's habit was to think very much and observe very little. The same criticism may be seen in T. H. Huxley's comment that Spencer's idea of a tragedy was a "deduction killed by a fact."

Spencer Jones, Sir Harold

(1890–1960)

BRITISH ASTRONOMER

The son of a London accountant, Spencer Jones won a scholarship to Cambridge University, graduating in 1912. He was chief assistant to the Astronomer Royal from 1913 to 1923 and from 1923 to 1933 served as astronomer at the Royal Observatory at the Cape of Good Hope. In 1933 he returned to Greenwich to become Astronomer Royal, retaining this office until his retirement in 1955. He was knighted in 1943.

Spencer Jones made many contributions to astronomy both in terms of research and organizing ability. In 1931 the minor planet Eros, discovered in 1898, was due to come within 16 million miles (26 million km) of the Earth. The accurate determination of its position would allow an improved calculation of the solar parallax, i.e., the angle subtended by the Earth's radius at the center of the Sun. This in turn would give a more accurate value to the astronomical unit, the mean distance of the Earth from the Sun. Under the organization of Spencer Jones, astronomers all over the world cooperated in the collection of the appropriate data. Eventually over 3,000 photographs arrived at Greenwich and Spencer Jones, after nearly ten years unremitting calculation, announced in 1941 a new figure for the solar parallax of 8.7904 seconds of arc. Although a great improvement over previous results, and thus a great achievement, more recent radar measurements give a value of 8″.7941.

Spencer Jones's second major contribution to astronomy concerned the Earth's rotation. Using new quartz clocks accurate to a thousandth of a second per year, he found that the Earth did not rotate regularly but kept time like a "cheap watch." In 1939 he announced that the Earth was running slow by about a second per year, which was sufficient to explain a number of anomalies in the orbits of the Moon and the planets. As a result of this work a new system of measuring time, ephemeris time, independent of the Earth's rotation rate, was brought into use in 1958.

Finally, from 1948, Spencer Jones organized the move of the Royal Observatory from Greenwich to Herstmonceux in Sussex. In London the Milky Way could no longer be seen, the silvered mirrors were being corroded by sulfur dioxide, and street lighting precluded the taking of long-exposure photographs. The move was thus long overdue but was only completed in 1958 after his retirement.

Sperry, Elmer Ambrose

(1860–1930)

AMERICAN INVENTOR

No one American has contributed so much to our naval technical progress.
　　　　　　　　—Charles Francis Adams

Born in Cortland, New York, Sperry is best known for the gyroscopic compass and gyroscopic stabilizers, now crucial to marine navigation. From the age of 19 he developed various inventions, from an improved dynamo and an arc light to electric cutting machinery for mines. He founded his first company in 1880.

The gyrocompass, invented by him in 1896, was developed from a toy, the gyroscope. It was not until 1911 that one was installed in a U.S. Navy battleship. The gyro principle was also used in gyropilots (for steering ships) and in gyroscopic stabilizers.

Sperry, Roger Wolcott

(1913–1994)

AMERICAN NEUROBIOLOGIST

Sperry, who was born in Hartford, Connecticut, studied psychology at Oberlin College and zoology at the University of Chicago, where he obtained his PhD in 1941. He worked at Harvard, the Yerkes Primate Center, and at Chicago before he moved to the California Institute of Technology in 1954 as professor of psychobiology where he remained until 1984.

Sperry worked on the hemispheres of the brain. Architecturally the brain consists of two apparently identical halves constructed in such a way that each half controls the opposite side of the body. The language center of the human brain is located in most people in the left side alone. The two cerebral hemispheres are far from distinct anatomically, with a number of bands of nervous tissue (commissures) carrying many fibers from one side to the other. In the early 1950s Sperry set out to find how a creature would behave if all such commissures were severed resulting in a "split brain." To his surprise he found that monkeys and cats with split brains act much the same as normal animals. However, where learning was involved the creatures behaved as if they had two independent brains. Thus if a monkey was trained to discriminate between a square and a circle with one eye, the other being covered with a patch, then, if the situation was reversed the animal would have to relearn how to make the discrimination.

He also studied a 49-year-old man whose brain had been "split" to prevent the spread of severe epileptic convulsions from one side to the other. He found that, though normal in other ways, the patient showed the effect of cerebral disconnection in any situation that required judgment or interpretation based on language. Sperry's work immediately posed the problem of whether there is any comparable specialization inherent in the human right-hand brain. This topic is receiving much attention.

Sperry also performed some equally dramatic experiments on nerve regeneration in amphibians. Although in mammals a severed optic nerve remains permanently severed, in certain amphibians such as the salamander it will regenerate. Sperry wondered if the nerves regenerate along the old pathway or whether a new one is formed. He found that whatever obstacles were placed before the nerve fiber it would invariably, however tortuous the path might be, find its way back to its original synaptic connection in the brain. This was shown most convincingly when, after severing the optic nerve, Sperry removed the eye, rotated it through 180° and replaced it. When food was presented to the right of the animal it would aim to the left, thus clearly showing the fibers had made their old functional connection. Sperry shared the 1981 Nobel Prize for physiology or medicine with David Hubel and Torsten Wiesel.

Spiegelman, Sol

(1914–)

AMERICAN MICROBIOLOGIST

Spiegelman was educated at the City College in his native New York, at Columbia, and at Washington University where he obtained his PhD in 1944. He initially taught physics and mathematics at Washington before moving to the University of Illinois, Urbana, in 1949 to serve as professor of microbiology. In 1969 he was appointed director of the Institute of Cancer Research and professor of human genetics and development at Columbia.

In 1958 Spiegelman, in collaboration with Masayasu Nomura and Benjamin Hall, introduced the techniques for the construction of hybrid nucleic acids. After considerable effort they finally succeeded in joining single-stranded DNA from the virus bacteriophage T2 with RNA from the bacteria *Escherichia coli* infected with T2 phage. They further demonstrated that the RNA would hybridize with DNA from no other source, not even DNA from the closely related phage, T5. Spiegelman concluded that the base sequence of *E. coli* RNA is complementary to at least one of the two strands in T2 DNA.

The significance of this work was to provide support for the existence of an "informational intermediary," an RNA template, between the DNA of the genes and the synthesis of the proteins. Such an intermediary, referred to as "translatable RNA" by Spiegelman but later known as messenger RNA, was incorporated in the detailed theory of protein synthesis of François Jacob and Jacques Monod in 1961.

Spitzer, Lyman Jr.

(1914–   )

AMERICAN ASTROPHYSICIST

Born at Toledo in Ohio, Spitzer gained his BA in 1935 from Yale University and then spent a year at Cambridge University, England. Returning to America he gained his PhD in 1938 from Princeton University. From Princeton he went back to Yale as an instructor in physics and astronomy, later (in 1946) to become an associate professor in astrophysics. World War II intervened, however, and in the years 1942–46 he was involved in sonar and undersea-warfare development at Columbia University.

From 1947 to 1979 Spitzer was professor of astronomy and director of the observatory at Princeton. His major research interest was the physical processes that occur in interstellar space, particularly those that lead to matter condensation and the formation of new stars. In considering how ionized matter behaves at very high temperatures inside stars he (and others) saw the possibility of creating suitable conditions for the fusion of hydrogen into helium here on Earth, thus liberating vast amounts of energy. In stars the ionized gases (plasma) are contained by intense gravitational fields but on Earth they must be contained by magnetic fields. Spitzer devised a system of magnetic containment in a figure-eight shaped loop. The machine, known as the "Stellerator," was built at Princeton's plasma physics laboratory and is one of a succession of machines by which physicists are still pursuing the goal of controlled thermonuclear fusion.

Spörer, Gustav Friedrich Wilhelm

(1822–1895)

GERMAN ASTRONOMER

Spörer (**shpu(r)**-rer) studied astronomy at the university in his native city of Berlin and wrote a thesis on comets. He became professor at the Aachen Gymnasium and in 1875 began work in the astrophysical laboratory at Potsdam. He showed, at the same time as Richard Carrington, that the Sun does not rotate as a rigid body. He also discovered the regular latitude variation of sunspots, known as *Spörer's law*. This showed that sunspots are restricted to latitudes 5°–35°. After the minimum phase, spots appear in high latitudes, gradually moving toward the equator where the old equatorial spots are just dying away.

Stahl, Franklin William

(1910–   )

AMERICAN MOLECULAR BIOLOGIST

Born in Boston, Massachusetts, Stahl was educated at Harvard and the University of Rochester where he obtained his PhD in 1956. After spending the period 1955–58 at the California Institute of Technology and a year at the University of Missouri, he moved in 1959 to the University of Oregon where he was later, in 1970, appointed to the chair of biology.

In 1958 Stahl published a joint paper with Matthew Meselson in which they reported the results of their classic experiment establishing the "semiconservative" nature of DNA replication.

Stahl, Georg Ernst

(1660–1734)

GERMAN CHEMIST AND PHYSICIAN

Where there is doubt, whatever the great majority of people hold to be true is wrong.
—His motto

Stahl (shtahl) was the son of a protestant minister from Ansbach in Germany. He studied medicine at Jena, graduating in 1684, and in 1687 was appointed physician to the duke of Sachsen-Weimar. He moved to Halle in 1694 where he became professor of medicine in the newly founded university. In 1716 he became physician to the king of Prussia.

Stahl developed phlogiston from the vague speculations of Johann Becher into a coherent theory, which dominated the chemistry of the latter part of the 18th century until replaced by that of Antoine Lavoisier. Phlogiston was the combustible element in substances. If substances contained phlogiston they would burn, and the fact that charcoal could be almost totally consumed meant that it was particularly rich in phlogiston. When a metal was heated it left a calx (a powdery substance) from which it was deduced that a metal was really calx plus phlogiston. The process could be reversed by heating the calx over charcoal, when the calx would take the phlogiston driven from the charcoal and return to its metallic form. It seemed to chemists that for the first time ever they could begin to understand the normal transformations that went on around them and the theory was the first rational explanation of combustion. It is no wonder that Stahl's theory was eagerly accepted and passionately supported.

As principles in addition to phlogiston Stahl accepted water, salt, and mercury. He also adopted the law of affinity that like reacts with like. However, there were difficulties with the theory for it seemed that, to explain some interactions, phlogiston must have no weight or even negative weight for the bodies that gain it, far from becoming heavier, sometimes become lighter.

Stanley, Wendell Meredith

(1904–1971)

AMERICAN BIOCHEMIST

Stanley, who was born in Ridgeville, Indiana, gained his doctorate in chemistry from the University of Illinois in 1929 and then traveled to Munich to work on sterols. On his return to America he joined the Rockefeller Institute for Medical Research in Princeton, New Jersey, where he began research with the tobacco mosaic virus (TMV).

Stanley was impressed by John Northrop's success in crystallizing proteins and applied Northrop's techniques to his extracts of TMV. By 1935 he had obtained thin rodlike crystals of the virus and demonstrated that TMV still retained its infectivity after crystallization. Initially this achievement met with skepticism from many scientists who had thought viruses were similar to conventional living organisms and thus incapable of existence in a crystalline form. In 1946 Stanley's research was recognized by the award of the Nobel Prize for chemistry, which he shared with Northrop and with James Sumner, who had crystallized the first enzyme.

During World War II Stanley worked on isolating the influenza virus and prepared a vaccine against it. From 1946 until his death he was director of the virus research laboratory at the University of California.

Stark, Johannes

(1874–1957)

GERMAN PHYSICIST AND SPECTROSCOPIST

The agents of Judaism in German intellectual life will have to disappear, just like the Jews themselves.
—*Das Schwarze Korps* (The Black Corps), magazine of the SS, 15 July 1937

Born at Schickenhof in Germany, Stark (shtark) was educated at the University of Munich where he obtained his doctorate and began his teaching career in 1897. Between 1906 and 1922 he taught successively at the universities of Göttingen, Hannover (where he first became a professor), Aachen, Griefswald, and Würzburg. At this point his academic career came to an end. He first tried to start a porcelain industry in northern Germany but the years following World War I were not generous to new businesses. Despite the award of the Nobel Prize for physics in 1919 his attempt to return to academic life was not successful and he had been rejected by six German universities by 1928.

This was due to his general unpopularity and because he had become somewhat extreme in his denunciation of quantum theory and the theories of Albert Einstein as being the product of "Jewish" science. Thus Stark, like Philipp Lenard, began to drift into Nazi circles and in 1930 joined the party. Unlike Lenard, who was content merely to rewrite the history of physics in the Aryan mode, Stark made a real bid for the control of German science. In 1933, although he was rejected by the Prussian Academy of Science, he succeeded in obtaining the presidency of the Imperial Institute of Physics and Technology, which he tried to use as a power base in his attempt to gain control of German physics. His attempt brought him into conflict with senior politicians and civil servants at the Reich Education Ministry, who saw him as too erratic and disruptive a force to be of much use to them, and consequently forced his resignation in 1939. Stark's final humiliation came in 1947, when he was sentenced to four years in a labor camp by a German de-Nazification court.

Stark first observed (1905) a shift of frequency in the radiation emitted by fast-moving charged particles (i.e., a Doppler effect). His other main scientific achievement was his discovery in 1913 of the spectral effect now known as the *Stark effect*, which won him the Nobel Prize. In this, following Pieter Zeeman's demonstration of the splitting of the spectral lines of a substance in a magnetic field, Stark succeeded in obtaining a similar phenomenon in an electric field. This is a quantum effect but Stark, although an early supporter of quantum theory, began to argue, with typical perversity, against the new theory as evidence for it mounted.

Starling, Ernest Henry

(1866–1927)

BRITISH PHYSIOLOGIST

A Londoner by birth, Starling studied medicine at Guy's Hospital, London, where he obtained his MB in 1889 and eventually became head of the department of physiology. In 1899 he moved to University College, London, to become Jodrell Professor of Physiology, a position he held until his death.

In 1896 Starling introduced the concept of the *Starling equilibrium*, which tried to relate the pressure of the blood to its behavior in the capillary system. He realized that the high pressure of the arterial system is enough to force fluids through the thin-walled capillaries into the tissues. But as the blood is divided through more and more capillaries its pressure falls. By the time it reaches the venous system the pressure of the fluid in the surrounding tissues is higher than that of blood in the venous capillaries, allowing much of the fluid lost from the arterial side to be regained. In theory the two systems should be in a state of equilibrium. In reality the system is complicated by the hydrostatic pressure of the blood and the osmotic pressure arising from the various salts and proteins dissolved in it.

In 1915 Starling formulated the important law (*Starling's law*) stating that the energy of contraction of the heart is a function of the length of the muscle fiber. As the heart fills with blood the muscle is forced to expand and stretch; the force with which the muscle contracts to expel the blood from the heart is simply a function of the extent to which it has been stretched. The curve that relates the two variables of the heart – pressure and volume – is known as *Starling's curve*.

Starling's best-known work was his collaboration with William Bayliss in the discovery of the hormone secretin in 1902. The normal pancreas releases a number of juices into the duodenum to aid in the process of digestion. By cutting all the pancreatic nerves and noting the continuing secretion of the pancreatic juices Starling and Bayliss showed that the release of the juices was not under nervous control. They concluded that a chemical, rather than a nervous, message must be sent to the pancreas through the blood when food enters the duodenum. They proposed to call the chemical messenger secretin. For the general class of such chemicals Starling proposed, in 1905, the term "hormone," from the Greek root meaning to excite. Thus endocrinology – a major branch of medicine and physiology – had been created.

It was widely known before the outbreak of World War I that Starling and Bayliss had been the strongest of the candidates for the Nobel Prize for physiology and medicine. However, as no awards were made during the war, they missed out completely; the prizes after 1918 were awarded for more recent work. As for honors from his own country, Starling was far too outspoken about the incompetent direction of the war even to be considered.

Stas, Jean Servais

(1813–1891)

BELGIAN CHEMIST

Stas (stahs), who was born at Louvain in Belgium, trained initially as a physician. He later switched to chemistry, serving as assistant to Jean Dumas before being appointed to the chair of chemistry at the Royal

Military School in Brussels in 1840. He had to retire in 1869 because of trouble with his voice through a throat ailment and became instead commissioner of the mint, but retired from this in 1872.

Stas was well known in his time for his extremely accurate determination of atomic weights. At first he supported William Prout's hypothesis that the weight of all elements is an exact multiple of that of the hydrogen atom. All his early measurements seemed to agree with this theory, but as his work progressed he seemed to be getting more and more fractional numbers and this turned him into the most articulate and damaging opponent of Prout. His work laid the foundations for the eventual formation of the periodic system.

Stas also carried out chemical analysis on potato blight and nicotine poisoning.

Staudinger, Hermann

(1881–1965)

GERMAN CHEMIST

Staudinger (**shtow**-ding-er), was born in Worms, Germany, the son of a philosophy professor; he was educated at the universities of Darmstadt, Munich, and Halle where, in 1903, he obtained his doctorate. He taught at the University of Strasbourg, the Karlsruhe Technical College, and the Federal Institute of Technology in Zurich before taking up an appointment at the University of Freiburg in 1926, where he remained until his retirement in 1951.

In 1922 Staudinger introduced the term "macromolecule" into chemistry and went on to propound the unorthodox view that there was no reason why molecules could not reach any size whatever. He argued that chain molecules could be constructed of almost any length in which the atoms were joined together by the normal valence bonds. Innocuous as such a view may now sound, at the time it was considered very strange and, by some, quite absurd.

The accepted view, the aggregate theory, regarded molecules in excess of a molecular weight of 5,000 as aggregates of much smaller molecules joined together by the secondary valence (nebenvalenzen) of Alfred Werner. Staudinger argued for his theory at length at a stormy meeting of the Zurich Chemical Society in 1926 in front of his most important critics. Within a few years the issue would be decisively settled in favor of Staudinger by the development of the ultracentrifuge by Theodor Svedberg. Consequently Staudinger was awarded the Nobel Prize for chemistry in 1953.

Stebbins, George Ledyard

(1906–   )

AMERICAN GENETICIST

Born in Lawrence, New York, Stebbins studied biology at Harvard where he obtained his PhD in 1931. After working at Colgate University he moved to Berkeley in 1935 and to Davis in 1950, where he established the department of genetics, holding the chair until his retirement in 1973.

In his *Variation and Evolution in Plants* (1950) Stebbins was the first to apply the modern synthesis of evolution, as expounded by Julian Huxley, Ernst Mayr, and others to plants. In collaboration with Ernest Babcock, Stebbins also studied polyploidy – the occurrence of three or more times the basic (haploid) number of chromosomes. When an artificial means of inducing polyploidy was developed Stebbins applied it to wild grasses and in 1944 managed to establish an artificially created species in a natural environment. He also used the technique to double the chromosome number of sterile interspecific hybrids and in so doing created fertile polyploid hybrids. Fertility tends to be restored in polyploid hybrids because the two different sets of chromosomes from the parent species will each have an identical set to pair with at meiosis and so the formation of gametes is not disturbed. Polyploids have proved extremely useful in plant-breeding work. Knowledge of naturally occurring polyploid systems has also helped greatly in understanding the relationships and consequently in classifying difficult genera such as *Taraxacum* (the dandelions).

Stebbins also studied gene action and proposed that mutations that result in a change in morphology act by regulating the rate of cell division in specific areas of the plant.

Steenstrup, Johann Japetus Smith

(1813–1897)

NORWEGIAN–DANISH ZOOLOGIST

> We may consider the bogs as annual reviews in which we can see how the flora and fauna of our country have developed and changed...The further we go back in time, the colder was the climate.
> —*Geognostik-geologisk Undersögelse af Skovmoserne Vidnesdam og Lillemose i det nordlige Sjaeland* (1842; Geological Examination of Forest Bogs and Small Bogs in the North of Zealand)

Born at Vang in Norway, Steenstrup (**steen**-struup) was educated in Copenhagen and obtained his first academic post as lecturer in botany and mineralogy at the Zealand Academy at Soro. After explorative expeditions to Jutland, Norway, Scotland, and Ireland (1836–44) he became professor of zoology at the University of Copenhagen Museum of Natural History. Steenstrup's most important contribution to zoology lies in his discovery and recognition, independently of Adelbert von Chamisso, of the alternation of sexual and asexual generations in certain animals, for example, the coelenterates, which produce both sexual (medusa) and asexual (polyp) forms. He also carried out anatomical and embryological studies of various marine animals, demonstrating hermaphroditism (bisexuality) in cephalopods and other organisms and investigating vision in flounders. His findings are published in such works as *Researches on the Existence of Hermaphrodites in Nature* (1846) and *Propagation and Development of Animals through Alternate Generations* (1892). Steenstrup also carried out pioneering studies of peat mosses as an aid to archeological dating and made investigations of prehistoric Danish kitchen middens.

Stefan, Josef

(1835–1893)

AUSTRIAN PHYSICIST

Stefan (**shte**-fahn) was educated in his native Klagenfurt and at the University of Vienna. In 1863 he became professor of mathematics and physics at Vienna University and remained there for the rest of his life.

Stefan's wide-ranging work included investigations into electromagnetic induction, thermomagnetic effects, optical interference, thermal conductivity, diffusion, capillarity, and the kinetic theory of gases. However, he is best remembered for his work on heat radiation in 1879. After examining the heat losses from platinum wire he concluded that the rate of loss was proportional to the fourth power of the absolute temperature; i.e., rate of loss = σT^4. In 1884 one of his students, Ludwig Boltzmann, showed that this law was exact only for black bodies (ones that radiate all wavelengths) and could be deduced from theoretical principles. The law is now known as the *Stefan–Boltzmann law*; the constant of proportionality, σ, as *Stefan's constant*.

Stefan was a good experimental physicist and a well-liked teacher. During his lifetime he held various important positions, including *Rector Magnificus* of the University (1876) and secretary (1875) then vice-president (1885) of the Vienna Academy of Sciences.

Stein, William Howard

(1911–1980)

AMERICAN BIOCHEMIST

Stein, who was born in New York City, graduated in chemistry from Harvard in 1933 and obtained his PhD in biochemistry from Columbia in 1938. He moved to the Rockefeller Institute being appointed professor of biochemistry in 1954.

From 1950 onward Stein, with his colleague Stanford Moore, worked on the problem of determining the amino-acid sequence of the enzyme ribonuclease – work which took them most of the decade. For their success in being the first to work out the complete sequence of an enzyme they shared the 1972 Nobel Prize for physiology or medicine with Christian Anfinsen.

Steinberger, Jack

(1921–)

AMERICAN PHYSICIST

Steinberger, who was born at Bad Kissingen in Germany, emigrated with his family to America in 1934 as Jewish refugees. He studied chemistry at the University of Chicago and spent World War II working in the Radiation Laboratory at the Massachusetts Institute of Technology. After the war he switched to physics and moved to Columbia, New York, where he was appointed professor of physics in 1950. In 1968 Steinberger returned to Europe to work as a senior physicist at the European Laboratory for Particle Physics in Geneva.

In the early 1960s Steinberger collaborated with his Columbia colleagues Leon Lederman and Melvin Schwartz on the two-neutrino experiment, which won for them the 1988 Nobel Prize for physics. To win the prize, Steinberger noted, for an experiment performed a quarter of a century earlier, you needed not only significant results but longevity as well.

Steno, Nicolaus

(1638–1686)

DANISH ANATOMIST AND
GEOLOGIST

The son of a goldsmith, Steno (**stee**-noh) was educated in his native city of Copenhagen before beginning his travels and studies abroad in 1660. While studying anatomy in Amsterdam he discovered the parotid salivary duct, also called *Stensen's duct* after the Danish form of his name. Other important anatomical findings included his realization that muscles are composed of fibrils and his demonstration that the pineal gland exists in animals other than man. (René Descartes had considered the pineal gland the location of the soul, believing that both were found only in man.)

Steno obtained his medical degree from Leiden in 1664 and the following year went to Florence, where he became physician to the grand duke Ferdinand II. In the field of geology he made important contributions to the study of crystals and fossils. His observations on quartz crystals showed that, though the crystals differ greatly in physical appearance, they all have the same angles between corresponding faces. This led to the formulation of *Steno's law*, which states that the angles between two corresponding faces on the crystals of any chemical or mineral species are constant and characteristic of the species. It is now known that this is a consequence of the internal regular ordered arrangement of the atoms or molecules.

Steno's geological and mineralogical views were expressed in his *De solido intra solidum naturaliter contento dissertationis prodromus* (1669; An Introductory Discourse on a Solid Body Contained Naturally within a Solid). The curious title refers to the solid bodies we refer to as fossils found in other solid bodies. Steno was particularly concerned with the common Mediterranean fossils known at the time as "glossipetrae" (tongue stones), thought by some to have fallen from the sky and by others to have grown in the earth like plants. They were triangular, flat, hard, and with discernible crenellations along two sides.

In 1666 Steno was presented with the head of a giant shark. He was immediately struck by the close similarity between the glossipetrae and sharks' teeth. In attempting to understand this correlation Steno formulated two important principles to explain how solids form in solids. By the first, an ordering rule, it proved possible to tell which solidified first by noting which solid was impressed on the other. As glossipetrae left their imprint in the surrounding rocks they must have been formed first. Therefore it made no sense to suppose that they grew in the strata.

Steno's second rule proclaimed that if two solids were similar in all observed respects then they were likely to have been produced in the same way. It followed that the similarity between the glossipetrae and sharks' teeth revealed them as fossilized teeth, a revolutionary claim at the time. But *Steno's rules* offered more than an explanation of glossipetrae; they in fact offered a novel way of interpreting the fossil record, one which would be followed increasingly by later geologists.

Steno was brought up a Lutheran but converted to Catholicism in 1667, taking holy orders in 1675. In 1677 he was appointed Titular Bishop of Titopolis (in Turkey), catering for the spiritual needs of the few Catholics surviving in Scandinavia and Northern Germany.

Stephenson, George

(1781–1848)

BRITISH ENGINEER AND INVENTOR

He could no more explain to others what he meant to do and how he meant to do it than he could fly; and therefore members of the House of Commons, after saying, "There is rock to be excavated to a depth of more than sixty feet...there is a swamp of five miles in length to be traversed...how will you do this?" and receiving no answer but a broad Northumbrian "I can't tell you how I'll do it, but I can tell you I *will* do it," dismissed Stephenson as a visionary.
—Fanny Kemble, *Records of a Girlhood* (1878)

Stephenson, who was born at Wylam, Northumberland, in the north of England, started adult life as the operator of a steam pump in a coal mine in Newcastle. He attended night school to learn to read and write.

He married and had one son, Robert, from whom he learned mathematics as they went over school homework together.

In 1813, when Stephenson was an enginewright in a coal mine, he had the idea of improving a "steam boiler on wheels" that he had seen on a neighboring mine. By introducing a steam blast, and exhausting steam into a chimney, more air could be drawn in. He built several locomotives for his colliery and in 1821, when he heard that there was to be a horse-drawn railroad to carry coal from Stockton to Darlington, he persuaded the project's sponsors to let him build a locomotive for the line. The first train traveled on the line on 27 September 1825 and carried 450 people at 15 miles (24 km) per hour.

Stephenson was then commissioned to build a 40-mile line from Liverpool to Manchester. On the line's completion, his locomotive design the *Rocket* won the famous Rainhill trials (at Rainhill near Liverpool in 1829) by achieving a speed of 36 miles (58 km) per hour. For the rest of his life Stephenson continued to design and advise on railroads throughout the world.

Stern, Curt

(1902–1981)

GERMAN–AMERICAN GENETICIST

Born at Hamburg in Germany, Stern received his PhD in zoology from the University of Berlin in 1923. He spent two years as a postdoctoral fellow with T. H. Morgan at Columbia before being appointed *Privatdozent* at the University of Berlin in 1928. Stern returned to America as a refugee from Nazi Germany in 1933 and settled first at the University of Rochester, serving as professor of zoology from 1941 until 1947. He then moved to the chair of zoology and genetics at the University of California, Berkeley, from which post he retired in 1970.

Stern, in 1931, was the first geneticist actually to demonstrate the phenomenon of crossing over in the chromosomes of *Drosophila*. That crossing over did occur had been assumed and widely used by Morgan and his school since about 1914. It was, however, only when Stern managed to get flies with a pair of homologous chromosomes that were structurally markedly different from each other at both ends that experimental support could be produced. (Normally chromosomes that pair together are structurally identical.) Stern knew that the longer chromosome (long–long) carried the genes AB while the shorter chromosome (short–short) carried the genes A^1B^1. Cytological examination of the off-spring revealed that those carrying the genes AB^1 or A^1B had long–short and short–long chromosomes respectively, showing that crossing over had indeed occurred. In the same year comparable evidence was provided by Harriett Creighton and Barbara McClintock from their work with maize.

Stern later worked on problems concerned with genetic mosaics and demonstrated that crossing over can occur in the somatic (nonreproductive) cells as well as the germ cells. He also produced the widely read textbook *Principles of Human Genetics* (1949).

Stern, Otto

(1888–1969)

GERMAN–AMERICAN PHYSICIST

Stern, who was born at Sohrau (now in Poland), was educated at the University of Breslau where he obtained his doctorate in 1912. He joined Einstein at the University of Prague and later followed him to Zurich (1913). After teaching at a number of German universities he was appointed an associate professor of theoretical physics at Rostock in 1921. He later moved (1923) to the University of Hamburg as professor of physical chemistry, but resigned in opposition to Hitler in 1933 and emigrated to America, where he took up an appointment with the Carnegie Institute of Technology at Pittsburgh. He retired in 1945.

Stern's main research came from his work with molecular beams of atoms and molecules (beams of atoms traveling in the same direction at low pressure, with no collisions occurring within the beam). Using such beams it is possible to measure directly the speeds of molecules in a gas. In 1920 Stern used a molecular beam of silver atoms to test an important prediction of quantum theory – namely, that certain atoms have magnetic moments (behave like small magnets) and that in a magnetic field these magnets take only certain orientations to the field direction.

The phenomenon is known as space quantization, and it could be predicted theoretically that silver atoms could have only two orientations in an external field. To test this, Stern with Walter Gerlach passed a beam of silver atoms through a nonuniform magnetic field and observed that it split into two separate beams. This, the famous *Stern–Gerlach experiment*, was a striking piece of evidence for the validity of the quantum theory and Stern received the 1943 Nobel Prize for physics for this work.

Stern used molecular beams for other measurements. Thus he was able to measure the magnetic moment of the proton by this technique. He also succeeded in demonstrating that atoms and molecules had wavelike properties by diffracting them in experiments similar to those of Clinton J. Davisson on the electron.

Stevin, Simon

(1548–1620)

FLEMISH MATHEMATICIAN AND ENGINEER

What appears to be a marvel is no marvel at all.
—Motto, expressing Stevin's view that everything is logically intelligible

Stevin (ste-**vĭn**) was also known as Stevinus, the Latinized form of his name. Born in the city of Bruges, he worked for a time as a clerk in Antwerp, eventually working his way up to become quartermaster of the army under Prince Maurice of Nassau. While in this post he devised a system of sluices, which could flood the land as a defense should Holland be attacked.

Stevin was a versatile man who contributed to several areas of science. Mathematics owes to him the introduction of the decimal system of notating fractions. This system was perfected when John Napier invented the decimal point. Stevin helped to popularize the practice of writing scientific works in modern languages (in his case Dutch) rather than Latin, which for so long had been the traditional European language of learning. However such was the hold of the old ways that Willebrord Snell thought it was worthwhile to translate some of Stevin's work into Latin. To hydrostatics he contributed the discovery that the shape of a vessel containing liquid is irrelevant to the pressure that liquid exerts. He also did some important experimental work in statics and in the study of the Earth's magnetism.

Stewart, Balfour

(1828–1887)

BRITISH PHYSICIST

Stewart was educated at the universities of St. Andrews and Edinburgh (his native city). He spent the years between 1846 and 1856 in the business world, but from 1856, when he joined the staff of Kew Observatory, he devoted himself to science. In 1856 he became assistant to J. D. Forbes at Edinburgh. He was appointed director of Kew Observatory in 1859. In 1870 he was made professor of natural philosophy at Owens College, Manchester, remaining there until his death.

Stewart's most original contributions to science were his researches into radiant heat. He extended Pierre Prévost's work on heat exchange and investigated absorption and radiation. However, Stewart's work did not become widely known and when, two years later, Kirchhoff independently made similar investigations his more rigorous treatment and the practical applications suggested by his work had the decisive influence on subsequent developments. After 1859 Stewart devoted himself mainly to meteorology, his investigations including terrestrial magnetism and sunspots. One of his suggestions (1882) was that daily variations in the Earth's magnetic field were caused by electric currents in the upper atmosphere.

Stibitz, George Robert

(1904–1995)

AMERICAN COMPUTER PIONEER

The son of a theologian, Stibitz was born in York, Pennsylvania, and educated at Cornell where he gained his PhD in 1930. He worked at the Bell Telephone Laboratories in New York as a mathematical engineer from 1930 to 1945, when he moved to the Vermont firm Burlington and Underhill as consultant in applied mathematics. Finally, from 1964 until his retirement in 1972, he worked as a research associate at the Dartmouth Medical School, New Hampshire.

At Bell Stibitz worked on the design of relay switches and in 1937 he was struck by the thought that relays could be used to represent binary numbers. Thus a lighted bulb could represent 1 and an unlighted bulb 0. Using this simple idea any number could be represented. So, with a "scrap of board, some snips of metal from a tobacco can, 2 relays, 2 flashlight bulbs, and a couple of dry cells," Stibitz built his first calculator.

Stibitz was asked if he could extend his work to deal with complex numbers. The result was his Model I at a cost of $20,000, based on about 450 electromagnetic relays. It was slow, limited by the speed of the relays, not programmable, and very restricted in its use. With the outbreak of war, Stibitz undertook to prepare a Mark II version for the NDRC (National Defense Research Committee) for use by the artillery. Two further models were developed during the war for military use.

Finally, in 1945, Model V appeared, an all-purpose machine containing 9,000 relays. It was the first to incorporate a floating-point decimal, that is, to represent a number by a fraction multiplied by a power of ten. Two copies of the model were built, both for military use.

Stirling, Robert

(1790–1878)

SCOTTISH INVENTOR

Stirling was born at Cloag in Scotland and attended the universities of Glasgow and Edinburgh. Having been ordained in the Church of Scotland in 1816, he spent most of his life from 1837 until his retirement in 1876 as minister at Galston, Ayrshire.

As engineers of today search for a reasonably efficient, nonpolluting, and silent engine, they seem unaware that precisely such an engine had been developed by a Scottish clergyman in 1816. A *Stirling engine* consists of a closed cylinder with a regenerator separating two opposing pistons. The compression space is kept at a low temperature by an external cooling system; the expansion chamber at a high temperature by an external heat supply. At the beginning of the cycle air, the working fluid, is compressed by the piston and moves into the expansion space while absorbing heat stored in the regenerator in the previous cycle. As the air expands and drives the piston work is done. The motion of the pistons and the gas is then reversed as heat is supplied to the expansion space from an external source.

As the source of heat is external, any fuel can be used and sited wherever convenient. Stirling's first engine generated about two horsepower and ran for about two years pumping water out of a quarry. A later model in 1843 was a modified steam engine that produced 37 horsepower more efficiently than a steam engine. Because the cylinders tended to burn out rather quickly, a common fault of Stirling engines, it was converted to steam use. In drawing up the patent, Robert Stirling was assisted by his brother James – a mechanical engineer who managed the foundry in Dundee where the engine was constructed.

In more recent years with improved materials major industrialists have investigated the possibility of developing the Stirling engine. It has, however, found only marginal use to power small generators and certain specialized engines.

Stock, Alfred

(1876–1946)

GERMAN CHEMIST

Stock (shtok) was born at Danzig (now Gdańsk in Poland) and educated at the University of Berlin, where he worked for some time as assistant to Emil Fischer. In 1909 he joined the staff of the Inorganic Chemistry Institute at Breslau, later moving to the Kaiser Wilhelm Institute in Berlin. He then served as director of the Chemical Institute at the Karlsruhe Technical Institute (1926–36).

Stock began studying boron hydrides in 1909. Boron had previously been little studied and was thought only to react with strongly electronegative elements, such as oxygen. However Stock found that magnesium boride and acid produced B_4H_{10}, the first of the several boron hydrides he discovered. It was clear from this and the other hydrides, B_2H_6 and $B_{10}H_{14}$, that the bond between boron and hydrogen could not be the familiar covalent bond which holds between carbon and hydrogen. Its actual form was not solved until the work of William Lipscomb in the 1950s. The boranes have since become useful in rocket fuels.

Stock is also remembered as being the first working chemist to be fully aware that he was suffering from mercury poisoning. By 1923 he was complaining of a large number of such distressing symptoms as deafness, vertigo, headaches, and amnesia, which he traced to mercury. Not only did he give his findings maximum publicity, broadcasting his infirmities to the chemical world, but he also devised techniques of laboratory practice to reduce the risk of such poisoning and introduced tests for the presence of mercury.

Stokes, Adrian

(1887–1927)

ANGLO-IRISH BACTERIOLOGIST

Stokes, whose father worked in the Indian Civil Service, was born at Lausanne in Switzerland and educated at Trinity College, Dublin, where he obtained his MD in 1911. After serving in the Royal Army Medical Corps during the war, in which he was awarded the DSO, he returned to Dublin in 1919 as professor of bacteriology but soon moved to London, where in 1922 he became professor of pathology at Guy's Hospital.

In 1920 Stokes visited Lagos to study yellow fever. He was anxious to test the suggestion of the Japanese bacteriologist Hideyo Noguchi that yellow fever was caused by the bacillus *Leptospira icteroides*, but it was not until his second visit to Lagos in 1927 that he made the vital breakthrough.

Stokes succeeded, for the first time, in infecting an experimental animal (the rhesus monkey) with the disease. He went on to show that while he could pass yellow fever from monkey to monkey there was no evidence that Noguchi's bacillus was also transmitted. But before he could proceed further Stokes, who was daily handling infected monkey blood, contracted the disease and joined the growing list of bacteriologists who had fallen victim to the virus.

Stokes, Sir George Gabriel

(1819–1903)

BRITISH MATHEMATICIAN AND PHYSICIST

Stokes was born at Skreen (now in the Republic of Ireland) and studied at Cambridge, remaining there throughout his life. In 1849 he became Lucasian Professor of Mathematics, but he found it necessary to supplement his slender income from this post by teaching at the Government School of Mines in London. He held his Cambridge chair until his death aged 84. He was the member of parliament for the university and among his many honors were a baronetcy conferred on him in 1889.

Stokes was equally interested in the theoretical and experimental sides of physics and did important work in a wide area of fields, including hydrodynamics, elasticity, and the diffraction of light. In hydrodynamics he derived the formula now known as *Stokes's law*, giving the force resisting motion of a spherical body through a viscous fluid. Among Stokes's other fields of study was fluorescence – one of his experimental discoveries was the transparency of quartz to ultraviolet light. He was also much interested in the then influential concept of the ether as an explanation of the propagation of light. Stokes became aware of some inherent difficulties with the concept, but rather than rejecting the whole idea of an ether he tried to explain these problems away by using work he had done on elastic solids, though naturally enough problems arose with his own ideas.

Stokes was perceptive in his views of other physicists' work. For example, he was among the first to appreciate the importance of the work of James Joule and to see the true meaning of the spectral lines discovered by Joseph von Fraunhofer.

Stoney, George Johnstone

(1826–1911)

IRISH PHYSICIST

Stoney, the son of an impoverished landowner, was born at Oakley Park (now in the Republic of Ireland) and educated at Trinity College, Dublin. After graduation in 1848 he worked as an assistant to the astronomer, Lord Rosse, at his observatory at Parsonstown until 1853 when he was appointed professor of natural philosophy at Queen's College, Galway. However, from 1857 onwards Stoney worked as an administrator, first as secretary of Queen's University, Belfast, and finally, from 1882 until 1893, as superintendent of civil service examinations.

Stoney is best known for his introduction of the term "electron" into science. Although he is reported to have spoken of "an absolute unit of electricity" as early as 1874, his first public use of the term in print was in 1891 when he spoke of "these charges, which it will be convenient to call electrons" before the Royal Society of Dublin.

He did however make more substantial contributions to science than this and in early spectroscopy his work was of considerable significance. He began, in 1868, by making a crucial distinction between two types of molecular motion. There was the motion of a molecule in a gas relative to other molecules, which Stoney was able to exclude as the cause of spectra. There was also internal motion of a molecule, which according to Stoney produces the spectral lines. He went on to tackle, with little real success, the difficult problem of establishing an exact formula for the numerical relationship between the lines in the hydrogen spectrum. This problem was solved by the quantum theory of Niels Bohr.

Strabo

(*c.* 63 BC–*c.* 23 AD)

GREEK GEOGRAPHER AND HISTORIAN

> The poets were not alone in sponsoring myths. Long before them cities and lawmakers had found them a useful expedient...They needed to control the people by superstitious fears, and these cannot be aroused without myths and marvels.
>
> —*Geography*, Book I

Strabo (**stray**-boh), who was born at Amaseia (now Amasya in Turkey), traveled to Rome in 44 BC and remained there until about 31 BC. He visited Corinth in 29 BC and in about 24 BC sailed up the Nile.

Although the historical writings of Strabo, including his *Historical Sketches*, in 47 books, have been almost entirely lost, his *Geography*, in 17 books, has survived virtually intact. This major geographical work is an important source of information on the ancient world. In it Strabo accepted the traditional description of the Earth as divided into five zones with the *oikoumene*, or inhabited part, represented as a parallelogram spread over eight lines of latitude and seven meridians of longitude. Where he excelled, however, was in the field of historical and cultural geography and he gave a detailed account of the history and culture of the lands and people of the Roman Empire and of such areas as India, which lay beyond the dominion of Augustus. In this he quoted much from the earlier Greeks, including Eratosthenes and Artemidorus.

Strabo, not content merely to describe the lands of the civilized world, also wished to understand its enormous diversity. He rejected the simple climatic determinism that he attributed to the Stoic Poseidonius, arguing in its place for the role of institutions and education. Despite the value of this work Strabo seemed to exercise little influence until Byzantine times.

Strachey, Christopher

(1916–1975)

BRITISH COMPUTER SCIENTIST

The son of a cryptographer and a nephew of the writer Lytton Strachey, Christopher Strachey was born at Hampstead in north London and educated at Cambridge. After graduating in 1939 he spent the war working on the development of radar. On demobilization in 1945 he became a schoolmaster. During this time he developed an interest in large computers.

In 1951 he wrote a successful checkers program for ACE (Automatic Computing Engine), one of the three computers then in use in Britain. Soon after he moved to the National Research and Development Corporation where he worked on the design of the new Ferranti computer, Pegasus. He also worked on computer models of the St. Lawrence Seaway, one of the great postwar engineering projects.

After spending some time as a private consultant, Strachey opted for academic life, accepting an appointment at Cambridge in 1962. He moved to Oxford in 1966 where he became professor of computation in 1971, a post he held until his death in 1975.

During this latter academic period Strachey worked on the design of the new high level computer language, CPL, later developed into BCPL (Basic Computer Programming Language).

Strasburger, Eduard Adolf

(1844–1912)

GERMAN BOTANIST

Strasburger (**shtrahs**-buur-ger) was born in the Polish capital Warsaw and educated at the universities of Paris, Bonn, and Jena, where he received his PhD in 1866. In 1868 he taught at Warsaw but in 1869 returned to Jena, where he became professor of botany in the same year and director of the botanical gardens in 1873.

His early work extended the researches of Wilhelm Hofmeister into the regular alternation of generations in the plant kingdom. Strasburger was the first to describe accurately the embryo sac in gymnosperms (conifers and their allies) and angiosperms (flowering plants) and to demonstrate the process of double fertilization in angiosperms. In 1875 he laid down the basic principles of mitosis in his *Cell Formation and Cell Division*. The third edition of this work contained one of the now well-established laws of cytology: that new nuclei can arise only from the division of existing nuclei.

From 1880 until his death Strasburger worked at Bonn, establishing it as one of the world's leading centers for cytological research. In 1891 he demonstrated that physical forces (e.g., capillarity), and not physiological forces, are primarily responsible for the movement of liquids up the plant stem. In 1894, together with three other eminent botanists, he founded the famous *Strasburger's Textbook of Botany*, which was run to 30 editions and is still important as a general course book today.

Strassmann, Fritz

(1902–)

GERMAN CHEMIST

Strassmann (**shtrahs**-mahn) was born at Boppard in Germany and educated at the Technical University at Hannover. He taught at Hannover and at the Kaiser Wilhelm Institute before being appointed to the chair of inorganic and nuclear chemistry at the University of Mainz in 1946. In 1953 he became director of chemistry at the Max Planck Institute.

In 1938 Strassmann collaborated with Otto Hahn on the experiment that first clearly revealed the phenomenon of nuclear fission.

Strato of Lampsacus

(about 287 BC)

GREEK PHILOSOPHER

Little is known about the life of Strato (or Straton; **stray**-toh or **stray**-ton). Born at Lampsacus in Greece, he probably studied under Theophrastus at the Lyceum and later became tutor in Alexandria to the son of the first king Ptolemy of Egypt. He succeeded Theophrastus as head of the Peripatetic school of philosophy in 287 BC and remained in Athens until his death in about 269. Although only fragments of his writings remain, Diogenes Laertius names about 40 of his works.

Many of Strato's ideas were developments of Aristotelianism with some resemblances to atomism. He believed that all bodies, even light rays, consisted of tiny particles separated by a void; this void existed as discrete interstices where the particles did not fit together exactly; space is always filled with some kind of matter. Strato gave explanations of the nature of light and sound, and had a considerable reputation as an experimenter.

Strato, held in high esteem by later writers, represents a link between the Lyceum of Athens and its offshoot, the Museum of Alexandria. He was known in antiquity as Strato the physicist.

Strohmeyer, Friedrich

(1776–1835)

GERMAN CHEMIST

Strohmeyer (**shtroh**-mI-er) was educated at the university in his native city of Göttingen, where his father was a professor of medicine, and also studied in Paris under Louis Vauquelin. He started teaching in 1802 at

Göttingen, becoming professor of chemistry in 1810. He was appointed inspector-general of the apothecaries of Hanover in 1817.

In 1817 while working with what he thought was zinc carbonate he found that it turned yellow when heated. At first he thought this indicated the presence of iron, but after failing to discover this he traced the color to a new element, which he named cadmium after the Latin name for zinc ore, cadmia.

Strömgren, Bengt Georg Daniel

(1908–1987)

SWEDISH–DANISH ASTRONOMER

Elis Strömgren (**stru(r)m**-grayn), father of Bengt, was an astronomer of distinction who served as director of the Copenhagen Observatory. His son was born at Gothenburg in Sweden and studied at the University of Copenhagen. After obtaining his PhD there in 1929 he joined the staff and was appointed professor of astronomy in 1938. He succeeded his father as director in 1940. He later moved to America, serving from 1951 to 1957 as professor at the University of Chicago and director of the Yerkes and McDonald observatories. He was a member of the Institute for Advanced Study, Princeton, from 1957 until 1967, when he returned to Copenhagen as professor of astrophysics.

In the 1930s and 1940s Strömgren engaged in pioneering work on emission nebulae – huge clouds of interstellar gas and dust shining by their own light. He showed that they consist largely of ionized hydrogen, H II to the spectroscopist. If hot young stars were embedded in uniformly but thinly distributed neutral hydrogen, then the emission by them of ultraviolet radiation would virtually ionize the gas completely. To meet this condition the stars would need a surface temperature of some 25,000 kelvin. At a certain distance from the star, the *Strömgren radius*, the emitted photons of radiation would no longer possess sufficient energy to ionize the hydrogen, leading to a sharp boundary between ionized and cooler nonionized regions. Strömgren showed that this distance would depend on the density of the hydrogen and the stellar temperature.

A typical example of the process described by Strömgren is to be found in the Orion nebula. Later work has however shown that there are three types of emission nebulae, two of which are produced by different mechanisms.

Struve, Friedrich Georg Wilhelm von

(1793–1864)

GERMAN–RUSSIAN ASTRONOMER

> A magnificent work ranking among the greatest performed by astronomical observers in recent times.
>
> —Friedrich W. Bessel, reviewing Struve's *Stellarum Duplicium Mensurae Micrometricae* (1837; Micrometric Measurements of Double Stars)

Struve (**shtroo**-ve), who was born at Altona in Germany, moved to Dorpat in Latvia in 1808 in order to escape conscription into the Napoleonic army then in control of Germany. He took a degree in philology in 1811 before becoming professor of astronomy and mathematics in Dorpat in 1813. In 1817 he became director of the Dorpat Observatory, which he equipped with a 9.5-inch (24-cm) refractor that he used in a massive survey of binary stars from the north celestial pole to 15°S. He measured 3,112 binaries – discovering well over 2,000 – and cataloged his results in *Stellarum Duplicium Mensurae Micrometricae* (1837; Micrometric Measurements of Double Stars).

In 1835 Czar Nicholas I persuaded Struve to set up a new observatory at Pulkovo, near St. Petersburg. There in 1840 Struve became, with Friedrich Bessel and Thomas Henderson, one of the first astronomers to detect parallax. He chose Vega, a bright star with a larger-than-normal proper motion and soon established a parallactic measurement (that was, however, too high).

Struve founded a dynasty of astronomers that is still in existence. He was succeeded by his son Otto at Pulkovo, his grandson Hermann became director of the Berlin Observatory, and his great-grandson, Otto Struve, became director of the Yerkes Observatory in Wisconsin.

Struve, Otto

(1897–1963)

RUSSIAN–AMERICAN ASTRONOMER

It is not an exaggeration to say that almost all our knowledge of the structure of the Milky Way which has developed during the past quarter of a century has come from the Mount Wilson discovery of spectroscopic luminosity criteria.

—*The Science Counselor* (1948)

Struve (**stroo**-ve), who was born at Kharkov in Russia, came from a long line of distinguished astronomers, being the great grandson of its founder Friedrich Georg von Struve. His father was the professor of astronomy and director of the observatory at the University of Kharkov and he had two uncles who were directors of German observatories. His studies at the university were interrupted by World War I but he finally graduated in 1919. Called up again in 1919 after the revolution, he ended up destitute in Turkey in 1920. Following a journey of some difficulty he finally arrived in America in 1921 where he attended the University of Chicago, obtaining his PhD in 1923. He worked at the Yerkes Observatory, serving as director from 1932 to 1947 as well as professor of astrophysics at Chicago for the same period. He played an important role in the founding of the McDonald Observatory on Mount Locke in Texas and the planning of its 82-inch (2.1-m) reflecting telescope, then the second largest in the world. He served as McDonald's first director from 1939 to 1950. Struve moved to a less demanding position at the University of California at Berkeley in 1950 but agreed in 1959 to become the first director of the National Radio Astronomy Observatory at Green Bank in West Virginia. Forced to resign in 1962 owing to ill health, he died shortly after.

Although Struve spent much of his time in administration and organization, he was able to conduct some major observational work. He made spectroscopic studies of binary and variable stars, stellar rotation, stellar atmospheres, and, possibly most important, of interstellar matter.

One of the problems facing astronomers at the beginning of the century was whether there was any interstellar matter and if so, did it significantly absorb or distort distant starlight. This was no trivial question for the answer could make nonsense of many accounts of the distribution of stars. In 1904 Johannes Hartmann had argued for the presence of interstellar calcium by pointing out that the calcium spectral lines associated with the binary system Delta Orionis did not oscillate with the other spectral lines as the stars orbited each other. This work was extended by Vesto Slipher in 1908 and 1912.

Struve produced evidence on the next crucial point as to whether the interstellar matter was diffuse and pervasive or only local and associated with individual star systems. In 1929, in collaboration with B. P. Gerasimovic, he showed that it exists throughout the Galaxy. This work was also done independently by John Plaskett. In 1937 Struve discovered the presence of interstellar hydrogen, in ionized form, which though much more prevalent than calcium was initially more difficult to detect.

Sturgeon, William

(1783–1850)

BRITISH PHYSICIST

Sturgeon's father, a shoemaker of Whittington, England, has been described as an "idle poacher who neglected his family." Seeing little future as an apprentice cobbler, Sturgeon enlisted in the army in 1802. While serving in Newfoundland his interest in science was aroused while watching a violent thunderstorm. Finding that no one seemed able to explain satisfactorily to him the cause and nature of lightning, he started reading whatever science books were available. This led him to the study of mathematics and Latin. When he left the army in 1820 he had acquired a considerable amount of scientific knowledge and skill. He began to write popular articles, joined the Woolwich Literary Society, and must have so impressed his associates that a move was made to find him a more suitable job than the shoemaking he was being forced back into. Thus in 1824 he was appointed to a lectureship in experimental philosophy at the East India Company's Royal Military College at Addiscombe.

In 1840 he moved to Manchester as the superintendent of the Royal Victoria Gallery of Practical Science. In 1836 he began the publication of the *Annals of Electricity*, the first periodical of its kind to be issued in Britain.

After various further appointments as an itinerant lecturer he was awarded a government pension of £200 a year for his services to science. His collected papers, *Scientific Researches*, were published in 1850.

Sturgeon made several fundamental contributions to the new science of electricity. The cell devised by Alessandro Volta had certain inherent weaknesses – any impurity in the zinc plates used caused erosion of the electrode. In 1828 Sturgeon found that amalgamating the plate with mercury made it resistant to the electrolyte. More important was his construction in about 1821 of the first electromagnet. Following the work of François Arago he wound 16 turns of copper wire around a one-foot iron bar, which, when bent into the shape of a horseshoe, was powerful enough to lift a weight of 9 pounds when the wire was connected to a single voltaic cell. He demonstrated his magnets in 1825 in London. More powerful ones were soon built by Joseph Henry and Michael Faraday.

In later years Sturgeon also made improvements to the design of the galvanometer, inventing the moving-coil galvanometer in 1836. In the same year he introduced the first commutator for a workable electric motor (1836).

Sturtevant, Alfred Henry

(1891–1970)

AMERICAN GENETICIST

I went home, and spent most of the night (to the neglect of my undergraduate homework) in producing the first chromosome map.
—On his early work on chromosomes,
c. 1910. *History of Genetics* (1965)

Born in Jacksonville, Illinois, Sturtevant graduated at Columbia University in 1912 and continued there, working for his PhD under the supervision of T. H. Morgan. His thesis dealt with certain aspects of fruit fly (*Drosophila*) genetics, the research being conducted in the famous "fly room" at Columbia.

During this period Sturtevant developed a method for finding the linear arrangement of genes along the chromosome. This technique, termed "chromosome mapping," relies on the analysis of groups of linked genes. His paper, published in 1913, describes the location of six sex-linked genes as deduced by the way in which they associate with each other: it is one of the classic papers in genetics.

Sturtevant later discovered the so-called "position effect," in which the expression of a gene depends on its position in relation to other genes. He also demonstrated that crossing over between chromosomes is prevented in regions where a part of the chromosome material is inserted the wrong way round. This had important implications for genetic analysis. Although employed by the Carnegie Institution in 1915, Sturtevant continued working at Columbia until 1928. He then moved to the California Institute of Technology, where he was professor of genetics and biology until his death. He wrote many important papers and books and was one of the authors of *The Mechanism of Mendelian Heredity* (1915).

Suess, Eduard

(1831–1914)

AUSTRIAN GEOLOGIST

The history of the continents results from that of the seas.
—*The Face of the Earth*, Vol. II

Suess (zoos), born the son of a businessman in London, was educated at the University of Prague. He began work, in 1852, in the Hofmuseum, Vienna, before moving to the University of Vienna in 1856 where he became professor of geology in 1861. Besides being an academic Suess served as a member of the Reichsrat (parliament) from 1872 to 1896. He was responsible for the provision of pure water to Vienna by the construction of an aqueduct in 1873 and the prevention of frequent flooding by the opening of the Danube canal in 1875.

His major work as a geologist was his publication of *Das Antlitz der Erde* (1883–88), translated into English as *The Face of the Earth* (5 vols., 1904–24). This was not a particularly original work but acquired significance as being the great synthesis of the achievements of the later 19th-century geologists, geographers, paleontologists, and so on. He also published, in 1857, a classic work on the origin of the Alps.

Suess was the first to propose the existence of the great early southern continent, Gondwanaland. He was impressed by the distribution of a fern, *Glossopteris*, present during the Carboniferous period. It was found in such widely scattered lands as Australia, India, South Africa, and South America. Suess therefore proposed that these lands had once formed part of one great continent, which he named for the Gonds, the supposed aboriginal Indians.

Sugden, Samuel

(1892–1950)

BRITISH CHEMIST

Born in Leeds, England, Sugden was educated at the Royal College of Science, London, where he was awarded a DSc in 1924. He joined the staff of Birkbeck College, London, where he served as professor of chemistry (1932–37) before moving to University College, London. During World War II he served in the Ministry of Supply and although he returned to his chair after the war his ill health virtually ended his research career.

Sugden worked on the physical properties of liquids, particularly surface tension. He introduced the measure that he named the "parachor" (1924) – a formula involving the molecular weight of a substance, its surface tension, and its densities in the liquid and vapor states. The parachor was a standard measure of molecular volume – i.e., a measure of the volume of molecules independent of attractive forces between molecules within the liquid. As such it was hoped that it could be used for determining the structures of organic compounds by adding values for different atoms and types of bond. Although the idea aroused much interest at the time it had little practical success, and the technique is now obsolete. Sugden also worked on radioactive tracers and on the magnetic properties of chemical compounds. In 1930 he published *The Parachor and Valency*.

Sugita, Genpaku

(1738–1818)

JAPANESE PHYSICIAN

The son of a physician, Sugita (suu-**gee**-ta) learned surgery in Edo. While there he saw a Dutch translation of a German anatomical text, *Anatomische Tabellen* (1722; Anatomical Tables) by Johan Kulmus. He was surprised to see how radically the anatomical illustrations differed from those contained in Chinese texts. Some time soon after he attended a postmortem dissection of a prisoner executed by decapitation. He took with him the illustrations from Kulmus and was amazed to note the agreement between its diagrams and the body. No such concord could be found with Chinese texts. Consequently Sugita decided to translate a Dutch version of the text into Japanese. It was published in 1774 as *Kaito Shinso* (New Book of Anatomy) and was the first translation of a European medical text into Japanese.

The influence of Sugita's work was considerable. It created a demand for further Dutch texts, as well as a new school of "Dutch medicine" called Ranpo, which was openly critical of traditional Chinese-style medicine.

Sumner, James Batcheller

(1877–1955)

AMERICAN BIOCHEMIST

Nothing can take the place of intelligence.
—TIBS, July 1981

Sumner, a wealthy cotton manufacturer's son from Canton, Massachusetts, was educated at Harvard, where he obtained his PhD in 1914. In the same year he took up an appointment at the Cornell Medical School where, in 1929, he became professor of biochemistry.

Despite having lost an arm in a shooting accident at 17, Sumner persisted in his desire to become an experimental chemist. In 1917 he began his attempt to isolate a pure enzyme. He chose for his attempt urease, which catalyzes the breakdown of urea into ammonia and carbon dioxide and is found in large quantities in the jack bean. After much effort he found, in 1926, that if he dissolved urease in 30% acetone and then chilled it, crystals formed. The crystal had high urease activity. Moreover Sumner's crystals were clearly protein and however hard he tried to separate the protein from them he always failed. He was therefore forced to conclude that urease, an enzyme, was a protein. However, this ran against the authority of Richard Willstätter who had earlier isolated enzymes in which no protein was detectable. In fact, protein was in Willstätter's samples, but in such small quantities as to be undetected by his techniques.

Consequently little attention was paid to Sumner's announcement and it was only when John Northrop succeeded in crystallizing further protein enzymes in the early 1930s that his work was properly acknowledged. In 1946 for "his discovery that enzymes can be crystallized" he was awarded the Nobel Prize for chemistry jointly with Northrop and Wendell Stanley.

Su Sung

(1020–1101)

CHINESE INVENTOR

Su Sung (soo suung), who was born at Nan-an in the Fujian province of China, was a mandarin and, like others of his class, he had considerable scientific knowledge and insight. In 1086 the emperor, Che Tsung, issued instructions for the construction of an astronomical clock that would surpass those of earlier dynasties. By clock the emperor meant a celestial globe or armillary sphere, that is, a set of connected rings corresponding to the main circles of the celestial sphere, which revolved in harmony with the heavens. There is a long tradition of such instruments in China going back as far as Chang Heng in the second century AD and including major improvements by I-Hsing in the eighth century.

By 1090 Su Sung had built his clock, details of which he revealed in his *New Design for an Astronomical Clock* (1094), which were clear enough to permit the construction of a working model in 1961. The clocktower was 30 feet tall and contained a revolutionary mechanism.

The problem facing clock makers is how to release the power in the mechanism, whether it be a falling weight or water, gradually, measurably, and under control. The early water clocks avoided the problem by using a continuous flow of water on the surface of which a pointer could float. The great advance beyond this was the escapement, which only appeared in Europe with Giovanni Dondi in the 14th century but which was first introduced by Su Sung. Water poured into scoops on a waterwheel, which when full tripped a lever that allowed the wheel to turn a measurable amount. The next scoop then filled and repeated the process. This turned the main drive shaft that worked the celestial globes, spheres, and chiming bells.

There is no direct evidence supporting the claim that Su Sung's work was known to the European clockmakers. The fate of the clock itself is obscure. It appears to have been damaged in a storm and finally destroyed in the Mongol invasion of the 13th century. The tradition of celestial clockwork survived only until the Ming dynasty in the 14th century, for when Matteo Ricci arrived in China in 1600 he could find no one who could still understand the astronomical instruments of their ancestors.

Sutherland, Earl

(1915–1974)

AMERICAN PHYSIOLOGIST

Born in Burlingame, Kansas, Sutherland was educated at Washington University, St. Louis. After serving in World War II as an army doctor he returned to St. Louis but in 1963 moved to Vanderbilt University, Tennessee, as professor of physiology. In the year before his death Sutherland joined the University of Miami Medical School in Florida.

In 1957 Sutherland discovered a molecule of great biological significance – 3,5–adenosine monophosphate, more familiarly known as cyclic AMP. At that time he was working with T. Rall on the way in which the hormone adrenaline (epinephrine) effects an increase in the amount of glucose in the blood. They found that the hormone stimulated the release of the enzyme adenyl cyclase into liver cells. This in turn converts adenosine triphosphate (ATP) into cyclic AMP, which then initiates the complex chain converting the glycogen stored in the liver into glucose in the blood. The significance of this reaction is that adrenaline does not act directly on the molecules in the liver cell; it apparently needs and "calls for" what soon became described as a "second messenger," cyclic AMP.

Sutherland went on to show that other hormones, such as insulin, also used cyclic AMP as a second messenger and that it was in fact used to control many processes of the cell. For his discovery of cyclic AMP Sutherland was awarded the 1971 Nobel Prize for physiology or medicine.

Svedberg, Theodor

(1884–1971)

SWEDISH CHEMIST

Svedberg (**sved**-berg or **svayd**-bar-ye), born the son of a civil engineer in Fleräng, Sweden, was educated at the University of Uppsala, where he obtained his doctorate in 1908. He spent his whole career at the university, becoming a lecturer in physical chemistry in 1907, a professor (1912–49), and finally, in 1949, director of the Institute of Nuclear Chemistry.

In 1924 he introduced the ultracentrifuge as a technique for investigating the molecular weights of very large molecules. In a suspension of particles, there is a tendency for the particles to settle (under the influence of gravity); this is opposed by Brownian motion, i.e., by collision with molecules. The rate of sedimentation depends on the size and weight of the particles, and can be used to measure these.

Svedberg applied this to measuring the sedimentation of proteins in solution, using an ultracentrifuge that generated forces much greater than that of the Earth's gravitational field. Using this, he could measure the molecular weights of proteins and was able to show that these were much higher than originally thought (hemoglobin, for instance, has a molecular weight of about 68,000).

Apart from confirming the claim made by Hermann Staudinger for the existence of giant molecules, Svedberg's invention also settled one further question. The same protein invariably yielded the same weight, thus implying that they did have a definite size and composition and were not, as Wilhelm Ostwald had earlier maintained, irregular assemblies of smaller molecules. For his work on the ultracentrifuge Svedberg was awarded the Nobel Prize for chemistry in 1926.

Svedberg was less successful with the inference he drew from his measurements of protein molecular weights. He thought that the molecular weight of egg albumin formed the basic protein unit of which all the other proteins were multiples. Following later research by crystallographers in the 1930s this view was disproved.

Swammerdam, Jan

(1637–1680)

DUTCH NATURALIST AND MICROSCOPIST

> The matter being properly considered, a worm or caterpillar does not change into a pupa, but becomes a pupa by the growing of parts.
> —*Historia insectorum* (1669; Account of Insects)

Swammerdam (**svahm**-er-dahm), an Amsterdam apothecary's son, studied medicine at Leiden University, graduating in 1667. However, he never practiced and instead devoted his life to microscopical studies of a widely varying nature. His most important work, namely the discovery and description of red blood corpuscles in 1658, was completed before he went to university. He later demonstrated experimentally that muscular contraction involves a change in the shape but not volume of the muscle. He also studied movements of the heart and lungs and discovered the valves in the lymph vessels that are named for him.

Swammerdam is also remembered for his pioneering work on insects. He collected some 3,000 different species and illustrated and described the anatomy, reproductive processes, and life histories of many of these. This work, together with his system of insect classification, laid the foundations of modern entomology. Swammerdam's *Biblia naturae* (Book of Nature), published long after his death (1737–38), still stands as one of the finest one-man collections of microscopical observations.

At the theoretical level Swammerdam developed a new argument in support of the preformationist position, the view that organisms are born already formed. His argument, first presented in his *Historia insectorum* (1669; Account of Insects), was based upon the nature of insect metamorphosis. At first sight it might appear that the metamorphic process supported the alternative view of development, epigenesis, the claim that organisms develop gradually and in sequence. Swammerdam, however, revealed a different picture when, with the aid of a microscope, he succeeded in identifying structures belonging to butterflies in pupae and caterpillars. The caterpillar, Swammerdam insisted, was not changed into a butterfly, rather it grew by the expansion of parts already formed. Nor does the tadpole change into a frog; it becomes a frog "by the infolding and increasing of some of its parts." In proof of his position Swammerdam would display a silkworm to his critics, peel off the outer skin, and display the rudiments of the wings within.

In the same work Swammerdam added one more piece of evidence against the claim that organisms can generate spontaneously. Insects found in plant galls, he pointed out, developed from eggs laid therein by visiting flies.

Swan, Sir Joseph Wilson

(1828–1914)

BRITISH INVENTOR AND
INDUSTRIALIST

Swan, the son of a dealer in anchors and chains from Sunderland in the northeast of England, was educated at local schools and apprenticed to an apothecary at the age of 14. After three years he left to work for a chemical supplier, John Mawson, eventually becoming his partner. One part of their business was supplying chemicals to photographers and Swan made an early improvement in the new collodion process when, in

1864, he patented the carbon process for producing permanent photographic prints.

But long before this, in 1848, he had already become interested in the construction of electric lights – the development for which he is best known. Early patent specifications on platinum filaments heated in a vacuum, led him to construct similar lamps with carbon filaments. He failed, however, to solve the problem of all the early bulbs – the filament rapidly oxidized at the high temperatures necessary for incandescence. The obvious solution – to exclude oxygen by using a better vacuum tube – was technically beyond him. So, after about 1860, he put the problem to one side.

He was fortunate in that in 1865 Hermann Sprengel invented an efficient mercury vacuum pump. Swan seems not to have heard of this basic tool until about 1877 but then lost little time in fitting a carbon filament into one of the improved vacuum tubes and in December 1878 he demonstrated his new invention to the Newcastle Chemical Society. He patented his discovery in 1880, forming the Swan Electric Company the following year. The House of Commons tried the new bulbs almost immediately, the British Museum in 1882. His work was an instant success and he stood to make a vast fortune.

The one drawback was that Thomas Edison had made a similar discovery in America and was intent on developing it exclusively for the use of his own company. Both men eventually came to an agreement and merged to set up a joint company, the Edison and Swan United Electric Light Company. Swan's discovery brought him considerable renown and he was knighted in 1904.

Sydenham, Thomas

(1624–1689)

ENGLISH PHYSICIAN

Born at Wynford Eagle in Dorset, England, Sydenham studied medicine at Oxford University. Although his education was interrupted by the English Civil War, in which he fought for the Parliamentarians, he returned to Oxford to gain his MB in 1648 and became a fellow of All Souls College. He later moved to London where he spent the rest of his life in private practice.

For his insistence on painstaking observation and careful recording, expressed in his *Observationes medica* (1676; Medical Observations), Sydenham became known as the English Hippocrates. He rejected speculative theories in medicine, the justification for this resting heavily on a frequently used analogy between diseases and plants. Sydenham saw similarities between the life cycle of a plant and the course of a disease, declaring that, by careful observation, one could predict the course of a disease in the same way as a botanist can predict the time of flowering, leaf fall, etc. He was one of the first to describe scarlet fever and Sydenham's chorea.

By way of therapy Sydenham followed such traditional practices as bleeding and purging while making full use of such newly introduced drugs as quinine for malaria and the mercury and laudanum of Paracelsus. He is, however, more accurately represented by his own statement, "I have consulted my patient's safety and my own reputation most effectually by doing nothing at all."

Sylvester, James Joseph

(1814–1897)

BRITISH MATHEMATICIAN

As the prerogative of Natural Science is to cultivate a taste for observation, so that of Mathematics is, almost from the starting point, to stimulate the faculty of invention.
—*The Collected Mathematical Papers of James Joseph Sylvester* (1904–12)

Born in London, Sylvester studied mathematics at Cambridge but was not granted his BA degree since he was a practicing Jew. The relevant statute was later revoked and Sylvester was granted both his BA and MA in 1871. He was widely read in a number of languages and was a keen amateur musician and a prolific poet. Feeling unable to keep an academic post as a mathematician Sylvester worked first in an insurance company and later as a lawyer. In 1876 he went to America to become the first professor of mathematics at Johns Hopkins University. He became the first editor of the *American Journal of Mathematics* and did much to develop mathematics in America. He returned to England in 1883 to become Savilian Professor of Geometry at Oxford University.

Sylvester's best mathematical work was in the theory of invariants and number theory. With his lifelong friend the British mathematician Arthur Cayley, he was one of the creators of the theory of algebraic invariants, which proved to be of great importance for mathematical physics.

Sylvius, Franciscus

(1614–1672)

DUTCH PHYSICIAN

Sylvius (**sil**-vee-us) was born at Hannau in Prussia (now in Germany), where his parents had fled from the Dutch struggles for independence from Spain. He Latinized his name from Franz de le Boë and attended the University of Basel where he qualified as a doctor in 1637. He later returned to the (independent) Netherlands and practiced medicine in Amsterdam from 1641 until 1658 when he was appointed professor of medicine at the University of Leiden, a post he held until his death.

Much influenced by Paracelsus and Jan van Helmont, he attempted to break away from the traditional theories of disease and tried to formulate a straightforward chemical account. His system, no less simplistic than that of the traditional humoral theory of Hippocrates, began with the fermentation of food into blood. From this process arose acids and alkalis, which could balance each other or lead to an acid- or an alkali-dominated disturbance of the body. Although the acid–alkali theory of disease had a short life, it was important in showing that there were alternatives to classical theory.

Sylvius was also an anatomist and described the division between the temporal and frontal lobes of the brain (the *fissure of Sylvius*). He also described the *aqueduct of Sylvius*, connecting the third and fourth ventricles of the brain while the ordinarily named middle cerebral artery is more accurately and impressively known as *arteria cerebri media Sylvii*.

Synge, Richard Laurence Millington

(1914–1994)

BRITISH CHEMIST

Synge was born in Liverpool, where his father was a member of the Liverpool Stock Exchange, and educated at Cambridge University, obtaining his doctorate in 1941. He worked in a number of research institutes, including the Wool Industries Research Association at Leeds (1941–43) and the Lister Institute of Preventive Medicine (1943–48). From 1948 to 1967 he worked as a protein chemist at the Rowett Research Institute near Aberdeen and finally, from 1967 to 1976, at the Food Research Institute, Norwich.

Synge was jointly awarded the 1952 Nobel Prize for chemistry with Archer Martin for their development in 1941 of partition chromatography, especially paper chromatography, which was to become one of the basic analytical tools of the revolution in biochemistry and molecular biology. Synge used the method to find the structure of the simple protein gramicidin S, working out the sequence of the different amino acids in the molecule. This work soon proved of great use to Frederick Sanger in his elucidation of the sequence of amino acids in the insulin molecule.

Szent-Györgi, Albert von

(1893–1986)

HUNGARIAN–AMERICAN BIOCHEMIST

A substance that makes you ill if you don't eat it.
—His definition of a vitamin

Discovery consists of seeing what everybody has seen and thinking what nobody has thought.
—Quoted by I.-J. Good in *The Scientist Speculates*

Szent-Györgi (sent-**jur**-jee), who was born in the Hungarian capital Budapest, studied anatomy at the university there, obtaining his MD in 1917. He continued his studies in Hamburg, Groningen, and at Cambridge University where he received his PhD in 1927. He also spent some time at the Mayo Clinic, Minnesota, before returning to Hungary as professor of medical chemistry at the University of Szeged. In 1947, however, he emigrated to America, becoming director of the Institute for Muscle Research at the Marine Biological Station, Woods Hole, Massachusetts.

Szent-Györgi, a highly original and productive biochemist, first became widely known in the late 1920s for his work on the adrenal glands. In the usually fatal condition Addison's disease, where the adrenal glands cease to function, one symptom is a brown pigmentation of the skin. Szent-Györgi wondered if there was a connection between this and the browning of certain bruised fruits, which is due to the oxidation of phenolics to quinole. Some fruits, notably citrus, do not turn brown because they contain a substance that inhibits this reaction. Szent-Györgi isolated a substance from adrenal glands, which he named hexuronic acid, that also turned out to be present in nonbruising citrus fruits known for their high vitamin C content. He suspected he had finally succeeded in isolating the elusive vitamin but was anticipated in announcing his discovery by Charles King, who published his own results two weeks earlier. The main reason for Szent-Györgi's delay was the problem of supply. However, when he began work in Szeged, with its paprika milling industry, he found a rich supply of the vitamin in Hungarian paprika and was soon able to confirm his suppositions and further investigate the action of the vitamin in the body.

Szent-Györgi also studied the uptake of oxygen in isolated muscle tissue and found that he could maintain the rate of uptake by adding any one of the four acids – succinic, fumaric, malic, or oxaloacetic. This work was extended by Hans Krebs and led to the elucidation of the Krebs cycle. For his studies into "biological combustion processes" Szent-Györgi was awarded the 1937 Nobel Prize for physiology or medicine.

In addition to such work Szent-Györgi became widely known for his studies into the biochemistry of muscular contraction. It was known that the contractile part of muscle was made mainly from the two proteins, actin and myosin. In 1942, in collaboration with Ferenc Straub, Szent-Györgi showed that the two proteins can be encouraged to form fibers of actomyosin which, in the presence of ATP, the cell's energy source, will contract spontaneously. Just how the combining of the two proteins can lead to muscular contraction was a question pursued and illuminated by Hugh Huxley.

Szilard, Leo

(1898–1964)

HUNGARIAN–AMERICAN PHYSICIST

If you want to succeed in this world you don't have to be much cleverer than other people, you just have to be one day earlier.
—*Leo Szilard: His Version of the Facts* (1978)

Szilard (**sil**-ard), the son of an architect, studied engineering in his native city of Budapest before moving to the University of Berlin where he began the study of physics and obtained his doctorate in 1922. He remained there until 1933 when, after spending a few years in England working at the Clarendon Laboratory, Oxford, and at St. Bartholomew's Hospital, London, he emigrated to America in 1938. After the war Szilard moved into biology and in 1946 was appointed to the chair of biophysics at the University of Chicago, where he remained until his death. He became a naturalized American in 1943.

Szilard was one of the first men in the world to see the significance of nuclear fission and the first to bring it to the attention of Roosevelt. In

1934, after hearing of the dismissal of the possibility of atomic energy by Ernest Rutherford, he worked out that an element that is split by neutrons and that would emit two neutrons when it absorbed one neutron could, if assembled in sufficiently large mass, sustain a nuclear chain reaction. Szilard applied for a patent, which he assigned to the British Admiralty to preserve secrecy.

When in 1938–39 he heard of the work of Otto Hahn and Lise Meitner on the fission of uranium he was well prepared. After quickly confirming that the necessary neutrons would be present Szilard, fearing the consequences that would ensue from Hitler's possession of such a weapon, decided that the only sound policy was for America to develop such a weapon first. To this end he approached Albert Einstein, with whom he had worked earlier and who commanded sufficient authority to be heard by all, and invited him to write a letter to the President of the United States. This initiated the program that was to culminate in the dropping of the atomic bomb on Hiroshima six years later. During the war Szilard worked on the development of the bomb and, in particular, worked with Enrico Fermi on the development of the uranium–graphite pile.

If Szilard was one of the first to see the possibility and necessity to develop the bomb he was also one of the earliest to question the wisdom and justice of actually using it against the Japanese. He was the dominant spirit behind the report submitted by James Franck to the Secretary of War in 1945 forecasting the nuclear stalemate that would follow a failure to ban the bomb.

Although his early reputation was based on his work in physics he moved, after the war, into molecular biology. Szilard took his new subject seriously, attending classes at the Cold Spring Harbor laboratories in 1946. He was soon to develop a high degree of competence, designing an important new instrument, the chemostat, formulating new theories on the aging process, and stimulating Jacques Monod in his work on the operon and the repressor.

T

Takamine, Jokichi

(1854–1922)

JAPANESE–AMERICAN CHEMIST

Takamine (tah-kah-**mee**-nee) was born at Takaoka in Japan, the son of a physician. Although brought up along traditional lines, he nevertheless received a modern scientific education at the Tokyo College of Science and Engineering, where he graduated in chemical engineering in 1879. After two years' training at Anderson's College, Glasgow, he returned to Japan in 1883 and entered the government department of agriculture and commerce. In 1887 he left to establish the first factory for the manufacture of superphosphates in Japan.

In 1890, having married an American, he settled permanently in America. He set up a private laboratory and in 1894 produced Takadiastase, a starch-digesting enzyme, which had applications in medicine and the brewing industry.

It had been demonstrated in 1896 that an injection of an extract from the center of the suprarenal (adrenal) gland causes blood pressure to rise rapidly. In 1901 Takamine managed to isolate and purify the substance involved – adrenaline (epinephrine). This was the first isolation and purification of a hormone from a natural source.

Tamm, Igor Yevgenyevich

(1895–1971)

RUSSIAN PHYSICIST

Born the son of an engineer in Vladivostock, Tamm (tahm) was educated at the universities of Edinburgh and Moscow, where he graduated in 1918. After a short period at the Odessa Polytechnic, Tamm taught at Moscow University (1924–34) then moved to the Physics Institute of the Academy.

In 1958, in collaboration with Ilya Frank and Pavel Cherenkov, Tamm was awarded the Nobel Prize for physics for his work in explaining Cherenkov radiation.

Tansley, Sir Arthur George

(1871–1955)

BRITISH PLANT ECOLOGIST

Tansley was born in London. Having found his school science teaching "farcically inadequate," he attended lectures at University College, London, where he received his first proper tuition in botany from Francis Oliver. In 1890 he went to Cambridge University and on graduation returned to London as Oliver's assistant.

In the following years Tansley's thinking was greatly influenced by two major books, *Ecological Plant Geography* (1895) by E. Warming and *The Physiological Basis of Plant Geography* (1898) by Andreas Schimper. These – together with his travels in Ceylon, Malaya, and Egypt – stimulated his interest in different vegetation types.

In 1902 Tansley founded *The New Phytologist*, a journal designed to promote botanical communication and debate in Britain. In 1913 he founded and became the first president of the British Ecological Society and four years later founded and edited the *Journal of Ecology*. These activities, and his ecology courses at Cambridge, played a large part in establishing the science of ecology.

After World War I Tansley turned to psychology and resigned from Cambridge in 1923 to spend time studying under Sigmund Freud in Austria. In 1927 he became professor of botany at Oxford University, a position held until his retirement in 1937. He continued to exert much influence, however, becoming president of the Council for the Promotion of Field Studies in 1947 and chairman of the Nature Conservancy Council in 1949, both bodies that he had helped to create. Probably his most important book, *The British Islands and Their Vegetation* (1939), was also published after his retirement.

Tartaglia, Niccoló

(1500–1557)

ITALIAN MATHEMATICIAN, TOPOGRAPHER, AND MILITARY SCIENTIST

I...continued to labor by myself over the works of dead men, accompanied only by the daughter of poverty that is called industry.
—On teaching himself mathematics. *Quesiti et inventioni diverse* (1546; Various Inquiries and Discoveries)

Tartaglia (tar-**tah**-lya) was born Niccoló Fontana but as a boy he suffered a saber wound to his face during the French sack of Brescia (1512), his native city; this left him with a speech defect and he adopted the nickname Tartaglia (Stammerer) as a result. Tartaglia began his studies as a promising mathematician, but his interests soon became very wide-ranging. He held various posts, including school teacher, before he eventually became a professor of mathematics in Venice where he stayed.

Tartaglia is remembered chiefly for his work on solving the general cubic equation. He discovered a method in 1535 but did not publish it. Incautiously he revealed his new method to his friend the mathematician Girolamo Cardano, who published it in *Ars magna* (1545; The Great Skill). This, not surprisingly, was the end of their friendship and led to a violent controversy. Tartaglia eventually lost the quarrel and with it his post as lecturer at Brescia in 1548.

Tartaglia's other chief mathematical interests were in arithmetic and geometry. The pattern now known as "Pascal's triangle" appeared in a work of Tartaglia's. His geometrical work centered on problems connected with the tetrahedron and he helped further the diffusion of classical mathematics by making the first translation of Euclid's *Elements* into a modern European language. His chief published work was the three-volume *Trattato di numeri et misure* (1556–60; Treatise on Numbers and Measures), an encyclopedic work on elementary mathematics. Apart from these mathematical activities Tartaglia made notable innovations in topography and the military uses of science, such as ballistics.

Tatum, Edward Lawrie

(1909–1975)

AMERICAN BIOCHEMIST

Tatum, who was born in Boulder, Colorado, studied chemistry at the University of Wisconsin, where his father was professor of pharmacology. He obtained the BA degree in 1931, then undertook research in microbiology for his master's degree, conferred the following year. His PhD was more biochemically oriented and after receiving his doctorate he worked as a research assistant in biochemistry for a year. He studied bacteriological chemistry at Utrecht University from 1936 to 1937 and on returning to America was appointed research associate at Stanford University.

His early experiments at Stanford concentrated on the nutritional requirements of the fruit fly, *Drosophila melanogaster*, but in 1940, in collaboration with George Beadle, he began working on the pink bread mold, *Neurospora crassa*. They irradiated the mold with x-rays to induce mutations and were then able to isolate a number of lines with different nutritional deficiencies. These lines needed special supplements to the basic growth medium to enable growth to continue as normal. When a mutant mold was crossed with the normal wild-type mold, the dietary deficiency was inherited in accordance with expected Mendelian ratios. Such studies established that genes act by regulating specific chemical processes. During World War II this work was of use in maximizing penicillin production, and it has also made possible the introduction of new methods for assaying vitamins and amino acids in foods and tissues.

In 1945 Tatum moved to Yale University where he extended his techniques to yeast and bacteria. Through studying nutritional mutations of the bacterium *Escherichia coli*, he and Joshua Lederberg were able to demonstrate, in 1946, that bacteria can reproduce sexually. Following this work, bacteria have become the primary source of information on the genetic control of biochemical processes in the cell.

Tatum returned to Stanford in 1948 and in 1957 joined the Rockefeller Institute for Medical Research. In 1958, together with Beadle and Lederberg, he received the Nobel Prize for physiology or medicine in recognition of the work that helped create the modern science of biochemical genetics.

Taube, Henry

(1915–)

AMERICAN INORGANIC CHEMIST

Taube, who was born in Saskatchewan, Canada, moved to America in 1937 and became naturalized in 1942. He was educated at the University of Saskatchewan and the Berkeley campus of the University of California, where he gained his PhD in 1940. After working at Cornell University (1941–46), Taube moved to Chicago and in 1952 was appointed professor of chemistry, a post he held until 1962 when he accepted a comparable appointment at Stanford, California.

As a leading inorganic chemist Taube has succeeded in developing a range of experimental techniques for studying the kinetics and mechanism of inorganic reactions, in particular electron-transfer reactions. Transition metals such as iron, copper, cobalt and molybdenum form coordination compounds of a type first described by Alfred Werner. In a typical coordination compound a metal ion is attached to a number of ligands, such as water or ammonia. It was thought that the ligands would keep the ions apart and inhibit electron transfer between ions. Taube showed experimentally that ligand bridges form between interacting complexes, thus allowing electrons to be transferred.

For his work in this field Taube was awarded the 1983 Nobel Prize for chemistry.

Taylor, Brook

(1685–1731)

BRITISH MATHEMATICIAN

Born in Edmonton, near London, Taylor studied at Cambridge University, and was secretary to the Royal Society during the period 1714–18. He made important contributions to the development of the differential calculus in his *Methodus incrementorum directa et inversa* (1715; Direct and Indirect Methods of Incrementation). This contained the formula known as *Taylor's theorem*, which was recognized by Joseph Lagrange in 1772 as being the principle of differential calculus. The *Methodus* also contributed to the calculus of finite differences, which Taylor applied to the mathematical theory of vibrating strings.

Outside mathematics Taylor was an accomplished artist and this led him to an interest in the theory of perspective, publishing his work on this subject in *Linear Perspective* (1715). *Taylor expansions* are named for him.

Taylor, Sir Geoffrey Ingram

(1886–1975)

BRITISH PHYSICIST

Many of his scientific contributions opened up whole new fields; he had the knack of being first.

—Obituary notice in *The Times*, 30 June 1975

Taylor, a Londoner by birth, was educated at Cambridge University where, apart from absence on service in two wars, he spent the whole of his career. He served initially in 1911 as reader in dynamic meteorology and from 1923 until his retirement in 1952 as research professor in physics.

Taylor was an original researcher and a prolific author, publishing on a wide variety of topics. Studies by him over many years into fluid turbulence have yielded applications in fields as varied as meteorology, aerodynamics, and Jupiter's Great Red Spot. One of his most important ideas, that of dislocation in crystals, was first formulated in 1934. By introducing the idea of an edge dislocation in which one layer of atoms is slightly displaced relative to a neighboring layer he was able to explain much about the properties of metals. The same proposal was made independently by Michael Polanyi and E. Orowan.

Taylor, Sir Hugh (Stott)

(1890–1974)

BRITISH CHEMIST

Taylor, the son of a glass technologist, was born in St. Helens, in northwest England. He studied chemistry at the University of Liverpool (1906–12), where he obtained a DSc in 1914, and in Stockholm under Svante Arrhenius. In 1914 he moved to Princeton University, remaining there for the whole of his career and serving as professor of chemistry from 1922 until his retirement in 1958.

At the beginning of his career Taylor worked on problems of catalysis; during World War I he concentrated on the catalytic synthesis of ammonia from nitrogen and hydrogen (the Haber process). With Eric Rideal, he produced the comprehensive work *Catalysis in Theory and Practice* (1919). In 1925, in his paper *A Theory of the Solid Catalytic Surface* (1925), he suggested that catalyst surfaces could not be homogeneous, i.e., that only a fraction of the surface of the catalyst was important and that the catalyst, in effect, had "active centers."

During World War II Taylor worked on the Manhattan Project at the Columbia Nuclear Laboratory to develop the gaseous diffusion process introduced by John Dunning for the enrichment of uranium.

Taylor, Joseph Hooton

(1941–)

AMERICAN ASTROPHYSICIST

Born in Philadelphia, Taylor was educated at Haverford College, Pennsylvania, and at Harvard, where he gained his PhD in astronomy in 1968. He moved to the University of Massachusetts, Amherst, in 1969 and was appointed professor of astronomy in 1977, a post he held until 1980 when he was elected professor of physics at Princeton.

In 1974 Russell Hulse, a research student of Taylor, while working at the Arecibo Radio Telescope in Puerto Rico, discovered a binary pulsar. The pulsar orbited its invisible companion with a period of 7.75 hours, and rotated about its axis every 0.05903 seconds. Taylor and Hulse continued to observe the pulsar and to establish the details of its orbital behavior as precisely as possible.

Taylor also saw that the pulsar could provide an important observational test of Einstein's theory of general relativity. In 1916 Einstein had argued that an accelerating mass should radiate energy in the form of gravitational waves. Any such energy radiated by Hulse's pulsar, 16,000 light years away, would be so weak by the time it reached Earth as to be undetectable. In fact, so far no direct reproducible evidence has been obtained for the existence of gravitational waves, despite the experiments of Joseph Weber carried out since the 1960s.

Taylor realized there was another way for the

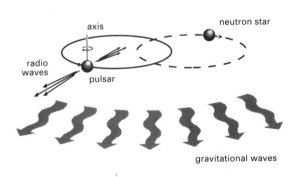

BINARY PULSAR The pulsar discovered by J. H. Taylor and Russell Hulse has a companion, which it orbits approximately every eight hours.

gravitational waves to be detected. Any system radiating gravitational waves will be losing energy. This loss of energy will cause the pulsar and its companion to approach closer to each other and a consequent decrease in the pulsar's orbital period. The orbital shrinkage would amount to only 3.5 meters a year, too small to be detected; a decrease of 75 millionth of a second per year in the orbital period, however, should be detectable. After four years careful observation and analysis Taylor announced in 1978 that he had detected just such a decrease in the orbital period. "Hence 66 years after Einstein predicted the existence of gravitational waves," Taylor concluded, "an experiment has been done that yields clear evidence for their existence." For his discovery of this evidence Taylor shared the 1993 Nobel Prize for physics with Hulse.

Taylor, Richard

(1929–)

CANADIAN PHYSICIST

Taylor, who was born in Medicine Hat, Alberta, was educated at the University of Alberta and at Stanford, California, where he obtained his PhD in 1962. After two years at the University of California, Berkeley, he returned to Stanford in 1964 and was appointed to the chair of physics in 1970.

In 1990 Taylor shared the Nobel Prize for physics with Jerome Friedman and Henry Kendall for their discovery in 1967 that the proton has an inner structure. Their work presented the first convincing experimental evidence for the existence of quarks.

Taylor, Stuart

(1937–)

AMERICAN PHYSIOLOGIST

The son of a physician, Taylor was educated at Cornell, Columbia, and New York University where he gained his PhD in 1966. From 1970 he has worked at the Mayo Medical School, Minnesota. Since the early 1990s he has also served as Distinguished Professor at Hunter College, New York.

During the mid-1950s physiologists began at last to understand in some detail the manner in which muscles contract. One of the leading workers in this field is Hugh Huxley, whom Taylor heard lecturing at Columbia in 1964. Taylor became so interested in the subject that he served a two-year postdoctoral fellowship in Huxley's laboratory at University College, London.

On his return to the United States, after a spell at the Brooklyn Downstate Medical Center teaching pharmacology, Taylor moved to the Mayo Medical School and set up a research project to enable physiologists to visualize in more detail the process of muscular contraction. To this end Taylor and his colleagues worked on the development of a technique known as CAMERA (Computer Assisted Measurement of Excitation-Response Activity). With the aid of CAMERA Taylor was able to obtain some 5,000 images per second of muscles contracting. He went on to investigate the role played by calcium in initiating muscle contraction.

Telford, Thomas

(1757–1834)

BRITISH ARCHITECT AND
ENGINEER

Telford was brought up in rural poverty in Westerkirk, Dumfriesshire, Scotland. When he was 15 years old and working as an apprentice stonemason, he was allowed access to the library of a local lady. He moved to Edinburgh in 1780 then to London in 1782 and in 1786 was appointed surveyor of Shropshire, where his work included the construction of bridges and buildings. Three bridges over the River Severn gained him notice and as a result he was appointed (1793) to plan and construct the Ellesmere Canal (1793–1805). His two great aqueducts, built to carry the canal, brought him national recognition. Many of his projects were noted for their architectural beauty.

In 1803 Telford presented a report on opening up access to the Scottish Highlands. The plan included extensive road and bridge building as well as a continuous channel from the North Sea to the Atlantic for warships and commercial ships – the Caledonian Canal. In 18 years 900 miles (1,450 km) of road and 120 bridges were built. He designed a system of locks for the Caledonian Canal to cope with a 90-foot (27-m) difference in water level.

Telford's other projects included the Göta Canal in Sweden, for which he received a Swedish knighthood, but his greatest achievement was the Menai Bridge between Wales and the Island of Anglesey. This was the first really successful suspension bridge in Britain. It took ten years to build and is still in use. He used wrought-iron chains, which were towed across the Menai Strait and hoisted, and from which the deck of the bridge was suspended.

Telford was the first president of the Institution of Civil Engineers, London.

Teller, Edward

(1908–   )

HUNGARIAN–AMERICAN PHYSICIST

Two paradoxes are better than one; they may even suggest a solution.
—Attributed remark

The son of a lawyer, Teller was born in the Hungarian capital Budapest. Having attended the Institute of Technology there, he continued his education in Germany at the universities of Karlsruhe, Munich, Leipzig (where he obtained his PhD in 1930), and Göttingen. He left Germany when Hitler came to power in 1933. After a short period in Denmark and London, he emigrated to America where in 1935 he took up an appointment as professor of physics at George Washington University. During the war he worked in the theoretical physics division at Los Alamos on the development of the atom bomb, resuming his academic career in 1946 at the University of Chicago. Teller moved in 1953 to the University of California at Berkeley, where he remained until his retirement in 1975.

Teller is often referred to as the "father of the hydrogen bomb." Insofar as he made the initial proposal in 1942, worked longest on the project, and campaigned most vigorously for its completion, the description is accurate. If, however, the phrase is taken to mean that the bomb exploded in 1951 was Teller's own design, the description is misleading.

From the mid-1940s Teller was working with three possible bomb designs, A, B, and C. By 1947 it was clear that B would fail and that C, though viable, would produce too small an explosion to be worthwhile. Research effort was therefore concentrated on design A which required horrendous amounts of calculation; these were carried out by the mathematician Stanislaw Ulam. In 1950 President Truman, following the Russian atomic bomb explosion, ordered the program to be speeded up. At this point Ulam revealed that option A was hopeless, requiring such massive amounts of tritium as to be virtually unworkable. At this point Teller found himself, after nearly a decade of intensive and costly research, without any viable design or idea in response to the President's urgent call.

By early 1951 Ulam and Teller had worked out a fourth and effective method, the origin of which remains a matter of dispute. The basic problem of the early designs was that the bomb would fly apart under the explosion of the fission device before the fusion material was sufficiently compressed. Ulam's solution was to use x-rays from the fission device to produce compression waves long before any shock waves could strangle the planned thermonuclear reaction. While Hans Bethe attributes the idea to Ulam, Teller has claimed the credit for himself, insisting that "Ulam triggered nothing."

After the successful explosion of the first thermonuclear device in 1951 Teller moved to the Livermore laboratories, which were performing research for the Atomic Energy Commission. Shortly afterward, loyalty hearings were held against Oppenheimer, who had been director of the Los Alamos laboratory while the atom bomb was developed. Teller, despite much pressure from the scientific community, decided to testify against him and although he did not accuse Oppenheimer of disloyalty, still less of treason, he did complain that "his actions frankly appeared to me confused and complicated...I would personally feel more secure if public matters could rest in other hands." In the charged atmosphere of the 1950s this contributed to the withdrawal of Oppenheimer's security status and to the ostracism of Teller by many of his old friends and colleagues. For ten years Teller was neither invited to nor visited Los Alamos.

Teller continued to be a powerful figure in American science after his retirement from Berkeley in 1975. In 1984, for example, he advised Washington that the influential paper of Carl Sagan and his colleagues on the dangers of a nuclear winter was far from convincing. At Livermore he worked on and campaigned vigorously for the Strategic Defense Initiative (SDI), better known as "Star Wars." The key ingredient of SDI was the x-ray laser, which would supposedly destroy enemy missiles in space. Teller had to face charges against the program from Hans Bethe that it was "unwieldy, costly, easily countered, destabilizing, and uncertain." Despite these and other charges, and despite a tendency for supporters of the SDI to promise more than they could ever hope to deliver, Teller's support for the project never wavered. He published a forthright defense of the program in his book *Better a Shield than a Sword* (1987). However, in 1993 the project was abandoned amid accusations that test results had been distorted. The SDI department was renamed the Ballistic Missile Defense Organization and now researches ways of eliminating enemy missiles nearer the ground.

Temin, Howard Martin

(1934–1994)

AMERICAN MOLECULAR
BIOLOGIST

Born in Philadelphia, Pennsylvania, Temin studied biology at Swarthmore College and at the California Institute of Technology, where he obtained his PhD in animal virology in 1959. He worked at the University of Wisconsin from 1960 onward, serving as professor of oncology there from 1969 until his death from lung cancer.

There are two classes of viruses, those with DNA and those with RNA genes. The former replicate by transforming their DNA into new DNA and transmit information from DNA through RNA into protein. The latter class of viruses replicate RNA into RNA and transmit information directly into protein without the need for DNA. That is, all such reactions fitted into the general sequence DNA to RNA to protein, the so-called Central Dogma of molecular biology. In the early 1960s Temin discovered a curious feature of the RNA Rous chicken sarcoma virus (RSV): he found that it would not grow in the presence of the antibiotic actinomycin D, a drug known to inhibit DNA synthesis. Temin realized that this might mean the RSV replicated through a DNA intermediate, which he called the provirus. That is, Temin was proposing the sequence RNA (of the RSV) to DNA (provirus) to RNA (replicated RSV) which, while not actually excluded by the Central Dogma, was not implied by it either.

If such a reaction did take place then it would certainly require the presence of an enzyme capable of transcribing RNA into DNA. It was not until 1970 that Temin identified the enzyme (discovered independently by David Baltimore) known variously as reverse transcriptase or RNA-directed DNA polymerase. It was for this work that Temin shared the 1975 Nobel Prize for physiology or medicine with Baltimore and Renato Dulbecco.

Tennant, Smithson

(1761–1815)

BRITISH CHEMIST

Tennant was born in Richmond, England, the son of a vicar. After studying medicine at Edinburgh University, where he attended the lectures of Joseph Black, he went on to study chemistry and botany at Cambridge University (1782). He received his medical degree in 1796 and was professor of chemistry at Cambridge from 1813 until his death.

Tennant was one of the first professional chemists to be seriously interested in chemistry's application to farming. He purchased land in Somerset where he farmed and showed, among other things, that lime from many parts of England contains magnesium and is positively harmful to crops. In pure chemistry he showed that diamond is a form of carbon (1797). While working with platinum minerals dissolved in aqua regia (1803–04) he discovered two new elements. The first he named iridium from the Greek for rainbow to mark the many colors its compounds form and the second he called osmium from the Greek for malodorous.

He died while on a visit to France when a drawbridge he was crossing on horseback broke, resulting in his drowning.

Tesla, Nikola

(1856–1943)

CROATIAN–AMERICAN PHYSICIST

It has been argued that the perfection of guns of great destructive power will stop warfare... On the contrary, I think that every new arm that is invented, every new departure that is made in this direction, merely...gives a fresh impetus to further development.
—Quoted by H. Bruce Franklin in *War Stars: The Superweapon and the American Imagination* (1988)

Tesla (**tes**-la) was born at Smiljan in Croatia, at that time within the Austro–Hungarian empire. He studied mathematics and physics at the University of Graz and philosophy at Prague. In 1884 he emigrated to America where he worked for Thomas Edison for a while before a bitter quarrel led to his resigning and joining the Westinghouse Company. After his invention of the first alternating current (a.c.) motor in 1887 he left to set up his own research laboratory.

Most commercially generated electricity at that time (including that of Edison) was direct current (d.c.). Tesla saw some fundamental weaknesses in the d.c. system: it required a commutator and needed costly maintenance. The main advantage of a.c. was that, with transformers, it was easier and cheaper to transmit very high voltages over long distances. Tesla's invention was soon taken up by Westinghouse and led to intense competition with Edison and the other d.c. users. Edison was not beyond suggesting that a.c. was inherently dangerous and when in 1889 the first criminal was electrocuted, Edison proposed that being "westinghoused" would be a good term to describe death by the electric chair.

In 1891 the transformer was first demonstrated at the Frankfurt fair when it was shown that 25,000 volts (alternating) could be transmitted for 109 miles (175 km) with an efficiency of 77%. The a.c. system soon replaced d.c. electricity, which was confined to specialized uses.

Thales

(*c.* 625 BC–*c.* 547 BC)

GREEK PHILOSOPHER, GEOMETER, AND ASTRONOMER

Water is the principle, or the element, of things. All things are water.
—Quoted by Plutarch in *Placita Philosophorum*

To Thales, the primary question was not what do we know, but how do we know it.

—Aristotle

It is with Thales (**thay**-leez) that physics, geometry, astronomy, and philosophy have long been thought to begin. However, little is known of the first supposed identifiable "scientist" apart from the fact that he was born at Miletus, now in Turkey, and a number of anecdotes that clearly originate in folklore.

Thus he is traditionally supposed to have acquired his learning from Egypt, an implausible claim when the modest mathematical skills of sixth-century Egypt are contrasted with the supposed achievements of Thales. To him is even attributed a proof of the proposition that the circle is divided into two equal parts by its diameter, a theorem not to be found in Euclid some 300 years later. It is also reported by the historian Herodotus that Thales gave a successful prediction of a solar eclipse in 585 BC.

The remaining claim for Thales rests on his introduction of naturalistic explanations of physical phenomena in opposition to the customary understanding of nature in terms of the behavior of the gods. Hence the importance of his claim that everything is water, perhaps the first recorded general physical principle in history.

Theiler, Max

(1899–1972)

SOUTH AFRICAN–AMERICAN VIROLOGIST

Theiler, the son of a physician from Pretoria in South Africa, was educated at the University of Cape Town; he received his MD in 1922 after attending St. Thomas's Hospital, London, and the London School of Tropical Medicine. The same year he left for America to take up a post at the Harvard Medical School. In 1930 Theiler moved to the Rockefeller Foundation in New York, where he later became director of the Virus Laboratory and where he spent the rest of his career.

When Theiler began at Harvard it was still a matter of controversy whether yellow fever was a viral infection, as Walter Reed had claimed in 1901, or whether it was due to *Leptospira icteroides*, the bacillus discovered by Hideyo Noguchi in 1919. Theiler's first contribution was to reject the latter claim by showing that *L. icteroides* is responsible for Weil's disease, an unrelated jaundice.

Little can normally be done in the development of a vaccine without an experimental animal in which the disease can be studied and in which the virus can spread. The breakthrough here came in 1927 when Adrian Stokes found that yellow fever could be induced in Rhesus monkeys from India. Within a year both Stokes and Noguchi had died from yellow fever and did not witness Theiler's next major advance. As monkeys tend to be expensive and difficult to handle, researchers much prefer to work with such animals as mice or guinea pigs. Attempts to infect mice had all failed when Theiler tried injecting the virus directly into their brains. Although the animals failed to develop yellow fever they did die of massive inflammation of the brain (encephalitis). In the course of this work Theiler himself contracted yellow fever but fortunately survived and developed immunity.

Although, he reported in 1930, the virus caused encephalitis when passed from mouse to mouse, if it was once more injected into the monkey it revealed itself still to be functioning and producing yellow fever. Yet there had been one crucial change: the virus had been attenuated and while it did indeed produce yellow fever it did so in a mild form and, equally important, endowed on the monkey immunity from a later attack of the normal lethal variety. All was thus set for Theiler to develop a vaccine against the disease. It was not however until 1937, after the particularly virulent Asibi strain from West Africa had passed through more than a hundred subcultures, that Theiler and his colleague Hugh Smith announced the development of the so-called 17-D vaccine. Between 1940 and 1947 Rockefeller produced more than 28 million doses of the vaccine and finally eliminated yellow fever as a major disease of man. For this work Theiler received the 1951 Nobel Prize for physiology or medicine.

Thénard, Louis-Jacques

(1777–1857)

FRENCH CHEMIST

Thénard (tay-**nar**) was the son of a peasant from Louptière in France. He studied pharmacy in Paris in poverty until he was befriended by Louis-Nicolas Vauquelin. He became assistant professor at the Ecole Polytechnique (1798) and succeeded Vauquelin as professor of chemistry at the Collège de France (1802). He also held a chair at the University of Paris where he became chancellor in 1832. In 1797 he made his fortune by his discovery of Thénard blue, a pigment that consisted of a fusion of cobalt oxide and alumina capable of withstanding the heat of furnaces used in porcelain production.

Thénard collaborated with his lifelong friend Joseph Gay-Lussac on studies of the alkali metals sodium and potassium, which they obtained by heating potash and soda with iron. However, it was not immediately clear whether these were indeed elements. Humphry Davy also discovered them in 1807 and competed with the French chemists to work out their properties. Thénard and Gay-Lussac heated potassium with ammonia and found more hydrogen liberated than could have come from the ammonia. They therefore concluded that potassium was a hydride but Davy showed that they had taken moist ammonia, the water in which could account for the excess hydrogen.

Working on his own Thénard discovered hydrogen peroxide (1818). He also produced a four-volume standard textbook, *Traité elémentaire de chimie* (Elementary Treatise on Chemistry), which remained a standard text for 25 years and by 1834 had gone into its sixth edition.

Theophrastus

(*c.* 372 BC–*c.* 287 BC)

GREEK BOTANIST AND PHILOSOPHER

It is manifest that Art imitates Nature and sometimes produces very peculiar things.
—*History of Stones*

Theophrastus (thee-oh-**fras**-tus), who was born at Eresus on Lesbos (now in Greece), attended the Academy at Athens as a pupil of Plato. After Plato's death he joined Aristotle and became his chief assistant when Aristotle founded the Lyceum at Athens. On Aristotle's retirement Theophrastus became head of the school. The school flourished under him and is said to have numbered two thousand pupils at this time.

Of Theophrastus's many works, his nine-volume *Enquiry into Plants* is considered the most important. This is a systematically arranged treatise that discusses the description and classification of plants and contains many personal observations. A second series of six books, the

Etiology of Plants, covers plant physiology. Theophrastus appreciated the connection between flowers and fruits and, from his description of germination, it is seen that he realized the difference between mono-cotyledons and dicotyledons.

Many of Theophrastus's pupils lived in distant regions of Greece and he encouraged them to make botanical observations near their homes. This practice probably helped him to conclude that plant distribution depends on soil and climate. Theophrastus was the first to invent and use botanical terms and is often called "the father of scientific botany."

Theorell, Axel Hugo Teodor

(1903–1982)

SWEDISH BIOCHEMIST

Theorell (**tay-oh-rel**), who was born at Linköping in Sweden, received his MD from the Karolinska Institute in Stockholm in 1930. However, he did not pursue a career in medicine because of a polio attack. Instead, he became assistant professor of biochemistry at Uppsala University (1932–33, 1935–36), spending the intervening years with Otto Warburg at the Kaiser Wilhelm Institute in Berlin.

Theorell found that the sugar-converting (yellow) enzyme isolated from yeast by Warburg consisted of two parts: a nonprotein enzyme (of vitamin B_2 plus a phosphate group) and the protein apoenzyme. He went further to show that the coenzyme oxidizes glucose by removing a hydrogen atom, which attaches at a specific point on the vitamin molecule. This was the first detailed account of enzyme action.

Theorell studied cytochrome *c* (important in the electron-transport chain) and was the first to isolate crystalline myoglobin. His research on alcohol dehydrogenase resulted in the development of blood tests that may be used to determine alcohol levels.

In 1937 Theorell became director of the biochemistry department of the Nobel Medical Institute, Stockholm, and in 1955 received the Nobel Prize for physiology or medicine.

Thiele, Friedrich Karl Johannes

(1865–1918)

GERMAN CHEMIST

Born at Ratibor (now Racibórz in Poland), Thiele (**tee**-le) studied mathematics at the University of Breslau but later turned to chemistry, receiving his doctorate from Halle in 1890. He taught at the University of Munich from 1893 to 1902, when he was appointed professor of chemistry at Strasbourg.

In 1899 Thiele proposed the idea of partial valence to deal with a problem that had been troubling theoretical chemists for some time. The structures produced by August Kekulé in 1858 and 1865 had revolutionized chemical thought but had also produced major problems. Double bonds in chemistry usually indicate reactivity but Kekulé's proposed structure for benzene, C_6H_6, contained three double bonds in its ring and yet benzene is comparatively unreactive. Thus it tends to undergo substitution reactions rather than addition reactions.

Thiele proposed that, when double and single bonds alternate, a pair of single bonds affect the intervening double bond in such a way as to give it some of the properties of a single bond. Given the ring structure of benzene, this occurs throughout the molecule and so neutralizes the activity of the double bonds. The same argument cannot be used with double bonds in a carbon chain for there the ends of the chain will be open to addition. Thiele's problem could not be completely solved until the development of quantum theory. Thiele's ideas are similar to the later concept of resonance structures – intermediate forms of molecules with bonding part way between conventional forms.

Thom, Alexander

(1894–1985)

BRITISH ENGINEER AND ARCHEOASTRONOMER

Thom (tom) studied at the University of Glasgow where he obtained his BSc in 1915 and his PhD in 1926. He lectured in engineering at Glasgow from 1922 until 1939 when he joined the Royal Aircraft Establishment at Farnborough. After the war he was appointed professor of engineering science at Oxford, a post he held until his retirement in 1961.

From 1934 Thom was engaged upon an investigation of the stone circles distributed so profusely throughout the British Isles and Brittany. He published two major works in this field after his retirement: *Megalithic Sites in Britain* (1967) and *Megalithic Lunar Observatories* (1971). The investigation of ancient remains for astronomical significance really begins with Norman Lockyer at the turn of the century. Thom's preeminence in this field was based upon his personal knowledge of hundreds of sites and his mathematical and surveying skills.

The twenty years he had spent making accurate surveys of stone circles allowed him to begin publishing in the 1950s some of his startling conclusions. That the stone circles clearly presupposed a considerable knowledge of the 19-year lunar cycle was not particularly original, although Thom produced an unprecedented amount of hard data in its favor. More original was his claim to have discovered certain widespread units of measurement used in the construction of the monuments.

These consist of a "megalithic yard" of 2.72 feet or 0.829 meter and a "megalithic inch," 0.816 of a modern inch, 40 of which made a megalithic yard. The evidence for the existence of such units is provided by a formidable statistical analysis of the rings themselves, which are not actually circles but more complicated geometrical figures with dimensions that are multiples of megalithic yards.

Although Thom's conclusions are not acceptable to all scholars and have been much exaggerated by others, there is no doubt of the importance and rigor of his work, which has raised many still unsolved problems.

Thomas, Edward Donnall

(1920–   )

AMERICAN PHYSICIAN

Thomas was born at Mart in Texas and educated at the University of Texas, receiving his BA in 1941 and MA two years later. In 1946 he was awarded his MD by Harvard University. He worked at the Peter Bent Brigham Hospital, Boston, from 1946, eventually specializing in hematology. After two years as a research associate with the Cancer Research Foundation at the Children's Medical Center, Boston (1953–55), he moved to the Mary Imogene Bassett Hospital as hematologist and assistant physician. In 1956 he became associate clinical professor of medicine at the College of Physicians and Surgeons, Columbia University, and from 1963 until 1990 he served with the University of Washington Medical School in Seattle as professor of medicine.

Although primarily a clinician rather than a research scientist, Thomas was instrumental in gaining new insights into how the body's immune system rejects tissue transplants. His expertise in hematology and cancer biology enabled him to develop the technique of bone-marrow transplantation to treat patients suffering from leukemia or other cancers of the blood. This involves the transfer of bone-marrow cells from a healthy donor to the bone marrow of the patient, so that the patient can resume production of healthy white blood cells to replace the cancerous cells.

In experiments using dogs, Thomas demonstrated the importance of matching donor tissue and the recipient's tissue as closely as possible, so as to minimize the risk of rejection of the transplanted tissue. He also showed that by treating the recipient with cell-killing drugs, it was possible to avoid another of the pitfalls associated with tissue transplantation, namely, the graft-versus-host reaction. This occurs when immune cells belonging to the donor and transferred with the transplant recognize the host's tissues as foreign and start to attack them.

Under Thomas's leadership the University of Washington Medical School became the preeminent North American center for bone-marrow transplants, where physicians from all over the world came to learn the pioneering technique. For his work Thomas was awarded the 1990 Nobel Prize for physiology or medicine, jointly with Joseph Murray.

Thomas, Sidney Gilchrist

(1850–1885)

BRITISH CHEMIST

Thomas came from a nonconformist background in London. Owing to the death of his father in 1866 he was unable to complete his education and instead became a clerk in a police court. In 1870 he started studying in the evenings at Birkbeck College, London, and passed exams in metallurgy and chemistry at the Royal College of Mines.

Thomas heard of the need to eliminate phosphorus from the steel-making process introduced by Henry Bessemer in 1856. If iron ores containing phosphorus were used the resulting steel was brittle and useless but large reserves of phosphorus-rich ores existed in France and Germany, and also in Britain, in Wales and Cleveland. Thomas began experimenting with various substances, including magnesium and lime. He made trial tests using a converter at the Blaenafon steel plant with the assistance of his cousin, Percy Carlyle Gilchrist, who was a chemist there.

In 1875 Thomas developed a lining for the Bessemer converter made of calcined dolomite with a lime binding, which eliminated the phosphorus and also produced a valuable fertilizer – basic slag – as a by-product. Demonstrated in 1879, the *Thomas–Gilchrist basic process* was an immediate success. Thomas resigned his job to manage the issue of licenses from his patents. He was awarded the Bessemer gold medal in 1883 and made a fortune but died young from tuberculosis. His money, inherited by his sister, was spent on the philanthropic works he was keen to promote. The new process made steel cheap and abundant; in 1879 world production of steel was about 4 million tons – by 1929 it was over 104 million tons, 90% of which was produced by the basic process.

Thompson, Sir D'Arcy Wentworth

(1860–1948)

BRITISH BIOLOGIST

> It behoves us always to remember that in physics it has taken great men to discover simple things. They are very great names indeed which we couple with the explanation of the path of a stone, the droop of a chain, the tints of a bubble, the shadows in a cup.
>
> —*On Growth and Form* (1917)

Thompson studied medicine at the university in his native city of Edinburgh, where he was greatly influenced by Charles Thomson, who had recently returned from the Challenger Expedition. In 1884 he became professor of biology (subsequently natural history) at University College, Dundee. In 1917, when he became senior professor, Thompson published *On Growth and Form*, in which he developed the notion of evolutionary changes in animal form in terms of physical forces acting upon the individual during its lifetime, rather than as the sum total of modifications made over successive generations – the latter being the traditional credo postulated by Darwinists. In a later edition (1942), however, Thompson admitted the difficulty of explaining away the cumulative effect of physical and mental adaptations, which can scarcely be accounted for in the experience of one generation. In addition to such theoretical work, Thompson was much involved in oceanographic studies, as well as fisheries and fur-seal conservation in northern Europe. He was one of the British representatives on the International Council for the Exploration of the Sea, from its foundation in 1902. He was also interested in classical science, publishing works on the natural history of ancient writers, including an edition of Aristotle's *Historia Animalium* (1910; History of Animals) and accounts of Greek birds and fishes.

Thompson, Sir Harold Warris

(1908–1989)

BRITISH PHYSICAL CHEMIST

Thompson, who was born at Wombwell in Yorkshire, England, was educated at the universities of Oxford and Berlin, where he obtained his PhD in 1930. He spent his entire career at Oxford, serving as professor of chemistry from 1964 until his retirement in 1975.

His early work was on chemical kinetics and photochemistry, later concentrating on absorption spectroscopy with ultraviolet radiation. In the 1930s he began to study absorption spectra taken in the infrared region. Absorption at a particular wavelength in the infrared corresponds to a change in vibrational energy of the molecule, and Thompson was able to use infrared spectra to measure the vibrational frequencies of bonds and the shapes and sizes of molecules.

During World War II he started to develop infrared spectroscopy as an analytical tool. Various bonds and groups in molecules have characteristic vibrational frequencies, and Thompson showed how analysis of the spectra could be used to work out the structures of complex organic molecules. Infrared spectroscopy is now a routine technique in organic chemistry for investigating and "fingerprinting" compounds.

Thompson also made significant advances in both the instrumentation used and in the theory of intensities of infrared absorption lines. He used infrared spectroscopy in studies of intermolecular forces and also investigated rotational spectra in the far infrared (at low frequencies).

Thomsen, Christian Jürgensen

(1788–1865)

DANISH ARCHEOLOGIST

> Mr. Thomsen is admittedly only a dilettante, but a dilettante with a wide range of knowledge. He has no university degree, but in the present state of scientific knowledge I hardly consider that fact as being a disqualification.
> —A member of the Royal Commission for the Preservation of Danish Antiquities, recommending Thomsen's employment as curator of the National Museum (1816)

Thomsen (**tom**-sen), the son of a Copenhagen merchant, was educated privately. He worked in the family business until 1840 and also, from 1816 until his death, served as curator of the Danish National Museum, first opened in 1819.

In a guide for the museum, *Ledetraad til nordisk Oldkyndighed* (A Guide to Northern Antiquities) published in 1836 but written much earlier, Thomsen introduced his revolutionary proposal on "the different periods to which the heathen antiquities may be referred," namely, the Stone, Bronze, and Iron ages. For Thomsen they represented probable technological stages; they were soon to become the essential basis for prehistory when shown by Jens Worsaae in the 1840s to correlate with the chronological sequence of artefacts found in the earth.

Although much modified and extended, complicated with subdivisions and insertions, the framework of Thomsen's three-age system, though not without its critics, is still very much part of the classification of prehistory.

Thomsen, Hans Peter Jörgen Julius

(1826–1909)

DANISH CHEMIST

Thomsen taught at the Technical University in his native city of Copen-hagen (1847–56) and at the Military High School (1856–66) before be-coming professor of chemistry at the University of Copenhagen (1866–91). He also served as director of the Technical University (1883–92).

Thomsen's main work was in thermochemistry, published over the years in four volumes of his *Thermochemische Untersuchungen* (1882–86; Thermochemical Analyses). He performed numerous calorimetric ex-periments and in 1854 stated his principle, namely, that every reaction of a purely chemical character, simple or complex, is accompanied by an evolution of heat. Marcellin Berthelot enunciated a similar principle in 1873 without acknowledgment, which led to an acrimonious dispute be-tween the two chemists. Thomsen did not go so far as Berthelot in ex-tending his principle but, by careful measurement of the heat liberated in different reactions, he hoped to be able to work out the affinity be-tween substances. Unfortunately both were wrong, and the emphasis on heat misled chemists for some time. There are reactions that absorb heat rather than liberate it.

Thomsen made a substantial fortune for himself by discovering in 1853 a method for manufacturing sodium carbonate from cryolite.

Thomson, Sir Charles Wyville

(1830–1882)

BRITISH MARINE BIOLOGIST

Thomson was born at Bonsyde in Scotland and educated at Edinburgh University; his first academic posts were as lecturer in botany at Aberdeen University (1850–51) and Marischal College (1851–52). He was then appointed to the chairs of natural history at Cork (1853) and Belfast (1854–68). From 1870 he was professor of natural history at Edinburgh.

Thomson is chiefly remembered for his extensive studies of deep-sea life, and particularly of marine invertebrates, in which he came to specialize. He made a number of oceanic expeditions to various parts of the world. In 1868–69 he led two deep-sea biological and depth-sounding expeditions off the north of Scotland, discovering, at a depth of some 650 fathoms, a wide variety of invertebrate forms, many of them previously unknown. To explain the variations in temperature that occurred at great depths he postulated the existence of oceanic circulation. After a further expedition to the Mediterranean (1870), Thomson published *The Depths of the Sea* (1872), in which he described his researches and findings. This culminated in his appointment as scientific head of the Challenger Expedition to the Atlantic, Pacific, and Antarctic oceans (1872–76), during which soundings and observations were made at 362 stations in a circumnavigation of some 70,000 miles. Using temperature variations as indicators, Thomson produced evidence to suggest the presence of a vast mountain range in the depths of the Atlantic – the Mid-Atlantic Ridge. His findings were later confirmed by a German expedition in 1925–27. Knighted on his return from the Challenger voyage, Thomson began preparation of the expedition's scientific reports – a work that eventually ran to 50 volumes – but had to resign in 1881 due to ill health. Thomson also wrote a general account of the expedition in *The Voyage of the Challenger* (1877).

Thomson, Elihu

(1853–1937)

AMERICAN ELECTRICAL ENGINEER

Although born at Manchester in England, Thomson moved to Philadelphia as a young child. He graduated from Philadelphia Central High School in 1870 and from 1870 to 1880 taught chemistry and physics there, gaining his MA in 1875.

It was with a fellow teacher, Edwin J. Houston, that he formed an innovative partnership, designing an arc-lighting system that attracted the financial backing to form the American Electric Company in New Britain, Connecticut. This was the precursor of the Thomson–Houston Electric Company of Lynn, Massachusetts, founded in 1883, which in 1892 merged with the Edison General Electric Company to become the General Electric Company – now the world's largest producer of electrical machinery. After the merger Thomson remained with General Electric as a consultant and was director of their Thomson Research Laboratory.

He was a prolific inventor and is associated with some 700 patents in the field of electrical engineering. General Electric operated under his patents, which, besides those for stable and efficient arc lighting, included ones for the three-phase alternating current generator, the high-frequency generator, the three-coil armature for dynamos and motors, electric welding by the incandescent method, the induction coil system of distribution, the induction motor, and meters for direct and alternating current.

Thomson also made his mark in the field of radiology, improving x-ray tubes and making stereoscopic x-ray pictures. He was also the first to suggest the use of a helium–oxygen breathing mixture for workers in underwater pressurized vessels to overcome caisson disease ("the bends"). He wrote many scientific papers and received awards and distinctions from scientific and engineering societies throughout the world.

Thomson, Sir George Paget

(1892–1975)

BRITISH PHYSICIST

George Thomson was the son of J. J. Thomson, the discoverer of the electron. He was born in Cambridge and educated at the university there, where he taught (1914–22). He was then appointed to the chair of physics at Aberdeen University. Thomson moved to take the chair of physics at Imperial College, London, in 1930. He remained there until 1952 when he returned to Cambridge as master of Corpus Christi College, a position he held until his retirement in 1962.

His early work was in investigating isotopic composition by a mass spectrograph method. In 1927 he also performed a classic experiment in which he passed electrons through a thin gold foil onto a photographic plate behind the foil. The plate revealed a diffraction pattern, a series of concentric circles with alternate darker and lighter rings. The experiment provided crucial evidence of the wave–particle duality of the electron. Thomson shared the 1937 Nobel Prize for physics for this work with Clinton J. Davisson who had made a similar discovery independently in the same year.

During the war Thomson was chairman of the "Maud committee" to advise the British government on the atom bomb. (The name of this committee arose from a telegram message that Niels Bohr had managed to convey to England shortly after the German invasion of Denmark. To assure his friends of his well-being he instructed: "Please inform Cockroft and Maud Ray, Kent," which was mistakenly interpreted as a secret message to "make uranium day and night"; Maud Ray was Bohr's former governess.) It was this committee that, in 1941, gave the crucial advice to Churchill that it was indeed possible to make an effective uranium bomb and elicited from him the minute: "Although personally I am quite content with existing explosives, I feel that we must not stand in the path of improvement."

Thomson, Sir Joseph John

(1856–1940)

BRITISH PHYSICIST

A research on the lines of applied science would doubtless have led to improvement and development of the older methods – the research in pure science has given us an entirely new and much more powerful method. In fact, research in applied science leads to reforms, research in pure science leads to revolutions, and revolutions, whether political or industrial, are exceedingly profitable things if you are on the winning side.

> —On his experimental work at the Cavendish Laboratory.
> Quoted by John Rayleigh in *J. J. Thomson*

Thomson, who was born at Manchester in England, entered Owens College (later Manchester University) at the age of 14. After studying engineering and then the sciences, he won a scholarship to Trinity College, Cambridge University. He graduated in 1876 and remained a member of the college in various capacities for the rest of his life. After graduating he worked at the Cavendish Laboratory under John Rayleigh, whom he succeeded as Cavendish Professor of Experimental Physics in 1884. As professor, Thomson built up the Cavendish Laboratory as a great and primarily experimental research school. Thomson was succeeded as professor in 1919 by his student Ernest Rutherford.

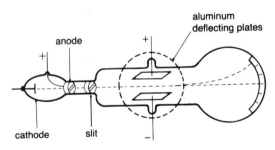

THOMSON'S APPARATUS   Diagram of the original apparatus used by J. J. Thomson to investigate cathode rays.

Thomson's most brilliant and famous scientific work was his investigations into cathode rays, in which he is considered to have discovered the electron. Using a highly evacuated discharge tube he calculated the velocity of the rays by balancing the opposing deflections caused by magnetic and electric fields. Knowing this

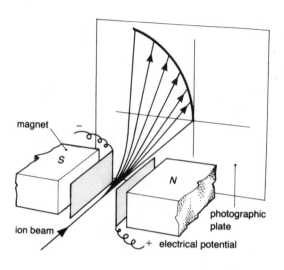

PARABOLIC MASS SPECTROMETER The *arrangement used by J. J. Thomson to produce a mass spectrum.*

velocity, and using a deflection from one of the fields, he was able to determine the ratio of electric charge (e) to mass (m) of the cathode rays. Thomson found that the ratio e/m was the same irrespective of the type of gas in the tube and the metal of the cathode, and was about a thousand times smaller than the value already obtained for hydrogen ions in the electrolysis of liquids. He later measured the charge of electricity carried by various negative ions and found it to be the same in gaseous discharge as in electrolysis. He thus finally established that cathode rays were negatively charged particles, fundamental to matter, and much smaller than the smallest atoms known. This opened up the way for new concepts of the atom and for the study of subatomic particles. Thomson announced his discovery of a body smaller than the hydrogen atom in April 1897.

His later researches included studies of Eugen Goldstein's canal rays, which he named positive rays. These studies gave a new method (1912) of separating atoms and molecules by deflecting positive rays in magnetic and electric fields. Ions of the same charge-to-mass ratio form a parabola on a photographic plate. Using this arrangement, Thomson first identified the isotope neon–22. This work was taken up by Francis W. Aston, who later developed the mass spectrograph.

Thomson's treatises were widely used in British universities. His *Conduction of Electricity through Gases* (1903) describes the work of his great days at the Cavendish; his autobiography, *Recollections and Reflections*, was published in 1936. He was awarded the 1906 Nobel Prize for physics for his work on the conduction of electricity through gases and was knighted in 1908.

Thorne, Kip

(1940–)

AMERICAN PHYSICIST

Born at Logan in Utah, Thorne was educated at the California Institute of Technology and at Princeton, where he obtained his PhD in 1965. He has been professor of theoretical physics at Cal Tech since 1970. He has been chiefly concerned with attempts to formulate a comprehensive and modern theory of gravitation. He coauthored *Gravitation Theory and Gravitational Collapse* (1965) and, with J. A. Wheeler and C. W. Misner, wrote an authoritative work, *Gravitation* (1973).

Thorne has also been involved in the search for a black hole. The technique, proposed by Y. B. Ze'ldovich and O. Gusyenov, is to search for binary systems that have an invisible companion with a large mass. It was also realized that a black hole could pull gas off its companion, which should heat up as it becomes attracted to the black hole and emit x-rays. It was only after the Uhuru satellite had identified 125 x-ray sources in 1972 that this proposal could be tested. This produced six x-ray binaries of which the most plausible candidate was the star known as Cygnus X-I. The launching of the Einstein X-ray Observatory in 1978 has produced new evidence showing that the mass of the companion of Cygnus X-I is greater than six solar masses. As it is too massive to be either a white dwarf or a neutron star, and it is also very compact, it may be a black hole. Thorne published his views on black holes, along with some more speculative material, in his *Black Holes and Time Warps* (1994).

Thorpe, Sir Thomas Edward

(1845–1925)

BRITISH CHEMIST

Thorpe was the son of a cotton merchant from Manchester, England. He was educated at Owens College, Manchester, and at the University of Heidelberg where he gained his doctorate in 1869. Having been appointed to the chemistry chair at Anderson's College, Glasgow, in 1870, he moved to the Yorkshire College of Science at Leeds four years later. He later became professor of chemistry at the Royal College of Science, London (1885–94, 1909–12), and also served as director of the British government laboratories (1894–1909).

Thorpe worked with Henry Roscoe on the new element vanadium, made some precise atomic weight measurements, and studied phosphorus compounds. In his work as a government chemist he managed to institute controls over such chemical hazards as white phosphorus, arsenic in beer, and lead glazes. He produced a number of works on the history of chemistry, including a biography of Joseph Priestley in 1906. He also published a multivolume *Dictionary of Applied Chemistry* (1890–93). He was knighted in 1909.

Tiemann, Johann Carl Wilhelm Ferdinand

(1848–1899)

GERMAN CHEMIST

Tiemann (**tee**-mahn) was born at Rubeland in Germany and started his career as an apprentice to an apothecary; he later studied chemistry at the University of Berlin, where he was appointed to the chair of chemistry in 1882.

Tiemann worked mainly on the chemistry of plant products, particularly glycosides and essential oils, which led to contacts with and commercial interests in the perfume industry. His work on ionone, the perfume of violets, led to protracted litigation.

Tilden, Sir William Augustus

(1842–1926)

BRITISH CHEMIST

Tilden, a Londoner by birth, was apprenticed to a pharmacist but allowed to attend the lectures of August Hofmann at the Royal College of Chemistry in his spare time. He worked as a demonstrator for the Pharmaceutical Society from 1863 until 1872. He then taught chemistry at

Clifton College until 1880, when he became professor of chemistry at Mason College, Birmingham. He finally moved to the Royal College of Science in London, where he held the chair of chemistry from 1894 until 1909.

Tilden's main work was in organic chemistry. He synthesized the compound nitrosyl chloride (1874) and discovered that it formed a crystalline derivative with turpentine. This led him into the study of terpenes – his main field of research. He made the important discovery in 1884 that, when heated, terpenes – hydrocarbons with the general formula $(C_5H_8)_n$ – decomposed to a mixture containing a closely related hydrocarbon, isoprene. The significance of this is that isoprene molecules can be polymerized (joined together in a long chain) to produce rubber. Tilden observed this when he made a sample of isoprene by passing turpentine through a heated tube and left part of it on a shelf. When he examined it several years later he found "a dense syrup in which was floating several large masses of solid." This was a form of rubber. Unfortunately the polymerization took place very slowly and attempts to speed up the process were unsuccessful at the time. Tilden also wrote on the history of chemistry.

Tinbergen, Nikolaas

(1907–1988)

DUTCH–BRITISH ZOOLOGIST AND ETHOLOGIST

Tinbergen (**tin**-ber-gen) was born in The Hague, the Dutch capital, and educated at Leiden University, where he gained his doctorate in 1932 for a thesis on insect behavior. Soon after he joined a Dutch meteorological expedition to East Greenland. The results of his Arctic year observing huskies, buntings, and phalaropes were later described in his *Curious Naturalists* (1958). In 1936 Tinbergen was appointed lecturer in experimental zoology at Leiden. Contact with Konrad Lorenz in 1937 led to an early collaboration. Tinbergen's work, however, was interrupted by the war. He refused to cooperate with plans to Nazify Leiden University and was consequently imprisoned in a concentration camp from 1942 to 1944. Although he was appointed a full professor by Leiden in 1947, Tinbergen chose to move to Oxford in 1947 to escape administrative duties. Here he took up the more junior post of lecturer in animal behavior. Tinbergen remained in Oxford until his retirement in 1974, having been appointed professor in animal behavior in 1966. He became a naturalized British subject in 1954.

Tinbergen demonstrated that ethology was basically an observational and experimental science. Unlike Lorenz, who tended to work with a large number of pets, Tinbergen worked with animals in their natural setting. Much of his early work dealt with identifying the mechanisms by which animals found their way around. How, for example, does a digger wasp recognize its burrow? In a few simple experiments with nothing more elaborate than a handful of pine cones, Tinbergen was able to show that the wasps were guided by the spatial arrangement of landmarks at the nest entrance. He also studied the social control of behavior in his work on the mating habits of sticklebacks.

Much of this early work was brought together in his classic text, *The Study of Instinct* (Oxford, 1951). In his other major work, *The Herring Gull's World* (London, 1953), Tinbergen began by recognizing the diversity of behavioral signals found in different species of gulls. Such a diversity had as much an evolutionary origin and history as more obvious anatomical features. Tinbergen set out to recover some of this history.

In his later years Tinbergen attempted to apply some of the principles of ethology to problems in human behavior. In particular, he worked with autistic children, publishing his results in *Autistic Children* (1983), a book he wrote in collaboration with his wife.

For his achievements in the field of animal behavior Tinbergen shared the 1973 Nobel Prize for physiology or medicine with Lorenz and Frisch. His brother Jan Tinbergen had been awarded the Nobel Prize for economics four years earlier.

Ting, Samuel Chao Chung

(1936–)

AMERICAN PHYSICIST

Although born at Ann Arbor, Michigan, Ting was educated at primary and secondary schools in China; he subsequently moved to Taiwan and returned to America to study at the University of Michigan. At Michigan he gained his bachelor's, master's, and doctoral degrees in the six years 1956–62.

His interest in elementary-particle physics, which was to lead to his sharing the Nobel Prize for the discovery of a significant new particle, took him to the European Organization for Nuclear Research (CERN) in Geneva (1963) and then Columbia University, New York (1964), where he became an associate professor in 1965. In 1966 Ting was given a group leader post at DESY, the German electron synchrotron project at Hamburg, and in 1967 joined the Massachusetts Institute of Technology; he was appointed professor of physics there in 1969.

Working at Long Island, New York, on the Brookhaven National Laboratory's alternating-gradient synchrotron, Ting and his collaborators performed experiments in which streams of protons were fired at a stationary beryllium target. In such an experiment a particle was observed that had a lifetime almost 1,000 times greater than could be expected from its observed mass. Announcement was made in a 14-author paper in the *Physical Review Letters* in 1974. The discovery was made independently and almost simultaneously by Burton Richter and his colleagues some 2,000 miles away at the Stanford Linear Accelerator Center. Ting called the new particle J, Richter named it psi (ψ); it is now known as the J/psi in recognition of the simultaneity of its discovery. Confirmation came quickly from other high-energy physics laboratories and a whole family of similar particles has since been created and detected.

Ting and Richter were very quickly honored for their discovery by the award, jointly, of the 1976 Nobel Prize for physics. By 1976 Ting was directing three research groups, at Brookhaven, CERN, and DESY.

Tiselius, Arne Wilhelm Kaurin

(1902–1971)

SWEDISH CHEMIST

Tiselius (tee-**say**-lee-uus) was born in Stockholm, Sweden, and educated at the University of Uppsala, where he became the assistant of Theodor Svedberg in 1925. He obtained his PhD in 1930 and his whole career was spent at Uppsala where, in 1938, a special research chair in biochemistry was created for him, which he occupied until 1968.

Tiselius's doctoral thesis was on electrophoresis – a method of separating chemically similar charged colloids. An electrical field is applied to the sample, and particles with different sizes migrate at different rates to the pole of opposite charge, enabling them to be detected and identified. The method was not initially very successful but by 1937 Tiselius had made a number of improvements to the apparatus. Using the technique on blood serum Tiselius confirmed the existence of four different groups of proteins – albumins and alpha, beta, and gamma globulins. Tiselius also conducted work on other methods for the separation of proteins and other complex substances in biochemistry including chromatography (from 1940) and partition and gel filtration (from the late 1950s).

In 1948 he was awarded the Nobel Prize for chemistry for his work on electrophoresis and other new methods of separating and detecting colloids and serum proteins. After the war Tiselius played an important role in the development and organization of science in Sweden, serving (1946–50) as chairman of the Swedish Natural Science Research Council.

Tishler, Max

(1906–1989)

AMERICAN PHARMACOLOGIST

Born in Boston, Massachusetts, Tishler was educated at Tufts University and Harvard, where he obtained his PhD in 1934. He taught at Harvard until 1937 when he joined Merck and Company, the pharmaceutical firm, rising to the position of head of the research division in 1956. He retired from Merck in 1970, joining Wesleyan University as professor of chemistry.

Tishler worked with Selman Waksman on the important antibiotic actinomycin and headed the research groups investigating the production of streptomycin and penicillin. He also did much to advance the commercial production of cortical steroids, developing a method whereby oxygen is introduced at a certain position in the steroid nucleus, which is vital to the antiinflammatory properties of such compounds. Tishler also contributed to vitamin chemistry, his investigations with Louis Fieser at Harvard leading to the syntheses of many important vitamins, such as vitamin A and riboflavin.

Tizard, Sir Henry (Thomas)

(1885–1959)

BRITISH CHEMIST AND ADMINISTRATOR

> The secret of science is to ask the right question, and it is the choice of problem more than anything else that marks the man of genius in the scientific world.
> —Quoted by C. P. Snow in *A Postscript to Science and Government* (1962)

Tizard, who was born at Gillingham in England, was the son of a naval officer who served as the navigator on the Challenger voyage. Barred from a similar career by an eye accident, Tizard instead went to Oxford University where he studied chemistry under Nevil Sidgwick. After spending a year in Berlin working under Walther Nernst, he returned to Oxford in 1911 to take a fellowship. It was in Berlin that he first met and became friendly with Frederick Lindemann, who was later to become his principal opponent for positions of power in British scientific government circles.

Tizard spent World War I in the Royal Flying Corps working on the development of bomb sights and the testing of new planes. After the war he realized, as he put it in his unpublished autobiography, that he "would never be outstanding as a pure scientist." Having developed a taste for the application of science to military problems, he took the post of assistant secretary at the Department of Scientific and Industrial Research (DSIR) in 1920 with specific responsibility for coordinating research relevant to the needs of the armed forces. In 1929, largely for financial reasons, Tizard accepted the position of rector of Imperial College, London, where he remained until 1942.

Tizard quickly established a reputation for having an expert and practical knowledge of service needs. He had the rare ability to distinguish between a crankish, totally unsound, idea and one that, though strange and new, was basically sound and could find practical military application. Thus it was that Tizard backed the young Frank Whittle in the development of jet propulsion of aircraft in 1937 and also Barnes Wallis in 1940 in his development of the bouncing bomb.

But, above all else, it was Tizard's support for the development of radar that will be remembered. In 1934 the Air Ministry set up the Committee for the Scientific Survey of Air Defence, under the chairmanship of Tizard. This was the famous "Tizard committee," which, in 1935, decided that radar was a workable means of air defense and should receive top priority.

The decision was not taken without dissent. In particular, Lindemann, then Churchill's scientific adviser, while recognizing the potential of radar, did not agree with the overriding priority demanded for it by Tizard and his associates. There was a further disagreement between the two men in that Lindemann advocated mass bombing of Germany while Tizard proposed instead (in 1942) a more balanced bombing policy with adequate aircraft being committed to the Battle of the Atlantic.

As a chemist Tizard's most significant work was on the ignition of gases in the internal combustion engine. He was editor of *Science of Petroleum* (1938), a standard multivolume work on the subject. He was knighted in 1937.

Todd, Alexander Robertus, Baron

(1907–   )

BRITISH BIOCHEMIST

Todd graduated from the university in his native city of Glasgow in 1928 and spent a further year there on a Carnegie Scholarship before going to the University of Frankfurt, Germany. He received doctorates from both Frankfurt (1931) and Oxford (1933) universities and in 1934 joined the medical faculty at Edinburgh University where he began work on thiamine (vitamin B_1). He continued this research at the Lister Institute of Preventive Medicine, London, and worked out the structure and synthesis of thiamine.

In 1938 Todd became professor of chemistry at Manchester University and continued vitamin studies on vitamins E and B_{12}. He also isolated the active principle from *Cannabis*, extracting the compound cannabinol from cannabis resin.

Todd transferred to Cambridge in 1944 to become professor of organic chemistry, a post he held until his retirement in 1971. At Cambridge he synthesized all the purine and pyrimidine bases that occur in nucleic acids (DNA and RNA) and found their structures. This was an important development in the understanding of the structure of the hereditary material and verified the formulae that Phoebus Levene had suggested for the nucleotide bases. Todd also synthesized various coenzymes related to these compounds, e.g., flavin adenine dinucleotide (FAD), and synthesized the energy-rich compounds adenosine di- and triphosphate (ADP and ATP) so important in energy transfer in living cells.

The 1957 Nobel Prize for chemistry was awarded to Todd for these contributions to biochemistry and the understanding of the gene. Todd was knighted in 1954, raised to the British peerage as Baron Todd of Trumpington in 1962, and from 1975 to 1980 was president of the Royal Society. He also published an account of his busy life in his autobiography *A Time to Remember* (1983).

Tombaugh, Clyde William

(1906–   )

AMERICAN ASTRONOMER

Tombaugh (**tom**-baw) came from a poor farming background in Streator, Illinois; although he never went to college he managed to teach himself enough of the basic observational skills to be taken on by the Lowell Observatory in Flagstaff, Arizona, in 1929. He transferred to New Mexico in 1955 and served as professor between 1965 and 1973.

Percival Lowell had begun his search for a planet lying beyond the orbit of Neptune in 1905 and this search continued at the Lowell Observatory after his death. Tombaugh was given the job of systematically photographing the sky along the ecliptic where it was thought any trans-Neptunian planet would be found. He used a specially designed wide-field telescope and for each region took two long-exposure photographs separated by several days. He then examined the pairs by means of a blink comparator, an instrument that allows two plates to be alternately observed in rapid succession. Any object that has moved against the background of the stars in the interval between the two exposures will appear to jump backward and forward. Methods were therefore devised for distinguishing asteroids and other moving bodies from the sought-for planet. After a year's observation Tombaugh was able to announce on 13 March 1930 the detection of the new planet, later named Pluto, at a point agreeing closely with the position predicted by Lowell.

The question naturally arose as to whether there were any further trans-Neptunian planets. Consequently Tombaugh continued the search but, although he examined 90 million star images and discovered 3,000 asteroids, no other new planet was detected. It is likely that Tombaugh has the honor of discovering the final planet of the solar system.

Tomonaga, Sin-Itiro

(1906–1979)

JAPANESE THEORETICAL PHYSICIST

Tomonaga (to-mo-**nah**-ga), who was born at Tokyo in Japan, graduated from Kyoto University in 1929 and then went to work in his native city. He remained there for the rest of his academic career, becoming professor of physics in 1941 and president of the university in 1956.

He was one of the first to develop a consistent theory of relativistic quantum electrodynamics. The problem at the time was that there was no quantum theory applicable to subatomic particles with very high energies. Tomonaga's first step in forming such a theory was his analysis of intermediate coupling – the idea that interactions between two particles take place through the exchange of a third (virtual particle), like one ship affecting another by firing a cannonball. Between 1941 and 1943 he used this concept to develop a quantum field theory that was consistent with the theory of special relativity. However, World War II prevented news of his work from reaching the West until 1947, at about the time that Richard Feynman and Julian Schwinger published their own independent solutions to the same problem. All three shared the Nobel Prize for physics for this work in 1965.

Tonegawa, Susumu

(1939–   )

JAPANESE IMMUNOLOGIST

Tonegawa (ton-e-**gah**-wa) was born at Nagoya in Japan and educated at Kyoto University and the University of California, San Diego. He worked at the Basle Institute for Immunology from 1971 and in 1981 was appointed professor of biology at the Center for Cancer Research and Department of Biology of the Massachusetts Institute of Technology.

Working at Basle in collaboration with Niels Jerne and Nobumichi Hozumi, Tonegawa revealed how the immune system is capable of generating the enormous diversity of antibodies required so that whatever the nature of the invading organism or "foreign" tissue a suitable antibody is available to bind specifically to it. This implies that the immune system's antibody-producing cells – the B-lymphocytes – can potentially manufacture billions of different antibodies; yet, even in humans, these cells carry only about 100,000 genes on their chromosomes.

Working with mouse cells, Tonegawa showed that during the development of the antibody-producing cell, the genes coding for antibody are shuffled at random, so that in the mature cell a cluster of functional genes is formed specific to that cell. Each individual mature cell thus produces its own specific antibody. This potential diversity is amplified by the fact that each antibody molecule comprises four protein chains, all with a highly variable terminal region. Hence the diversity of antibodies is a consequence of the huge numbers of lymphocytes present in the body, each with its own combination of functional antibody-producing genes. In recognition of the significance of his discovery Tonegawa was awarded the 1987 Nobel Prize for physiology or medicine.

Topchiev, Alexsandr Vasil'evich

(1907–1962)

RUSSIAN CHEMIST

Topchiev (**top**-chyef) was born in Russia and educated at the Moscow Chemical Technology Institute, graduating in 1930. After working at the Institute of Technology of the Food Industry he joined the Moscow Petroleum Institute in 1940, becoming director in 1943. Although Topchiev served as deputy minister of higher education (1947–49) and from 1949 held high office in the Soviet Academy of Sciences he continued to retain his link with the Petroleum Institute.

His work was mainly in the field of hydrocarbon chemistry and he was an important figure in the development of the Russian petroleum industry.

Torrey, John

(1796–1873)

AMERICAN BOTANIST

Torrey was the son of a New York alderman, who had responsibility for the city's prisons. This led to Torrey meeting Amos Eaton, a lawyer turned natural historian and imprisoned for forgery, who encouraged

Torrey's early interest in botany. He obtained an MD in 1818 from the College of Physicians and Surgeons, to which he returned in 1827 as professor of chemistry after a spell (1824–27) at the Military Academy, West Point, as professor of chemistry, mineralogy, and geology. Torrey also held from 1830 a professorship of chemistry at Cornell but in 1855 he resigned both chairs to become assayer of the New York branch of the Mint, a post he retained until his death.

However, it little mattered what post Torrey held for his life was exclusively devoted to the description and classification of the flora of America. In 1824 he published *Flora of the Northern and Middle Sections of the United States* and continued, in collaboration with his pupil Asa Gray, with *A Flora of North America* (2 vols., 1838–43) and his own *Flora of the State of New York* (1843).

In later life Torrey devoted himself to the description in numerous monographs of the flora sent him by the explorers of the North American continent. From such a source he built up a collection of some 40,000 species, which was given to the New York Botanical Gardens in 1899, forming the nucleus of their herbarium.

Nor was Torrey simply a collector for, against considerable opposition, he discarded the sexual classification of Linnaeus and introduced into North America the "natural" system of Antoine de Jussieu and Alphonse de Candolle. A genus of ornamental trees and shrubs, *Torreya*, in the yew family is named for him, and his name is also remembered with the Torrey Botanical Club.

Torricelli, Evangelista

(1608–1647)

ITALIAN PHYSICIST

A Galileist by profession and sect.
—Describing himself in a letter to Galileo
Galilei, 11 September 1632

Born at Faenza in Italy, Torricelli (tor-i-**chel**-ee) was educated at the Sapienza College, Rome. His *De motu* (1641; On Movement) attracted the attention of Galileo, who invited him to come to Florence to work and live with him. After the death of Galileo in 1642 Torricelli was appointed professor of mathematics in Florence, where he remained until his death.

He had been introduced by Galileo to the problem of why water, in the duke of Tuscany's well, could not be raised higher than 30 feet (9 m). Dissatisfied with earlier explanations, he used Galileo's earlier demonstration that the atmosphere has weight to offer a more satisfactory account. He argued that as the atmosphere has weight, it must also have pressure that can force water up a pipe but only until the weight of the water produced an equivalent counterpressure. Thirty feet of water was equal to the pressure exerted by the atmosphere.

Torricelli realized that he could test this argument by substituting mercury for water. A tube of mercury inverted over a dish – given that mercury is 14 times heavier than water – should be supported by the atmosphere to only one-fourteenth the height of an equivalent amount of water. This was confirmed by his pupil Viviani in 1643. Torricelli noticed that over time there was a variation in the height of the mercury in the tube, and reasoned that this was due to variations in the pressure of the atmosphere. This led to his construction of the barometer in 1644. The vacuum above the mercury in a closed tube is called a *Torricellian vacuum* and the unit of pressure, the *torr*, was named in his honor. Torricelli also made advances in pure mathematics and geometry, in particular in his calculations on the cycloid.

Toscanelli, Paolo

(1397–1482)

ITALIAN ASTRONOMER AND CARTOGRAPHER

Toscanelli (tos-kah-**nel**-ee), who was born at Florence in Italy, studied medicine at Padua and had a reputation among his contemporaries as being the most learned man of his time. Only a few extracts of his work have survived. He is best known for having convinced Columbus that the

East Indies could be reached by sailing a moderate distance across the Atlantic. He mistakenly thought (as did many others) that Asia was a mere 3,000 miles west of Europe and drew up a map showing this. Columbus saw a copy of this and, not satisfied with a distance of 3,000 miles to Japan, convinced himself that it was even less.

Toscanelli also made careful recordings of the comets of 1433, 1449, 1456 (Halley's comet), 1457, and 1472.

Tousey, Richard

(1908–   )

AMERICAN PHYSICIST

Born in Somerville, Massachusetts, Tousey was educated at Tufts, where he graduated in physics and mathematics (1928), and Harvard, where he gained his PhD (1933). After holding junior appointments at Harvard (1933–36) and Tufts (1936–41), he joined the U.S. Naval Research Laboratory, serving in the Optics Division until 1958 when he was appointed head of the spectroscopy branch, a post he retained until his retirement in 1978.

In 1946 Tousey initiated a new era in astronomy by launching a German V-2 rocket into the upper atmosphere with a spectrograph in its nose cone. With it he succeeded in photographing the solar spectrum from above the ozone layer and observing the extreme short-wavelength ultraviolet region down to a wavelength of 2,200 angstroms. Such a pioneering attempt was quickly followed in the 1960s by more sophisticated and powerful orbiting solar observatories (OSOs) launched by NASA.

Tousey was also involved in NASA's Skylab program, in which he conducted experiments using powerful solar instruments operated by the astronauts. He was awarded the Exceptional Scientific Achievement Medal of NASA in 1974.

Townes, Charles Hard

(1915–   )

AMERICAN PHYSICIST

Born in Greenville, South Carolina, Townes was educated at Furman and Duke universities in his home state and at the California Institute of Technology, where he obtained his PhD in 1939. He worked at the Bell Telephone Laboratories (1939–47) before he took up an appointment at Columbia University, New York, where he became a full professor in 1950. He moved to the Massachusetts Institute of Technology in 1961 and then served as professor of physics at the University of California at Berkeley from 1967 until 1986.

In 1953 Townes designed the first maser (*m*icrowave *a*mplification by *s*timulated *e*mission of *r*adiation). The maser works on the realization in quantum theory that molecules can only adopt a certain number of discrete characteristic energy states and that in their movement from one energy level to another they emit or absorb precisely determined amounts of radiation. Townes knew that the ammonia molecule (NH_3) could occupy one of two energy levels, the difference between them equaling a particular energy of a photon.

The question Townes went on to ask is, what happens if the ammonia molecule absorbs the photon of the appropriate frequency while it is at its higher energy level? Albert Einstein had answered the question in 1917 and shown that the molecule would fall to its lower state emitting a photon of the same frequency. There would then in fact be two photons of the right frequency to repeat the process and produce four photons. This is a rapid and powerful amplification producing a narrow beam of radiation with a single frequency. In this case the radiation emitted would have a frequency of 1.25 centimeters and thus fall in the microwave band, hence the name maser.

In any normal sample of ammonia only a few of the molecules would be in the higher energy state. Townes's problem was to devise a technique for the separation of molecules of the higher energy level ("population inversion") and he did this using a nonuniform electric field; molecules in the higher state were repelled and focused into the resonator while those in the lower state were attracted to it. By 1953 Townes had a working model of a maser.

Masers quickly found use in atomic clocks, receivers in radio telescopes, and numerous other uses. The maser led to the development of the laser, where light is amplified rather than microwave radiation and which was known in its earlier days as an "optical maser." Townes, in fact, published a paper with A. L. Schawlow in 1958 showing the theoretical possibility of the laser. He was, however, beaten in the race to construct it by Theodore Maiman in 1960.

For his work on the maser Townes shared the 1964 Nobel Prize for physics with the Russians Nicolai Basov and Aleksandr Prokhorov, who had independently produced a maser in the Soviet Union in 1955.

Townsend, Sir John Sealy Edward

(1868–1957)

IRISH PHYSICIST

Townsend, the son of a professor of civil engineering from Galway (now in the Republic of Ireland), was educated at Trinity College, Dublin. In 1895 he took advantage of a change in the Cambridge examination statutes and, together with Ernest Rutherford, entered the Cavendish Laboratory as one of the first two non-Cambridge graduates. There they worked as research students of J. J. Thomson. In 1900 Townsend moved to Oxford as the first Wykeham Professor of Experimental Physics, a post he retained until his retirement in 1941.

In 1898 Townsend achieved his first major scientific success when he measured the fundamental unit of electric charge (the charge of the electron). The previous year Thomson had reported the discovery of the electron, whose mass he estimated at about 1/1,000 that of the hydrogen atom. Townsend, working with gases released by electrolysis, was able to form charged clouds of water droplets and, by measuring the rate of fall of a water drop in the cloud, he could calculate the charge on each drop. More accurate work of this type was done by Robert Millikan in 1911.

Townsend's main work however was on, to take the title of his important book, *Electricity in Gases* (1915). He formulated a theory of ionization by collision, showing that the motion of electrons in an electric field would release more electrons by collision. These in turn would release even more electrons, and so on. This multiplication of charges, known as an avalanche, allowed him to explain the passage of currents through gases where the electric field was thought to be too weak.

Townsend was knighted in 1941.

Traube, Moritz

(1826–1894)

GERMAN CHEMIST

Born at Ratibor (now Racibórz in Poland), Traube (**trow**-be) studied at the universities of Berlin and Giessen, where he worked on fermentation under Justus von Liebig. Owing to the deaths of his two older brothers he was forced to give up his chemical career to run the family wine business but he carried on his research privately at the University of Breslau, producing over 50 papers.

Although having worked under Liebig, Traube differed from him in his dispute with Louis Pasteur over the nature of fermentation. He showed that it was caused by what he called "a nonliving unorganized ferment" produced by a yeast organism. He tried unsuccessfully to isolate this "ferment" (which later became better known as an enzyme). Traube also worked on osmosis, investigated first by Jean Nollet in 1748, and introduced various semipermeable membranes, which could serve as models for transfer in living cells.

Travers, Morris William

(1872–1961)

BRITISH CHEMIST

The son of a London physician, Travers was educated at University College, London, where he obtained a DSc in 1898, and in Nancy, France. He worked with William Ramsay in London (1894–1904) and then moved to Bristol as professor of chemistry. Travers served in India as the director of the Indian Institute for Science at Bangalore (1906–14). On returning to England he worked in the glass industry for some years before returning to Bristol in 1927 as honorary professor and Nash Lecturer in Chemistry and remained there until his retirement in 1937.

Travers was associated with Ramsay in his work on the rare gases, discovering in 1898 krypton, neon, and xenon, and later gave a full account of their work in *The Discovery of the Rare Gases* (1928). He also carried out research into low-temperature phenomena and into gas reactions.

Trembley, Abraham

(1710–1784)

SWISS ZOOLOGIST

Trembley (trahn-**blay**) was born at Geneva in Switzerland. In the uprising of 1733, however, his father Jean, a leading politician and soldier, was driven from office and into exile. The fall in the family's fortune forced Trembley to seek employment. He moved to Holland in 1733 and served as tutor to the children of various noblemen. While working for Count Bentinck he read the *Mémoires* of René Réaumur, which so stimulated him that he began to observe nature himself. During the next few years he made a number of discoveries which were to astound Europe.

At first he worked on parthenogenesis in aphids. Though he achieved some interesting results the work was basically derivative, having already been carried out by Réaumur and Charles Bonnet. At the same time he was studying polyps or, in modern terminology, hydra, of the species *Chlorohydra viridissima*. They were assumed to be plants but one day in the summer of 1740 Trembley observed them to move their "arms." At first he assumed that the movement was caused by currents in the water. When he swirled the jar around, expecting to see the hydra sway with the vortex, he noted that they suddenly contracted to a point, their tentacles seeming to disappear in the process. As the water calmed, the polyps stretched and once more revealed their tentacles. He was still unsure, however, whether they were plants or animals. There was, he realized, a simple procedure he could carry out to resolve the dilemma. If they were animals, then they would surely die if cut into two; plants would continue to grow.

In late 1740 he divided a number of polyps transversely. To his surprise he found that within a few days the two parts had not merely grown, but had developed into two perfect polyps: the tail grew a head, and the head a tail. He published his results in his *Mémoires...à l'histoire d'un genre de polypes d'eau douce* (1744; Memoirs on the Natural History of Freshwater Polyps). Polyp samples were also dispatched to scholars and institutions throughout Europe. Some, particularly vitalists, found Trembley's work difficult to accept. What happened to the animal's soul? Was that also divided into two? Others saw it as evidence for the oneness of nature, the "Great Chain of Being," with the polyp being the link between plants and animals. Embryologists saw in the polyp conclusive proof against the preformationists who claimed that embryos were minute but preformed individuals. These and other issues were endlessly debated throughout the century, and Trembley's polyps became the best-known invertebrates in Europe.

Trembley himself had little more to contribute to science. He left his post with Bentinck in 1747. Thereafter he traveled around Europe, engaged in some kind of diplomatic activity for Britain, for which he received a pension of 300 pounds per annum for life, and wrote a number of books on education, politics, and philosophy.

Trumpler, Robert Julius

(1886–1956)

SWISS–AMERICAN ASTRONOMER

Trumpler was the son of an industrialist. He studied at the university in his native city of Zurich in Switzerland (1906–08) and then at the University of Göttingen in Germany, where he obtained his PhD in 1910. After spending four years with the Swiss Geodetic Survey he emigrated to America in 1915, where he worked first at the Allegheny Observatory near Pittsburgh before moving to the Lick Observatory in California in 1919. He remained there until his retirement in 1951, also holding from 1938 to 1951 a chair of astronomy at Berkeley.

Trumpler's most important work was his discovery in 1930 of conclusive evidence for interstellar absorption. He had examined over 300 open clusters of stars and found that remote clusters seemed to be about twice the size of nearer ones. He could find no observational error nor could he believe that he was witnessing a real phenomenon. He did, however, appreciate that this could be due to the presence of an absorbing medium occurring between the clusters and the observer on Earth. Trumpler assumed correctly that the quantity of absorbing medium increased with distance so that this would cause more distant clusters to appear fainter and would lead to an overestimate of their distance and size. For nearby objects only a small correction would be needed but for distant ones it could be quite considerable. He went on to estimate the effect of the absorbing medium, which was interstellar dust, on the dimming of the received light as 0.2 of a magnitude per thousand light-years. This means that the brightness of a star is decreased by interstellar dust by a factor of 1.208 for every thousand light-years that the starlight travels toward Earth. This had far-reaching implications for the work of such astronomers as Harlow Shapley who had been working on the size and structure of our Galaxy. It forced him to reduce the scale of his model by a factor of three.

Trumpler was also involved in 1922 in a test of Einstein's general theory of relativity. Einstein had predicted the amount by which starlight would be bent when it passed close to the Sun's limb. Trumpler assisted W. W. Campbell of the Lick Observatory to make the relevant measurements at Wallal in Australia during the total solar eclipse of 1922. The value they obtained for the deflection, 1.75 ± 0.09 seconds of arc, was much more accurate than the value Arthur Eddington had found in 1919 and was very close to Einstein's prediction of 1″.745.

Tsiolkovsky, Konstantin Eduardovich

(1857–1935)

RUSSIAN PHYSICIST

> The Earth is the cradle of mankind. But one does not live in the cradle forever.
> —Quoted by Alan L. Mackay in *A Dictionary of Scientific Quotations* (1991)

Tsiolkovsky (tsyol-**kof**-skee), who was born at Ryazan in Russia, was the son of a forester whom he described as being an "impractical inventor and philosopher." He was educated at local schools but when nine years old became almost completely deaf. He was to a large extent self-educated, his deafness driving him to a solitary life of reading. He studied science for three years in Moscow (1873–76), returned home and took his teacher's examination in 1879, and in 1880 obtained a post at a school in Borovsk. In 1892 he moved to a school and later to a college in Kaluga where he remained until his retirement in 1920.

Such was Tsiolkovsky's isolation from the world of science that when he submitted some of his work to the St. Petersburg Society of Physics and Chemistry in 1880 he had to be told that his results on the gas laws and the speed of light were by no means new. What was new, however, were the thoughts that he was beginning to have about space travel.

Tsiolkovsky had worked for many years on various problems in aeronautics, including the design and testing, in a wind tunnel, of an all-metal airship. These investigations led him in the late 1890s to consider and write about the possibility of space flight and he is thus considered the pioneer in this field. In 1896 he began to write his famous work, published in 1903, *Exploration of Cosmic Space by Means of Reaction Devices*, in which he clearly stated most of the basic principles of rocketry and space travel. He realized that a reaction engine was required and discussed the problems of using such engines in space and here and in subsequent articles described the basic theory and design of a liquid-fuel rocket engine. Tsiolkovsky had no funds or means to test his theories, unlike the American Robert Goddard, who actually built and launched the first liquid-fuel rocket. He still continued into late life to put forward his ideas. His main method of giving them wider circulation was to write science-fiction stories.

After his death he was much honored as a Soviet pioneer of the space age. Appropriately enough the launching of the first satellite, Sputnik 1, was planned (although not realized) for the 22nd anniversary of his death and a giant crater on the reverse side of the Moon, unseen by all until recently, has been named for him.

Tsui, Lap-Chee

(1950–   )

CHINESE–CANADIAN MOLECULAR BIOLOGIST

Tsui (**tsoo**-ee) was born at Shanghai in China and educated at the Chinese University, Hong Kong, and at the University of Pittsburgh, where he obtained his PhD in 1979. He joined the staff of the Hospital for Sick Children, Toronto, in 1980 and has continued to work there while also holding (since 1990) a professorship of medical genetics at the University of Toronto.

In 1989, in collaboration with his Toronto colleagues Jack Riordan and Francis Collins of the University of Michigan and against strong competition, Tsui announced that he had located the cystic fibrosis gene. Cystic fibrosis (CF) is caused by a recessive gene widely distributed among Caucasians; about 1,000 children with CF are born in the United States each year. The disease affects secretory epithelia and, until recently, patients tended to die from lung infections and heart failure in their twenties.

When Tsui arrived in Toronto in 1980 new techniques were being proposed which, if effective, should allow defective genes to be identified. The procedure, introduced by Ray White and his colleagues, involved identifying an appropriate RFLP (restriction fragment length polymorphism), i.e., a fragment of DNA for use as a genetic marker to locate the site of the defective gene. The difficulty was that the human genome contains 3 billion base pairs of DNA; it was, therefore, a very remote possibility that any genetic marker would be within a reasonable distance of the CF gene. The chances would, however, be much improved if it was known on which chromosome the gene was sited. This was established as chromosome 7 by a Massachusetts biotechnology firm, Collaborative Research Inc (CRI), in 1985.

Thereafter it was a matter of using the available probes to focus on the area in which the gene could be found. By 1989 it had been narrowed to 300,000 base pairs. Further work demonstrated that the defective gene encoded a membrane protein of 1,480 amino acids and has been dubbed the CF transmembrane conductance regulator (CFTR). Tsui and his colleagues have shown that a loss of one amino acid one third of the way along the gene is responsible for 68% of cases of CF. He has continued to search for the mutations responsible for the other cases and has also sought to understand at the molecular level variations in the severity of the disease.

Sources and Further Reading

SALK

Radetsky, Peter. *The Invisible Invaders: Viruses and the Scientists Who Pursue Them.* Boston, MA: Little, Brown and Co., 1994.

SARICH

Gribbin, John, and Jeremy Cherfas. *The Monkey Puzzle.* New York: Pantheon Books, 1982.

SCHRIEFFER

Vidali, Gianfranco. *Superconductivity: The Next Revolution?.* New York: Cambridge University Press, 1993.

SCHRÖDINGER

Moore, Walter. *Schrödinger: Life and Thought.* New York: Cambridge University Press, 1989.

SCHWINGER

Schweber, Silvan S. *QED – The Men Who Made It; Dyson, Feynman, Schwinger and Tomonaga.* Princeton, NJ: Princeton University Press, 1994.

SEABORG

Seaborg, G. T. *The Transuranium Elements.* New Haven, CT: Yale University Press, 1958.

——. *Nuclear Milestones.* San Francisco, CA: Freeman, 1972.

SEGRÉ

Segré, Emilio. *A Mind Always in Motion: The Autobiography of Emilio Segré.* Berkeley, CA: University of California Press, 1993.

SEMMELWEIS

Slaughter, Frank G. *Immortal Magyar: Semmelweis, Conqueror of Childbed Fever.* New York: Henry Schuman, 1950.

SHAPLEY

Shapley, Harlow. *Galaxies.* Cambridge, MA: Harvard University Press, 1943.

Smith, R. W. *The Expanding Universe: Astronomy's Great Debate.* New York: Cambridge University Press, 1982.

SHERRINGTON

Eccles, J. C., and W. C. Gibson. *Sherrington: His Life and Thought.* Berlin: Springer-Verlag, 1979.

Granit, Ragnar. *C. S. Sherrington: An Appraisal.* London: Nelson, 1966.

SMALLEY

Baggot, Jim. *Perfect Symmetry: The Accidental Discovery of Buckminsterfullerene*. New York: Oxford University Press, 1994.

SMOOT

Smoot, George, and Keay Davidson. *Wrinkles in Time: The Imprint of Creation*. New York: Little, Brown and Co., 1993.

SMYTH

Brück, H. A., and M. T. Brück. *The Peripatetic Astronomer: The Life of Charles Piazzi Smyth*. Philadelphia, PA: Adam Hilger, 1988.

SNYDER

Kanigel, Robert. *Apprentice to Genius: The Making of a Scientific Discovery*. Baltimore, MD: Johns Hopkins University Press, 1993.

SODDY

Tren, Thaddeus J. *The Self Splitting Atom: The History of the Rutherford–Soddy Collaboration*. London: Taylor and Francis, 1977.

SOMERVILLE

Patterson, Elizabeth C. *Mary Somerville and the Cultivation of Science 1815–40*. Boston, MA: Nijhoff, 1983

SPALLANZANI

Gasking, Elizabeth. *Investigations into Generation 1651–1828*. Baltimore, MD: Johns Hopkins University Press, 1967.

STENO

Gould, Stephen Jay. *Time's Arrow, Time's Cycle*. Cambridge, MA: Harvard University Press, 1987.

STERN, Otto

Harré, Rom. *Great Scientific Experiments*. Oxford: Phaidon Press, 1981.

SU SUNG

Needham, J., Wang Ling, and D. J. de S. Price. *Heavenly Clockwork: The Great Astronomical Clocks of Medieval China*. New York: Cambridge University Press, 1959.

SZILARD

Weart, S. R., and G. W. Szilard, eds. *Leo Szilard: His Version of the Facts*. Cambridge, MA: MIT Press, 1978.

TELLER

Blumberg, S. A., and L. G. Panos. *Edward Teller: Giant of the Golden Age of Physics*. New York: Scribners, 1990.

TESLA

Cheney, Margaret. *Tesla: Man Out of Time*. New York: Prentice Hall, 1981.

THOMPSON, Sir D'Arcy Wentworth

Thompson, D'Arcy Ruth. *D'Arcy Wentworth Thompson: The Scholar-Naturalist 1860–1948*. New York: Oxford University Press, 1958.

THOMSON, J. J.

Thomson, G. P. *J. J. Thomson and the Cavendish Laboratory*. London: Nelson, 1964.

THORNE

Thorne, Kip. *Black Holes and Time Warps: Einstein's Outrageous Legacy*. New York: W. W. Norton, 1994.

TINBERGEN

Tinbergen, Nikolaas. *Curious Naturalists*. Amherst, MA: University of Massachusetts Press, 1984.

TIZARD

Clark, R. W. *Tizard*. Cambridge, MA: MIT Press, 1965.

TODD

Todd, A. *A Time to Remember: The Autobiography of a Chemist*. New York: Cambridge University Press, 1983.

TOMBAUGH

Simon, Tony. *The Search for Planet X*. New York: Scholastic Book Services, 1962.

TREMBLEY

Baker, John R. *Abraham Trembley: Scientist and Philosopher 1710–1784*. London: Edward Arnold, 1952.

TURING

Hodges, Andrew. *Alan Turing: The Enigma of Intelligence*. Boston, MA: Counterpoint, 1985.

TWORT

Twort, Antony. *In Focus, Out of Step: A Biography of Frederick W. Twort 1877–1950*. Dover, NH: Alan Sutton, 1993.

Glossary

absolute zero The zero value of thermodynamic temperature, equal to 0 kelvin or $-273.15°C$.

acceleration of free fall The acceleration of a body falling freely, at a specified point on the Earth's surface, as a result of the gravitational attraction of the Earth. The standard value is 9.80665 m s^{-2} (32.174 ft s^{-2}).

acetylcholine A chemical compound that is secreted at the endings of some nerve cells and transmits a nerve impulse from one nerve cell to the next or to a muscle, gland, etc.

acquired characteristics Characteristics developed during the life of an organism, but not inherited, as a result of use and disuse of organs.

adrenaline (epinephrine) A hormone, secreted by the adrenal gland, that increases metabolic activity in conditions of stress.

aldehyde Any of a class of organic compounds containing the group $-CHO$.

aliphatic Denoting an organic compound that is not aromatic, including the alkanes, alkenes, alkynes, cycloalkanes, and their derivatives.

alkane Any of the saturated hydrocarbons with the general formula C_nH_{2n+2}.

alkene Any one of a class of hydrocarbons characterized by the presence of double bonds between carbon atoms and having the general formula C_nH_{2n}. The simplest example is ethylene (ethene).

alkyne Any one of a class of hydrocarbons characterized by the presence of triple bonds between carbon atoms. The simplest example is ethyne (acetylene).

allele One of two or more alternative forms of a particular gene.

amino acid Any one of a class of organic compounds that contain both an amino group ($-NH_2$) and a carboxyl group ($-COOH$) in their molecules. Amino acids are the units present in peptides and proteins.

amount of substance A measure of quantity proportional to the number of particles of substance present.

anabolism The sum of the processes involved in the synthesis of the constituents of living cells.

androgen Any of a group of steroid hormones with masculinizing properties, produced by the testes in all vertebrate animals.

antibody A protein produced by certain white blood cells (lymphocytes) in response to the presence of an antigen. An antibody forms a complex with an antigen, which is thereby inactivated.

antigen A foreign or potentially harmful substance that, when introduced into the body, stimulates the production of a specific antibody.

aromatic Denoting a chemical compound that has the property of aromaticity, as characterized by benzene.

asteroid Any of a large number of small celestial bodies orbiting the Sun, mainly between Mars and Jupiter.

atomic orbital A region around the nucleus of an atom in which an electron moves. According to wave mechanics, the electron's location is described by a probability distribution in space, given by the wave function.

ATP Adenosine triphosphate: a compound, found in all living organisms, that functions as a carrier of chemical energy, which is released when required for metabolic reactions.

bacteriophage A virus that lives and reproduces as a parasite within a bacterium.

bacterium (*pl.* **bacteria**) Any one of a large group of microorganisms that all lack a membrane around the nucleus and have a cell wall of unique composition.

band theory The application of quantum mechanics to the energies of electrons in crystalline solids.

baryon Any of a class of elementary particles that have half-integral spin and take part in strong interactions. They consist of three quarks each.

beta decay A type of radioactive decay in which an unstable nucleus ejects either an electron and an antineutrino or a positron and a neutrino.

black body A hypothetical body that absorbs all the radiation falling on it.

bremsstrahlung Electromagnetic radiation produced by the deceleration of charged particles.

carbohydrate Any of a class of compounds with the formula $C_nH_{2m}O_m$. The carbohydrates include the sugars, starch, and cellulose.

carcinogen Any agent, such as a chemical or type of radiation, that causes cancer.

catabolism The sum of the processes involved in the breakdown of molecules in living cells in order to provide chemical energy for metabolic processes.

catalysis The process by which the rate of a chemical reaction is increased by the presence of another substance (the catalyst) that does not appear in the stoichiometric equation for the reaction.

cathode-ray oscilloscope An instrument for displaying changing electrical signals on a cathode-ray tube.

cellulose A white solid carbohydrate, $(C_6H_{10}O_5)_n$, found in all plants as the main constituent of the cell wall.

chelate An inorganic metal complex in which there is a closed ring of atoms, caused by attachment of a ligand to a metal atom at two points.

chlorophyll Any one of a group of green pigments, found in all plants, that absorb light for photosynthesis.

cholesterol A steroid alcohol occurring widely in animal cell membranes and tissues. Excess amounts in the blood are associated with atherosclerosis (obstruction of the arteries).

chromatography Any of several related techniques for separating and analyzing mixtures by selective adsorption or absorption in a flow system.

chromosome One of a number of threadlike structures, consisting mainly of DNA and protein, found in the nucleus of cells and constituting the genetic material of the cell.

codon The basic coding unit of DNA and RNA, consisting of a sequence of three nucleotides that specifies a particular amino acid in the synthesis of proteins in a cell.

collagen A fibrous protein that is a major constituent of the connective tissue in skin, tendons, and bone.

colligative property A property that depends on the number of particles of substance present in a substance, rather than on the nature of the particles.

continental drift The theory that the Earth's continents once formed a single mass, parts of which have drifted apart to their present positions.

cortisone A steroid hormone, produced by the cortex (outer part) of the adrenal gland, that regulates the metabolism of carbohydrate, fat, and protein and reduces inflammation.

critical mass The minimum mass of fissile material for which a chain reaction is self-sustaining.

cryogenics The branch of physics concerned with the production of very low temperatures and the study of phenomena occurring at these temperatures.

cyclotron A type of particle accelerator in which the particles move in spiral paths under the influence of a uniform vertical magnetic field and are accelerated by an electric field of fixed frequency.

cytoplasm The jellylike material that surrounds the nucleus of a living cell.

dendrochronology A method of dating wooden specimens based on the growth rings of trees. It depends on the assumption that trees grown in the same climatic conditions have a characteristic pattern of rings.

dialysis The separation of mixtures by selective diffusion through a semipermeable membrane.

diffraction The formation of light and dark bands (diffraction patterns) around the boundary of a shadow cast by an object or aperture.

diploid Describing a nucleus, cell, or organism with two sets of chromosomes, one set deriving from the male parent and the other from the female parent.

DNA Deoxyribonucleic acid: a nucleic acid that is a major constituent of the chromosomes and is the hereditary material of most organisms.

dissociation The breakdown of a molecule into radicals, ions, atoms, or simpler molecules.

distillation A process used to purify or separate liquids by evaporating them and recondensing the vapor.

ecology The study of living organisms in relation to their environment.

eigenfunction One of a set of allowed wave functions of a particle in a given system as determined by wave mechanics.

electrolysis Chemical change produced by passing an electric current through a conducting solution or fused ionic substance.

electromagnetic radiation Waves of energy (electromagnetic waves) consisting of electric and magnetic fields vibrating at right angles to the direction of propagation of the waves.

electromotive force The energy supplied by a source of current in driving unit charge around an electrical circuit. It is measured in volts.

electromotive series A series of the metals arranged in decreasing order of their tendency to form positive ions by a reaction of the type $M = M^+ + e$.

electron An elementary particle with a negative charge equal to that of the proton and a rest mass of 9.1095×10^{-31} kilograms (about 1/1836 that of the proton).

electron microscope A device in which a magnified image of a sample is produced by illuminating it with a beam of high-energy electrons rather than light.

electroweak theory A unified theory of the electromagnetic interaction and the weak interaction.

enthalpy A thermodynamic property of a system equal to the sum of its internal energy and the product of its pressure and its volume.

entomology The branch of zoology concerned with the study of insects.

entropy A measure of the disorder of a system. In any system undergoing a reversible change the change of entropy is defined as the energy absorbed divided by the thermodynamic temperature. The entropy of the system is thus a measure of the availability of its energy for performing useful work.

escape velocity The minimum velocity that would have to be given to an object for it to escape from a specified gravitational field. The escape velocity from the Earth is 25,054 mph (7 miles per second).

ester A compound formed by a reaction between an alcohol and a fatty acid.

estrogen Any one of a group of steroid hormones, produced mainly by the ovaries in all vertebrates, that stimulate the growth and maintenance of the female reproductive organs.

ethology The study of the behavior of animals in their natural surroundings.

excitation A change in the energy of an atom, ion, molecule, etc., from one energy level (usually the ground state) to a higher energy level.

fatty acid Any of a class of organic acids with the general formula R.CO.OH, where R is a hydrocarbon group.

fermentation A reaction in which compounds, such as sugar, are broken down by the action of microorganisms that form the enzymes required to catalyze the reaction.

flash photolysis A technique for investigating the spectra and reactions of free radicals.

free energy A thermodynamic function used to measure the ability of a system to perform work. A change in free energy is equal to the work done.

free radical An atom or group of atoms that has an independent existence without all its valences being satisfied.

fuel cell A type of electric cell in which electrical energy is produced directly by electrochemical reactions involving substances that are continuously added to the cell.

fungus Any one of a group of spore-producing organisms formerly classified as plants but now placed in a separate kingdom (Fungi). They include the mushrooms, molds, and yeasts.

galaxy Any of the innumerable aggregations of stars that, together with gas, dust, and other material, make up the universe.

gene The functional unit of heredity. A single gene contains the information required for the manufacture, by a living cell, of one particular polypeptide, protein, or type of RNA and is the vehicle by which such information is transmitted to subsequent generations. Genes correspond to discrete regions of the DNA (or RNA) making up the genome.

genetic code The system by which genetic material carries the information that directs the activities of a living cell. The code is contained in the sequence of nucleotides of DNA and/or RNA (*see* codon).

genome The sum total of an organism's genetic material, including all the genes carried by its chromosomes.

global warming *See* greenhouse effect.

glycolysis The series of reactions in which glucose is broken down with the release of energy in the form of ATP.

greenhouse effect An effect in the Earth's atmosphere resulting from the presence of such gases as CO_2, which absorb the infrared radiation produced by the reradiation of solar ultraviolet radiation at the Earth's surface. This causes a rise in the Earth's average temperature, known as "global warming."

half-life A measure of the stability of a radioactive substance, equal to the time taken for its activity to fall to one half of its original value.

halogens The nonmetallic elements fluorine, chlorine, bromine, iodine, and astatine.

haploid Describing a nucleus or cell that contains only a single set of chromosomes; haploid organisms consist exclusively of haploid cells. During sexual reproduction, two haploid sex cells fuse to form a single diploid cell.

heat death The state of a closed system when its total entropy has increased to its maximum value. Under these conditions there is no available energy.

histamine A substance released by various tissues of the body in response to invasion by microorganisms or other stimuli. It triggers inflammation and is responsible for some of the symptoms (e.g., sneezing) occurring in such allergies as hay fever.

histology The study of the tissues of living organisms.

hormone Any of various substances that are produced in small amounts by certain glands within the body (the endocrine glands) and released into the bloodstream to regulate the growth or activities of organs and tissues elsewhere in the body.

hydrocarbon Any organic compound composed only of carbon and hydrogen.

hydrogen bond A weak attraction between an electronegative atom, such as oxygen, nitrogen, or fluorine, and a hydrogen atom that is covalently linked to another electronegative atom.

hysteresis An apparent lag of an effect with respect to the magnitude of the agency producing the effect.

ideal gas An idealized gas composed of atoms that have a negligible volume and undergo perfectly elastic collisions. Such a gas would obey the gas laws under all conditions.

immunology The study of the body's mechanisms for defense against disease and the various ways in which these can be manipulated or enhanced.

insulin A hormone that is responsible for regulating the level of glucose in the blood, i.e., "blood sugar." It is produced by certain cells in the pancreas; deficiency causes the disease diabetes mellitus.

integrated circuit An electronic circuit made in a single small unit.

interferon Any one of a group of proteins, produced by various cells and tissues in the body, that increase resistance to invading viruses. Some types are synthesized for use in medicine as antiviral drugs.

internal energy The total energy possessed by a system on account of the kinetic and potential energies of its component molecules.

ion An atom or group of atoms with a net positive or negative charge. Positive ions (cations) have a deficiency of electrons and negative ions (anions) have an excess.

ionizing radiation Electromagnetic radiation or particles that cause ionization.

ionosphere A region of ionized air and free electrons around the Earth in the Earth's upper atmosphere, extending from a height of about 31 miles to 621 miles.

isomerism The existence of two or more chemical compounds with the same molecular formula but different arrangements of atoms in their molecules.

isotope Any of a number of forms of an element, all of which differ only in the number of neutrons in their atomic nuclei.

ketone Any of a class of organic compounds with the general formula RCOR′, where R and R′ are usually hydrocarbon groups.

kinetic energy The energy that a system has by

virtue of its motion, determined by the work necessary to bring it to rest.

kinetic theory Any theory for describing the physical properties of a system with reference to the motion of its constituent atoms or molecules.

laser A device for producing intense light or infrared or ultraviolet radiation by stimulated emission.

latent heat The total heat absorbed or produced during a change of phase (fusion, vaporization, etc.) at a constant temperature.

lepton Any of a class of elementary particles that have half-integral spin and take part in weak interactions; they include the electron, the muon, the neutrino, and their antiparticles.

lipid An ester of a fatty acid. Simple lipids include fats and oils; compound lipids include phospholipids and glycolipids; derived lipids include the steroids.

liquid crystal A state of certain molecules that flow like liquids but have an ordered arrangement of molecules.

macromolecule A very large molecule, as found in polymers or in such compounds as proteins.

magnetohydrodynamics The study of the motion of electrically conducting fluids and their behavior in magnetic fields.

meiosis A type of nuclear division, occurring only in certain cells of the reproductive organs, in which a diploid cell produces four haploid sex cells, or gametes.

meson Any member of a class of elementary particles characterized by a mass intermediate between those of the electron and the proton, an integral spin, and participation in strong interactions. They consist of two quarks each.

metabolism The totality of the chemical reactions taking place in a living cell or organism.

mitosis The type of nuclear division occurring in the body cells of most organisms, in which a diploid cell produces two diploid daughter cells.

moderator A substance used in fission reactors to slow down fast neutrons.

monoclonal antibody Any antibody produced by members of a group of genetically identical cells (which thus constitute a "clone"). Such antibodies have identical structures and each combines with the same antigen in precisely the same manner.

morphology The study of the form of organisms, especially their external shape and structure.

muon An elementary particle having a positive or negative charge and a mass equal to 206.77 times the mass of the electron.

mutation Any change in the structure of a gene, which can arise spontaneously or as a result of such agents as x-rays or certain chemicals. It may have a beneficial effect on the organism but most mutations are neutral, harmful, or even lethal. Mutations affecting the germ cells can be passed on to the organism's offspring.

natural selection The process by which the individuals of a population that are best adapted to life in a particular environment tend to enjoy greater reproductive success than members which are less well adapted. Hence, over successive generations, the descendants of the former constitute an increasing proportion of the population.

neutrino An elementary particle with zero rest mass, a velocity equal to that of light, and a spin of one half.

nuclear fission The process in which an atomic nucleus splits into fragment nuclei and one or more neutrons with the emission of energy.

nuclear fusion A nuclear reaction in which two light nuclei join together to form a heavier nucleus with the emission of energy.

nuclear winter The period of darkness and low temperature, predicted to follow a nuclear war, as a result of the obscuring of sunlight by dust and other debris.

nucleic acid Any of a class of large biologically important molecules consisting of one or more chains of nucleotides. There are two types: deoxyribonucleic acid (DNA) and ribonucleic acid (RNA).

nucleotide Any of a class of compounds consisting of a nitrogen-containing base (a purine or pyrimidine) combined with a sugar group (ribose or deoxyribose) bearing a phosphate group. Long chains of nucleotides form the nucleic acids, DNA and RNA.

nucleon A particle that is a constituent of an atomic nucleus; either a proton or a neutron.

nucleus 1. The positively charged part of the atom about which the electrons orbit. The nucleus is composed of neutrons and protons held together by strong interactions. **2.** A prominent body found in the cells of animals, plants, and other organisms (but not bacteria) that contains the chromosomes and is bounded by a double membrane.

oncogene A gene, introduced into a living cell by certain viruses, that disrupts normal metabolism and transforms the cell into a cancer cell.

optical activity The property of certain substances of rotating the plane of polarization of plane-polarized light.

osmosis Preferential flow of certain substances in solution through a semipermeable membrane. If the membrane separates a solution from a pure solvent, the solvent will flow through the membrane into the solution.

oxidation A process in which oxygen is combined with a substance or hydrogen is removed from a compound.

ozone layer A layer containing ozone in the Earth's atmosphere. It lies between heights of 9 and 19 miles and absorbs the Sun's higher-energy ultraviolet radiation.

parity A property of elementary particles depending on the symmetry of their wave function with respect to changes in sign of the coordinates.

parthenogenesis A form of reproduction in which a sex cell, usually an egg cell, develops into an embryo without fertilization. It occurs in certain plants and invertebrates and results in offspring that are genetically identical to the parent.

pathology The study of the nature and causes of disease.

peptide A compound formed by two or more amino acids linked together. The amino group ($-NH_2$) of one acid reacts with the carboxyl group ($-COOH$) of another to give the group $-NH-CO-$, known as the "peptide linkage."

periodic table A tabular arrangement of the elements in order of increasing atomic number such that similarities are displayed between groups of elements.

pH A measure of the acidity or alkalinity of a solution, equal to the logarithm to base 10 of the reciprocal of the concentration of hydrogen ions.

photocell Any device for converting light or other electromagnetic radiation directly into an electric current.

photoelectric effect The ejection of electrons from a solid as a result of irradiation by light or other electromagnetic radiation. The number of electrons emitted depends on the intensity of the light and not on its frequency.

photolysis The dissociation of a chemical compound into other compounds, atoms, and free radicals by irradiation with electromagnetic radiation.

photon A quantum of electromagnetic radiation.

photosynthesis The process by which plants, algae, and certain bacteria "fix" inorganic carbon, from carbon dioxide, as organic carbon in the form of carbohydrate using light as a source of energy and, in green plants and algae, water as a source of hydrogen. The light energy is trapped by special pigments, e.g., chlorophyll.

piezoelectric effect An effect observed in certain crystals in which they develop a potential difference across a pair of opposite faces when subjected to a stress.

pion A type of meson having either zero, positive, or negative charge and a mass 264.2 times that of the electron.

plankton The mass of microscopic plants and animals that drift passively at or near the surface of oceans and lakes.

plasma 1. An ionized gas consisting of free electrons and an approximately equal number of ions. 2. Blood plasma: the liquid component of blood, excluding the blood cells.

plate tectonics The theory that the Earth's surface consists of lithospheric plates, which have moved throughout geological time to their present positions.

polypeptide A chain of amino acids held together by peptide linkages. Polypeptides are found in proteins.

potential energy The energy that a system has by virtue of its position or state, determined by the work necessary to change the system from a reference position to its present state.

probability The likelihood that an event will occur. If an event is certain to occur its probability is 1; if it is certain not to occur the probability is 0. In any other circumstances the probability lies between 0 and 1.

protein Any of a large number of naturally occurring organic compounds found in all living matter. Proteins consist of chains of amino acids joined by peptide linkages.

proton A stable elementary particle with a positive electric charge equal to that of the electron. It is the nucleus of a hydrogen atom and weighs 1,836 times the mass of the electron.

protozoa A large group of minute single-celled organisms found widely in freshwater, marine, and damp terrestrial habitats. Unlike bacteria they possess a definite nucleus and are distinguished from plants in lacking cellulose.

pulsar A star that acts as a source of regularly fluctuating electromagnetic radiation, the period of the pulses usually being very rapid.

quantum electrodynamics The quantum theory of electromagnetic interactions between particles and between particles and electromagnetic radiation.

quantum theory A mathematical theory involving the idea that the energy of a system can change only in discrete amounts (quanta), rather than continuously.

quark Any of six elementary particles and their corresponding antiparticles with fractional charges that are the building blocks of baryons and mesons. Together with leptons they are the basis of all matter.

quasar A class of starlike astronomical objects with large redshifts, many of which emanate strong radio waves.

radioactive labeling The use of radioactive atoms in a compound to trace the path of the compound through a biological or mechanical system.

radioactivity The spontaneous disintegration of the nuclei of certain isotopes with emission of beta rays (electrons), alpha rays (helium nuclei), or gamma rays.

radio astronomy The branch of astronomy involving the use of radio telescopes.

radiocarbon dating A method of dating archeological specimens of wood, cotton, etc., based on the small amount of radioactive carbon (carbon–14) incorporated into the specimen when it was living and the extent to which this isotope has decayed since its death.

radioisotope A radioactive isotope of an element.

recombination The reassortment of maternally derived and paternally derived genes that occurs during meiosis preceding the formation of sex cells. Recombination is an important source of genetic variation.

redox reaction A reaction in which one reactant is oxidized and the other is reduced.

redshift The displacement of the spectral lines emitted by a moving body towards the red end of the visual spectrum. It is caused by the Doppler effect and, when observed in the spectrum of distant stars and galaxies, it indicates that the body is receding from the earth.

reduction A process in which oxygen is removed from or hydrogen is combined with a compound.

reflex An automatic response of an organism or body part to a stimulus, i.e., one that occurs without conscious control.

refractory A solid that has a high melting point and can withstand high temperatures.

relativistic mass The mass of a body as predicted by the theory of relativity. The relativistic mass of a particle moving at velocity v is $m_0(1 - v^2/c^2)^{-1/2}$, where m_0 is the rest mass.

rest mass The mass of a body when it is at rest relative to its observer, as distinguished from its relativistic mass.

retrovirus A type of virus whose genome, consisting of RNA, is transcribed into a DNA version and then inserted into the DNA of its host. The flow of genetic information, from RNA to DNA, is thus the reverse of that found in organisms generally.

RNA Ribonucleic acid: any one of several types of nucleic acid, including messenger RNA, that process the information carried by the genes and use it to direct the assembly of proteins in cells. In certain viruses RNA is the genetic material.

semiconductor A solid with an electrical conductivity that is intermediate between those of insulators and metals and that increases with increasing temperature. Examples are germanium, silicon, and lead telluride.

semipermeable membrane A barrier that permits the passage of some substances but is impermeable to others.

serum The fraction of blood plasma excluding the components of the blood-clotting system.

sex chromosome A chromosome that participates in determining the sex of individuals. Humans have two sex chromosomes, X and Y; females have two X chromosomes (XX) and males have one of each (XY).

sex hormone Any hormone that controls the development of sexual characteristics and regulates reproductive activity. The principal human sex hormones are progesterone and estrogens in females, testosterone and androsterone in males.

simple harmonic motion Motion of a point moving along a path so that its acceleration is directed towards a fixed point on the path and is directly proportional to the displacement from this fixed point.

SI units A system of units used, by international agreement, for all scientific purposes. It is based on the meter-kilogram-second (MKS) system and consists of seven base units and two supplementary units.

soap A salt of a fatty acid.

solar cell Any electrical device for converting solar energy directly into electrical energy.

solar constant The energy per unit area per unit time received from the Sun at a point that is the Earth's mean distance from the Sun away. It has the value 1,400 joules per square meter per second.

solar wind Streams of electrons and protons emitted by the Sun. The solar wind is responsible for the formation of the Van Allen belts and the aurora.

solid-state physics The experimental and theoretical study of the properties of the solid state, in particular the study of energy levels and the electrical and magnetic properties of metals and semiconductors.

speciation The process in which new species evolve from existing populations of organisms.

specific heat capacity The amount of heat required to raise the temperature of unit mass of a substance by unit temperature; it is usually measured in joules per kilogram per kelvin.

spectrometer Any of various instruments used for producing a spectrum (distribution of wavelengths of increasing magnitude) and measuring the wavelengths, energies, etc.

speed of light The speed at which all electromagnetic radiation travels; it is the highest speed attainable in the universe and has the value 2.998×10^8 meters per second in a vacuum.

standing wave A wave in which the wave profile remains stationary in the medium through which it is passing.

state of matter One of the three physical states – solid, liquid, or gas – in which matter may exist.

stereochemistry The arrangement in space of the groups in a molecule and the effect this has on the compound's properties and chemical behavior.

steroid Any of a group of complex lipids that occur widely in plants and animals and include various hormones, such as cortisone and the sex hormones.

stimulated emission The process in which a photon colliding with an excited atom causes emission of a second photon with the same energy as the first. It is the basis of lasers.

stoichiometric Involving chemical combination in exact ratios.

strangeness A property of certain hadrons that causes them to decay more slowly than expected from the energy released.

strong interaction A type of interaction between elementary particles occurring at short range (about 10^{-15} meter) and having a magnitude about 100 times greater than that of the electromagnetic interaction.

sublimation The passage of certain substances from the solid state into the gaseous state and then back into the solid state, without any intermediate liquid state being formed.

substrate A substance that is acted upon in some way, especially the compound acted on by a catalyst or the solid on which a compound is adsorbed.

sugar Any of a group of water-soluble simple carbohydrates, usually having a sweet taste.

sunspot A region of the Sun's surface that is much cooler and therefore darker than the surrounding area, having a temperature of about 4,000°C as opposed to 6,000°C for the rest of the photosphere.

superconductivity A phenomenon occurring

in certain metals and alloys at temperatures close to absolute zero, in which the electrical resistance of the solid vanishes below a certain temperature.

superfluid A fluid that flows without friction and has extremely high thermal conductivity.

supernova A star that suffers an explosion, becoming up to 10^8 times brighter in the process and forming a large cloud of expanding debris (the supernova remnant).

surfactant A substance used to increase the spreading or wetting properties of a liquid. Surfactants are often detergents, which act by lowering the surface tension.

symbiosis A long-term association between members of different species, especially where mutual benefit is derived by the participants.

taxonomy The science of classifying organisms into groups.

tensile strength The applied stress necessary to break a material under tension.

thermal conductivity A measure of the ability of a substance to conduct heat, equal to the rate of flow of heat per unit area resulting from unit temperature gradient.

thermal neutron A neutron with a low kinetic energy, of the same order of magnitude as the kinetic energies of atoms and molecules.

thermionic emission Emission of electrons from a hot solid. The effect occurs when significant numbers of electrons have enough kinetic energy to overcome the solid's work function.

thermodynamics The branch of science concerned with the relationship between heat, work, and other forms of energy.

thermodynamic temperature Temperature measured in kelvins that is a function of the internal energy possessed by a body, having a value of zero at absolute zero.

thixotropy A phenomenon shown by some fluids in which the viscosity decreases as the rate of shear increases, i.e., the fluid becomes less viscous the faster it moves.

transducer A device that is supplied with the energy of one system and converts it into the energy of a different system, so that the output signal is proportional to the input signal but is carried in a different form.

transistor A device made of semiconducting material in which a flow of current between two electrodes can be controlled by a potential applied to a third electrode.

tribology The study of friction between solid surfaces, including the origin of frictional forces and the lubrication of moving parts.

triple point The point at which the solid, liquid, and gas phases of a pure substance can all coexist in equilibrium.

tritiated Denoting a chemical compound containing tritium (^3H) atoms in place of hydrogen atoms.

ultracentrifuge A centrifuge designed to work at very high speeds, so that the force produced is large enough to cause sedimentation of colloids.

unified-field theory A theory that seeks to explain gravitational and electromagnetic interactions and the strong and weak nuclear interactions in terms of a single set of equations.

vaccine An antigenic preparation that is administered to a human or other animal to produce immunity against a specific disease-causing agent.

valence The combining power of an element, atom, ion, or radical, equal to the number of hydrogen atoms that the atom, ion, etc., could combine with or displace in forming a compound.

valence band The energy band of a solid that is occupied by the valence electrons of the atoms forming the solid.

valence electron An electron in the outer shell of an atom that participates in the chemical bonding when the atom forms compounds.

vector 1. A quantity that is specified both by its magnitude and its direction. **2.** An agent, such as an insect, that harbors disease-causing microorganisms and transmits them to humans, other animals, or plants.

virtual particle A particle thought of as existing for a very brief period in an interaction between two other particles.

virus A noncellular agent that can infect a living animal, plant, or bacterial cell and use the apparatus of the host cell to manufacture new virus particles. In some cases this causes disease in the host organism. Outside the host cell, viruses are totally inert.

viscosity The property of liquids and gases of resisting flow. It is caused by forces between the molecules of the fluid.

water of crystallization Water combined in the form of molecules in definite proportions in the crystals of many substances.

wave equation A partial differential equation relating the displacement of a wave to the time and the three spatial dimensions.

wave function A mathematical expression giving the probability of finding the particle associated with a wave at a specified point according to wave mechanics.

wave mechanics A form of quantum mechanics in which particles (electrons, protons, etc.) are regarded as waves, so that any system of particles can be described by a wave equation.

weak interaction A type of interaction between elementary particles, occurring at short range and having a magnitude about 10^{10} times weaker than the electromagnetic force.

work function The minimum energy necessary to remove an electron from a metal at absolute zero.

x-ray crystallography The determination of the structure of crystals and molecules by use of x-ray diffraction.

zero point energy The energy of vibration of atoms at the absolute zero of temperature.

zwitterion An ion that has both a positive and negative charge.

INDEX

Chinese pharmacologist: **6**: 121
Chittenden, Russell Henry **2**: 150
Chladni, Ernst Florens **2**: 151
Chlorophyll: **3**: 212; **8**: 19, 212; **10**: 142, 167
Cholera: **6**: 4; **9**: 90
Cholesterol: **1**: 204; **2**: 62, 87, 190; **4**: 134; **8**: 204; **10**: 150, 167
Chou Kung 2: 152
Christie, Sir William Henry Mahoney **2**: 152
Chromatography: **10**: 1
Chromosomes: **4**: 6; **7**: 103; **9**: 127, 145
Chu, Paul Ching-Wu **2**: 153
Chu Shih-Chieh 2: 154
Civil Engineer: **3**: 140
Clairaut, Alexis Claude **2**: 155
Claisen, Ludwig **2**: 156
Clark, Alvan Graham **2**: 157
Clarke, Sir Cyril Astley **2**: 158
Claude, Albert **2**: 159
Claude, Georges **2**: 160
Clausius, Rudolf **2**: 161
Clemence, Gerald Maurice **2**: 162
Cleve, Per Teodor **2**: 163
Climate: **3**: 14; **6**: 48
Cloud chamber: **1**: 198; **10**: 145
Cloud formation: **1**: 164
Coblentz, William Weber **2**: 164
Cockcroft, Sir John **2**: 164
Cocker, Edward **2**: 165
Coenzymes: **3**: 168; **4**: 207; **9**: 181, 205; **10**: 74
Cohen, Paul Joseph **2**: 166
Cohen, Seymour Stanley **2**: 166
Cohen, Stanley **2**: 167
Cohn, Ferdinand Julius **2**: 168
Cohnheim, Julius **2**: 169
Colloids: **4**: 153; **10**: 198
Colombo, Matteo Realdo **2**: 170
Comets: **7**: 195; **10**: 112
Compton, Arthur Holly **2**: 171
Computer Scientists: **1**: 18, 41, 76, 96; **2**: 49, 90; **3**: 116, 190; **4**: 15; **5**: 71, 76, 90, 153, 176, 204; **6**: 2, 106; **7**: 10, 24, 81, 151, 192; **9**: 12, 131, 138; **10**: 133, 151, 200
Comte, Auguste Isidore **2**: 172
Conant, James Bryant **2**: 174
Conon of Samos 2: 174
Continental drift: **1**: 198; **2**: 76; **3**: 109; **5**: 80, 148; **8**: 191; **10**: 88
Contraceptive pill: **8**: 48; **9**: 100
Conway, John Horton **2**: 175
Conybeare, William **2**: 177
Cook, James **2**: 178
Cooke, Sir William **2**: 179
Cooper, Leon Neil **2**: 180
Cope, Edward Drinker **2**: 181
Copernicus, Nicolaus **2**: 182
Corey, Elias James **2**: 184
Cori, Carl Ferdinand **2**: 185
Cori, Gerty Theresa **2**: 186
Coriolis, Gustave-Gaspard **2**: 187
Cormack, Allan Macleod **2**: 188
Corner, Edred **2**: 189
Cornforth, Sir John **2**: 190
Correns, Karl Erich **2**: 190

Cort, Henry **2**: 191
Corvisart, Jean-Nicolas **2**: 192
Cosmic background radiation: **3**: 69; **8**: 25
Cosmic rays: **1**: 198; **2**: 17, 171; **5**: 41; **7**: 73; **8**: 80
Cosmologists: **2**: 4; **3**: 3; **4**: 173; **5**: 2, 99; **6**: 102
Coster, Dirk **2**: 193
Cottrell, Sir Alan **2**: 193
Coulomb, Charles Augustin de **2**: 194
Coulson, Charles Alfred **2**: 196
Couper, Archibald Scott **2**: 197
Cournand, André **2**: 198
Courtois, Bernard **2**: 199
Cousteau, Jacques Yves **2**: 200
Crafts, James Mason **2**: 201
Craig, Lyman Creighton **2**: 201
Cram, Donald James **2**: 202
Crick, Francis **2**: 203
Croatian earth scientist: **7**: 88
Croatian mathematician: **7**: 68
Croll, James **2**: 205
Cronin, James Watson **2**: 206
Cronstedt, Axel Frederic **2**: 207
Crookes, Sir William **2**: 207
Cross, Charles Frederick **2**: 208
Crum Brown, Alexander **2**: 209
Crutzen, Paul **2**: 210
Crystallographers: **1**: 168; **5**: 178; **6**: 159; **10**: 179
Crystallography: **9**: 125
Cuban physician: **3**: 206
Cugnot, Nicolas-Joseph **2**: 211
Culpeper, Nicholas **2**: 211
Curie, Marie Skłodowska **2**: 212
Curie, Pierre **2**: 215
Curtis, Heber Doust **2**: 217
Curtius, Theodor **2**: 218
Cushing, Harvey **2**: 218
Cuvier, Baron Georges **2**: 219
Cybernetics: **10**: 125
Cytologists: **1**: 159; **2**: 114; **3**: 103; **4**: 6, 136; **7**: 56
Czech chemist: **5**: 47
Czech physiologist: **8**: 100

d'Abano, Pietro **3**: 1
Daguerre, Louis-Jacques-Mandé **3**: 2
d'Ailly, Pierre **3**: 3
Daimler, Gottlieb Wilhelm **3**: 4
Dainton, Frederick Sydney **3**: 5
Dale, Sir Henry Hallett **3**: 6
d'Alembert, Jean Le Rond **3**: 7
Dalén, Nils Gustaf **3**: 8
Dalton, John **3**: 9
Dam, Carl Peter Henrik **3**: 11
Dana, James Dwight **3**: 12
Daniell, John Frederic **3**: 13
Daniels, Farrington **3**: 14
Danish anatomist: **9**: 125
Danish archeologists: **9**: 188; **10**: 169
Danish astronomers: **2**: 35; **3**: 94; **5**: 36; **8**: 167; **9**: 141
Danish bacteriologist: **4**: 154
Danish biochemist: **3**: 11
Danish biologist: **9**: 122
Danish botanist: **5**: 154
Danish chemists: **1**: 195; **2**: 57; **5**: 216; **9**: 103, 189

Danish earth scientists: **6**: 96; **7**: 173; **9**: 125
Danish geneticist: **5**: 154
Danish immunologist: **5**: 152
Danish mathematicians: **1**: 129; **7**: 173
Danish meteorologist: **3**: 14
Danish physicians: **3**: 203, 207
Danish physicists: **1**: 215, 216; **7**: 112, 120, 184
Danish physiologist: **6**: 27
Danish zoologist: **9**: 122
Dansgaard, Willi **3**: 14
Darby, Abraham **3**: 15
Dark matter: **8**: 187
Darlington, Cyril Dean **3**: 16
Dart, Raymond Arthur **3**: 17
Darwin, Charles Robert **3**: 18
Darwin, Erasmus **3**: 21
Darwin, Sir George **3**: 22
Daubrée, Gabriel Auguste **3**: 23
Dausset, Jean **3**: 24
Davaine, Casimir Joseph **3**: 25
Davenport, Charles **3**: 26
Davis, Raymond **3**: 26
Davis, William Morris **3**: 27
Davisson, Clinton Joseph **3**: 28
Davy, Sir Humphry **3**: 29
Dawes, William Rutter **3**: 31
Dawkins, Richard **3**: 32
Day, David Talbot **3**: 33
Deacon, Henry **3**: 34
de Bary, Heinrich Anton **3**: 34
De Beer, Sir Gavin **3**: 35
Debierne, André Louis **3**: 36
de Broglie, Prince Louis Victor Pierre Raymond **3**: 37
Debye, Peter **3**: 38
Dedekind, (Julius Wilhelm) Richard **3**: 39
de Duve, Christian René **3**: 40
Deficiency diseases: **3**: 130; **4**: 56, 130; **6**: 131
De Forest, Lee **3**: 41
De Geer, Charles **3**: 42
Dehmelt, Hans Georg **3**: 43
De la Beche, Sir Henry **3**: 44
Delambre, Jean Baptiste **3**: 45
De la Rue, Warren **3**: 45
Delbrück, Max **3**: 46
D'Elhuyar, Don Fausto **3**: 48
DeLisi, Charles **3**: 49
Del Rio, Andrès Manuel **3**: 50
De Luc, Jean André **3**: 50
Demarçay, Eugene Anatole **3**: 52
Demerec, Milislav **3**: 52
Democritus of Abdera 3: 53
De Moivre, Abraham **3**: 54
Dempster, Arthur Jeffrey **3**: 55
Dendrochronologist: **3**: 90
Dentists: **7**: 107; **10**: 98
Derham, William **3**: 56
Desaguliers, John **3**: 57
Desargues, Girard **3**: 57
Descartes, René du Perron **3**: 58
Desch, Cyril Henry **3**: 60
de Sitter, Willem **3**: 61
Desmarest, Nicolas **3**: 61
Désormes, Charles Bernard **3**: 62
Deville, Henri **3**: 63
de Vries, Hugo **3**: 64
Dewar, Sir James **3**: 65

Goddard, Robert **4**: 121
Gödel, Kurt **4**: 122
Godwin, Sir Harry **4**: 124
Goeppert-Mayer, Maria **4**: 125
Goethe, Johann Wolfgang von
4: 126
Gold, Thomas **4**: 128
Goldberger, Joseph **4**: 130
Goldhaber, Maurice **4**: 131
Goldschmidt, Johann Wilhelm **4**: 132
Goldschmidt, Victor **4**: 132
Goldstein, Eugen **4**: 133
Goldstein, Joseph **4**: 134
Golgi, Camillo **4**: 136
Gomberg, Moses **4**: 137
Good, Robert Alan **4**: 138
Goodall, Jane **4**: 139
Goodman, Henry Nelson **4**: 141
Goodpasture, Ernest **4**: 142
Goodrich, Edwin Stephen **4**: 143
Goodricke, John **4**: 144
Gordan, Paul Albert **4**: 144
Gorer, Peter Alfred **4**: 145
Gorgas, William **4**: 146
Gossage, William **4**: 147
Goudsmit, Samuel **4**: 148
Gould, Benjamin **4**: 149
Gould, Stephen Jay **4**: 150
Graaf, Regnier de **4**: 151
Graebe, Karl **4**: 152
Graham, Thomas **4**: 152
Gram, Hans Christian **4**: 154
Granit, Ragnar Arthur **4**: 155
Grassi, Giovanni Battista **4**: 156
Gray, Asa **4**: 157
Gray, Harry Barkus **4**: 158
Gray, Stephen **4**: 159
Greek anatomists: **3**: 154; **5**: 25
Greek astronomers: **1**: 65; **2**: 93,
174; **3**: 155, 165; **5**: 23, 57; **7**:
57; **8**: 78, 102; **9**: 177
Greek botanist: **9**: 180
Greek earth scientists: **1**: 56; **9**:
177
Greek explorer: **8**: 102
Greek-French astronomer: **1**: 55
Greek geographers: **3**: 67; **5**: 7,
57; **9**: 137
Greek inventor: **5**: 25
Greek mathematicians: **1**: 56, 62;
2: 174; **3**: 73, 163, 165; **5**: 25,
131; **7**: 214; **8**: 101
Greek philosophers: **1**: 24, 45, 46,
65; **3**: 53, 67, 146, 152; **5**: 23;
6: 108; **7**: 219; **8**: 40, 55, 78,
91, 101; **9**: 93, 140, 177, 180;
10: 181, 192
Greek physicians: **1**: 24; **3**: 73,
154; **4**: 62; **5**: 25, 58; **8**: 82
Greek scientists: **1**: 65; **8**: 41
Green, George **4**: 159
Greenhouse effect: **8**: 134
Greenstein, Jesse Leonard **4**: 160
Gregor, William **4**: 160
Gregory, James **4**: 161
Griess, Johann Peter **4**: 162
Griffin, Donald Redfield **4**: 163
Griffith, Fred **4**: 164
Grignard, François **4**: 165
Grimaldi, Francesco **4**: 166
Group theory: **1**: 6; **4**: 72; **5**: 161
Grove, Sir William **4**: 166

Guericke, Otto von **4**: 167
Guettard, Jean Etienne **4**: 168
Guillaume, Charles **4**: 169
Guillemin, Roger **4**: 170
Guldberg, Cato **4**: 171
Gullstrand, Allvar **4**: 172
Gutenberg, Beno **4**: 172
Guth, Alan Harvey **4**: 173
Guthrie, Samuel **4**: 174
Guyot, Arnold Henry **4**: 175
Guyton de Morveau, Baron Louis
Bernard **4**: 176

Haber, Fritz **4**: 177
Hadamard, Jacques **4**: 178
Hadfield, Sir Robert **4**: 179
Hadley, George **4**: 180
Hadley, John **4**: 180
Haeckel, Ernst Heinrich **4**: 181
Hahn, Otto **4**: 183
Haken, Wolfgang **4**: 185
Haldane, John Burdon Sander-
son **4**: 186
Haldane, John Scott **4**: 187
Hale, George Ellery **4**: 189
Hales, Stephen **4**: 191
Hall, Asaph **4**: 192
Hall, Charles Martin **4**: 193
Hall, Edwin Herbert **4**: 194
Hall, James **4**: 195
Hall, Sir James **4**: 195
Hall, Marshall **4**: 196
Haller, Albrecht von **4**: 197
Halley, Edmond **4**: 198
Halsted, William Stewart **4**: 200
Hamilton, William **4**: 201
Hamilton, Sir William Rowan **4**:
202
Hämmerling, Joachim **4**: 203
Hammond, George Simms **4**: 204
Hansen, Gerhard Henrik **4**: 205
Hantzsch, Arthur Rudolf **4**: 206
Harcourt, Sir William **4**: 206
Harden, Sir Arthur **4**: 207
Hardy, Godfrey Harold **4**: 208
Hardy, Sir William Bate **4**: 209
Hare, Robert **4**: 210
Hargreaves, James **4**: 211
Hariot, Thomas **4**: 211
Harkins, William Draper **4**: 212
Harris, Geoffrey Wingfield **4**:
213
Harrison, Ross Granville **4**: 214
Hartline, Haldan Keffer **4**: 215
Hartmann, Johannes **4**: 215
Harvey, William **4**: 216
Hassell, Odd **4**: 218
Hatchett, Charles **4**: 219
Hauksbee, Francis **4**: 219
Hauptman, Herb Aaron **4**: 220
Haüy, René Just **5**: 1
Hawking, Stephen William **5**: 2
Haworth, Sir (Walter) Norman
5: 5
Hays, James Douglas **5**: 6
Heat: **1**: 197; **5**: 163; **8**: 190
Heaviside, Oliver **5**: 7
Hecataeus of Miletus **5**: 7
Hecht, Selig **5**: 8
Heezen, Bruce Charles **5**: 8
Heidelberger, Michael **5**: 9
Heisenberg, Werner Karl **5**: 10
Helmholtz, Hermann Ludwig

von **5**: 13
Helmont, Jan Baptista van **5**: 14
Hemoglobin: **2**: 174; **5**: 135; **8**:
33; **10**: 113
Hempel, Carl Gustav **5**: 15
Hench, Philip Showalter **5**: 17
Henderson, Thomas **5**: 18
Henle, Friedrich **5**: 19
Henry, Joseph **5**: 20
Henry, William **5**: 21
Hensen, Viktor **5**: 22
Heracleides of Pontus **5**: 23
Heraclitus of Ephesus **5**: 23
Herbalist: **4**: 101
Hermite, Charles **5**: 24
Hero of Alexandria **5**: 25
Herophilus of Chalcedon **5**: 25
Héroult, Paul **5**: 26
Herring, William Conyers **5**: 27
Herschbach, Dudley **5**: 28
Herschel, Caroline **5**: 29
Herschel, Sir (Frederick)
William **5**: 30
Herschel, Sir John Frederick
William **5**: 31
Hershey, Alfred Day **5**: 32
Hertz, Gustav **5**: 33
Hertz, Heinrich Rudolf **5**: 34
Hertzsprung, Ejnar **5**: 36
Herzberg, Gerhard **5**: 38
Hess, Germain Henri **5**: 39
Hess, Harry Hammond **5**: 39
Hess, Victor Francis **5**: 40
Hess, Walter Rudolf **5**: 42
Hevelius, Johannes **5**: 43
Hevesy, George Charles von **5**:
44
Hewish, Antony **5**: 45
Heymans, Corneille **5**: 46
Heyrovský, Jaroslav **5**: 47
Higgins, William **5**: 48
Higgs, Peter Ware **5**: 48
Hilbert, David **5**: 49
Hildebrand, Joel Henry **5**: 52
Hilditch, Thomas Percy **5**: 53
Hill, Archibald Vivian **5**: 54
Hill, James Peter **5**: 55
Hillier, James **5**: 55
Hinshelwood, Sir Cyril **5**: 56
Hipparchus **5**: 57
Hippocrates of Cos **5**: 58
Hirsch, Sir Peter Bernhard **5**: 60
Hirst, Sir Edmund **5**: 60
His, Wilhelm **5**: 61
Hisinger, Wilhelm **5**: 62
Histologists: **4**: 136; **6**: 11, 204; **8**:
108, 114; **9**: 106
Hitchings, George Herbert **5**: 63
Hittorf, Johann Wilhelm **5**: 64
Hitzig, Eduard **5**: 65
HIV: **4**: 70; **7**: 98
Hjelm, Peter Jacob **5**: 66
Hoagland, Mahlon Bush **5**: 66
Hodge, Sir William **5**: 67
Hodgkin, Sir Alan Lloyd **5**: 68
Hodgkin, Dorothy **5**: 69
Hodgkin, Thomas **5**: 70
Hoff, Marcian Edward **5**: 71
Hoffmann, Friedrich **5**: 72
Hoffmann, Roald **5**: 73
Hofmann, Johann Wilhelm **5**: 74
Hofmeister, Wilhelm **5**: 75
Hofstadter, Douglas **5**: 76

Index • 243

Metchnikoff, Elie **7**: 56
Meteorologists: 1: 1, 164, 193,
194; **2**: 88, 210; **3**: 13, 14, 50,
162, 196, 216; **4**: 180; **6**: 14,
48, 160, 163; **7**: 209; **8**: 122,
143, 173; **9**: 56, 72; **10**: 86
Metius, Jacobus **7**: 57
Meton 7: 57
Mexican chemist: 7: 90
Meyer, Julius Lothar **7**: 58
Meyer, Karl **7**: 59
Meyer, Viktor **7**: 60
Meyerhof, Otto Fritz **7**: 61
Michaelis, Leonor **7**: 61
Michel, Hartmut **7**: 62
Michell, John **7**: 63
Michelson, Albert Abraham **7**:
64
Microscope: 6: 145; **7**: 51; **10**:
193
Midgley, Thomas Jr. **7**: 66
Miescher, Johann Friedrich **7**:
67
Milankovich, Milutin **7**: 68
Military Scientists: 6: 206; **9**: 163
Miller, Dayton Clarence **7**: 69
Miller, Hugh **7**: 70
Miller, Jacques Francis Albert
Pierre **7**: 71
Miller, Stanley Lloyd **7**: 72
Millikan, Robert Andrews **7**: 73
Mills, Bernard Yarnton **7**: 74
Mills, William Hobson **7**: 75
Milne, Edward Arthur **7**: 76
Milne, John **7**: 77
Milstein, César **7**: 78
Mineralogists: 1: 147; **2**: 207; **3**:
12, 48, 50; **4**: 60, 160; **5**: 1, 62,
212; **7**: 89; **8**: 127; **10**: 100
Mining Engineer: 1: 127
Minkowski, Hermann **7**: 79
Minkowski, Rudolph Leo **7**: 80
Minot, George Richards **7**: 81
Minsky, Marvin Lee **7**: 81
Misner, Charles William **7**: 83
Mitchell, Maria **7**: 84
Mitchell, Peter Dennis **7**: 85
Mitscherlich, Eilhardt **7**: 86
Möbius, August Ferdinand **7**: 87
Mohl, Hugo von **7**: 87
Mohorovičić, Andrija **7**: 88
Mohs, Friedrich **7**: 89
Moissan, Ferdinand Frédéric
Henri **7**: 89
Molina, Mario José **7**: 90
Mond, Ludwig **7**: 91
Mondino de Luzzi 7: 93
Monge, Gaspard **7**: 94
Monod, Jacques Lucien **7**: 95
Monro, Alexander (Primus) **7**:
96
Monro, Alexander (Secundus) **7**:
97
Montagnier, Luc **7**: 98
Montgolfier, Etienne Jacques de
7: 99
Montgolfier, Michel Joseph de
7: 99
Moore, Stanford **7**: 100
Mordell, Louis Joel **7**: 101
Morgagni, Giovanni Batista **7**:
102
Morgan, Thomas Hunt **7**: 103

Morgan, William Wilson **7**: 104
Morley, Edward Williams **7**: 105
Morse, Samuel **7**: 106
Morton, William **7**: 107
Mosander, Carl Gustav **7**: 108
Moseley, Henry Gwyn Jeffreys
7: 109
Mössbauer, Rudolph Ludwig **7**:
110
Mott, Sir Nevill Francis **7**: 111
Mottelson, Benjamin Roy **7**: 112
Moulton, Forest Ray **7**: 113
Mueller, Erwin Wilhelm **7**: 114
Muller, Alex **7**: 115
Müller, Franz Joseph, Baron
von Reichenstein **7**: 116
Muller, Hermann Joseph **7**: 117
Müller, Johannes Peter **7**: 118
Müller, Otto Friedrich **7**: 120
Müller, Paul Hermann **7**: 120
Muller, Richard August **7**: 121
Mulliken, Robert Sanderson **7**:
122
Mullis, Kary Banks **7**: 123
Munk, Walter Heinrich **7**: 124
Murchison, Sir Roderick Impey
7: 125
Murphy, William Parry **7**: 126
Murray, Sir John **7**: 127
Murray, Joseph Edward **7**: 127
Muscle contraction: 5: 54, 90,
124; **9**: 159
Muspratt, James **7**: 129
Musschenbroek, Pieter van **7**:
130
Muybridge, Eadweard James **7**:
131

Naegeli, Karl Wilhelm von **7**:
133
Nagaoka, Hantaro **7**: 134
Nambu, Yoichipo **7**: 135
Nansen, Fridtjof **7**: 136
Napier, John **7**: 137
Nasmyth, James **7**: 138
Nathans, Daniel **7**: 139
Natta, Giulio **7**: 140
Naturalists: 1: 26, 51, 77, 133,
146, 156; **2**: 6, 32, 72, 74, 133;
3: 18; **4**: 13, 105; **7**: 142; **8**:
118, 188; **9**: 152; **10**: 66, 114
Naudin, Charles **7**: 141
Nebulae: 1: 124; **5**: 108; **7**: 55;
10: 159
Nebular hypothesis: 5: 147, 174;
6: 63; **10**: 95
Needham, Dorothy Mary Moyle
7: 142
Needham, John Turberville **7**:
142
Needham, Joseph **7**: 143
Néel, Louis Eugène Félix **7**: 144
Ne'eman, Yuval **7**: 145
Nef, John Ulric **7**: 146
Neher, Erwin **7**: 147
Neisser, Albert Ludwig Sieg-
mund **7**: 148
Nernst, Walther Hermann **7**:
148
Nerve action: 1: 15; **3**: 97, 157; **4**:
81; **5**: 68, 182; **6**: 178
Nerve cells: 3: 115; **7**: 119; **8**:
114, 132

Nervous system: 1: 152; **4**: 10, 79,
136; **6**: 200; **9**: 60
Newcomb, Simon **7**: 150
Newcomen, Thomas **7**: 151
Newell, Allan **7**: 151
Newlands, John Alexander
Reina **7**: 152
Newton, Alfred **7**: 153
Newton, Sir Isaac **7**: 154
New Zealand biochemist: 10: 143
New Zealand physicist: 8: 201
Nicholas of Cusa 7: 160
Nicholson, Seth Barnes **7**: 161
Nicholson, William **7**: 162
Nicol, William **7**: 163
Nicolle, Charles Jules Henri **7**:
164
Niepce, Joseph-Nicéphore **7**:
165
Nieuwland, Julius Arthur **7**: 166
Nilson, Lars Fredrick **7**: 166
Nirenberg, Marshall Warren **7**:
167
Nitrogen fixation: 1: 190; **4**: 177
Nobel, Alfred Bernhard **7**: 168
Nobili, Leopoldo **7**: 169
Noddack, Ida Eva Tacke **7**: 170
Noddack, Walter **7**: 170
Noguchi, (Seisako) Hideyo **7**:
171
Nollet, Abbé Jean Antoine **7**:
172
Nordenskiöld, Nils Adolf Eric **7**:
173
Norlund, Niels Erik **7**: 173
Norman, Robert **7**: 174
Norrish, Ronald **7**: 174
Northrop, John Howard **7**: 175
Norton, Thomas **7**: 176
Norwegian bacteriologist: 4: 205
Norwegian biologist: 7: 136
Norwegian chemists: 1: 190; **4**:
132, 171, 218; **10**: 57
Norwegian engineer: 3: 174
Norwegian explorer: 7: 136
Norwegian industrialist: 3: 174
Norwegian mathematicians: 1: 6;
6: 124; **9**: 76
Norwegian meteorologists: 1: 193,
194
Norwegian physicist: 1: 190
Noyce, Robert Norton **7**: 176
Noyes, William Albert **7**: 177
Nuclear fission: 4: 49, 184; **7**: 35,
170; **9**: 173; **10**: 12
Nuclear magnetic resonance: 1:
203; **6**: 209; **8**: 99
Nucleic acids: 2: 31; **6**: 17; **7**: 67
Nucleotide bases: 3: 210; **6**: 110;
9: 205
Nucleus: 1: 215; **4**: 125; **5**: 151; **7**:
112; **8**: 105
Nüsslein-Volhard, Christiane **7**:
178

Oakley, Kenneth Page **7**: 179
Oberth, Hermann Julius **7**: 180
Occhialini, Giuseppe Paolo
Stanislao **7**: 181
Ocean currents: 3: 140; **5**: 9, 113;
7: 17
Oceanography: 2: 200
Ochoa, Severo **7**: 182